101 Healing Stories

101 Healing Stories

Using Metaphors in Therapy

George W. Burns

John Wiley & Sons, Inc

New York • Chichester • Weinheim • Brisbane • Singapore • Toronto

Copyright © 2001 by John Wiley & Sons. All rights reserved.

Published simultaneously in Canada.

Library of Congress Cataloging-in-Publication Data

Burns, George W. (George William)
    101 healing stories : using metaphors in therapy / George W. Burns
      p. cm.
    Includes bibliographical references.
    ISBN 0-471-39589-7 (alk. paper)
    1. Counseling. 2. Psychotherapy. 3. Storytelling—Therapeutic use. I. Title: One hundred and one stories. II. Title: One hundred and one stories. III. Title
    BF637.C6 B828 2001
    616.89′14—dc21

                        00-065290

I dedicate this book with love, memories, and thanks to
My father, Reg, who taught me from his tales of life
My mother, Marge, who sat on my bed each night reading me stories
My children, Leah and Jurien, who created, and taught me to tell, stories of Fred Mouse
And my grandson, Thomas, who continues the stories into a new generation

It is also in memory of my very dear friend
Dr. Lok Wah (Ken) Woo
Whose life story was one of compassion, healing, and wisdom.

 # Acknowledgments

Nothing happens in isolation in this world and, consequently, our environment is full of metaphors of relationship and interaction. The computer at which I write is the product of many people's imaginative creativity and skilled technical abilities, and, though I don't know them, I benefit from their contributions. The stories retold in this volume have been penned because of the encouragement of friends, peers, and colleagues, and, as you read them, there is a relationship that evolves between you and me, my thoughts and the things that I have learned, collected, or experienced in my journey through life.

This interrelationship, I have discovered, is very apparent when writing a book. It, like any other activity in life, is not an act of isolation but the product of an interaction with many very special and highly valued people.

Julie Nayda, as a secretary, cheerful welcomer of clients to our practice, and warm friend, you are the best! Your patient keyboarding of my words, your creative talents, and that great sense of humor contribute immensely to my enjoyment of work . . . and life.

To Michael Yapko, PhD, I say "Thank you" for consenting to write the Foreword even before you saw the text. That confidence from a colleague is encouraging. I have valued your support over the years, the pragmatic style of your thinking, and the pleasure of our mateship.

Leah Burns, MSc, Rob Mc Neilly, MBBS, Peter Moss, MBBS, Graham Taylor, MA, Pam Wooding, BEd, and Michael Yapko, PhD (alphabetically). You guys are more than peer-reviewers. You are treasured colleagues *and* friends, for it is only to a *very* special friend that an author can hand his or her precious manuscript and ask for—and expect—the brutally honest criticisms you so generously gave. I thank you for your time, willingness, efforts, and honesty. Incorporated in the text you will find snippets of your grammatical suggestions, more eloquent words, and challenging ideas. Thanks.

Tracey Belmont, (plus all at John Wiley & Sons and at Graphic Composition) I have really enjoyed working with you as my editor. You have helped take my ideas and structured them into a shape that will be useful and readily accessible to readers. I love the way we bounced thoughts around, especially at the beginning of this project, and the conversations we have shared about our own corners of this beautiful world.

Ian Bytheway, PhD, for your encouragement, proofreading, and creative contributions—thanks and welcome to the family.

Claire Ash, how can I begin to express my gratitude to you for being such a wonderful and integral part of my life? I appreciate your support, encouragement, and the way you have selflessly tolerated my "other" relationship (with the computer) over the last several months. My story feels very complete with you as its main character.

I consider myself fortunate to have sat at the feet of very skilled storytellers from the beaches of Fiji to the coffee plantations of Vietnam and the mountain villages of the Himalaya. They have allowed a stranger privileged access to their age-old tales of wisdom and absorbing processes of communication.

I also thank my clients who have so willingly shared the intimate stories of their lives with me, especially those who have given their permission to reproduce their tales here. These stories I have deliberately distorted to protect the person while seeking to maintain the integrity of the message. Family and friends will also find themselves in these pages, often in ways that only they will recognize. I appreciate that you are not only part of my book, but also part of my life.

Just as writing a book is an act that highlights our interactions with others, so stories are processes of relationship. As each story is told and retold, as the message is spread, so the ripples of health, healing, and happiness radiate out in much the same way as when a stone is dropped into a pond.

Contents

Foreword

It rained and rained, and then rained some more, as if the sky had opened up and an ocean of rain fell to the earth. As the flood waters began to rise, the Holy Man looked all around him and wondered if the rains were a sign from God. He felt sure that even if they were, he was safe. He stood at his door, and as the water began to spill into his house, a man in a rowboat paddled up to him and said, "Holy Man, save yourself! Get into my rowboat." The Holy Man replied, "I am a man of God, and God will not let me drown. Give the place in your boat to some other deserving soul." The man paddled on.

The flood waters continued to rise above his home's first level, and so the Holy Man went up to his second-floor bedroom and waited and watched. Soon, another man in a rowboat floated up to his window and said, "Holy Man, you are in danger. Please, get into my boat so you won't drown." The Holy Man once again declined, saying, "God will not let me drown. I am His servant, His voice. Give the place in your boat to someone else who is worthy of saving." The man paddled on.

The rains continued, and the rising water level forced the Holy Man onto his roof. As the waters rose and began to cover his home, he climbed onto the chimney. Soon a helicopter flew by and hovered over him, and a booming voice coming over a loudspeaker said, "Holy Man, I will drop a rope to you and pull you from your chimney. Grab the rope and save yourself." The Holy Man replied, "God will not let me drown. Fly on and rescue another person needing your help." The helicopter flew on.

The rains continued, the waters rose, and . . . the Holy Man drowned.

When he encountered God in Heaven, he asked, "God, how could you let me drown? Have I not served you *faithfully all these years? Did I not devote my entire life to your greatness and bring others to know your word? I don't understand. Why did you let me drown?"*

And God replied, "Idiot! I sent you two rowboats and a helicopter!"

Sometimes, solutions are right in front of us, but we are too closed-minded or too unfocused to notice or apply them. For example, on an everyday basis, all around us there are wonderful people who can show us, simply from their very way of being, how to solve problems, relate well to others in positive and effective ways, and manage complex aspects of life well. Each person has *some* skills, *some* resources that can serve as models to us all as we try to learn to do what works in life. Each person's life is a story worth telling, if only we would take the time to notice—and to tell it.

George Burns, in sharing his many resources and skills with us through this book, has offered us a wonderful opportunity to learn and benefit from his wisdom. Burns is a keen observer of people, and his sensitivity and perceptiveness are immediately evident in the gentle way he talks to us through the stories he tells. He provides readers with a framework for understanding why storytelling is an invaluable means for communicating ideas, teaching skills, and providing relief to people burdened with the chains of despair, most often they created themselves. Freeing people to live life well is an obvious goal for Burns, and his stories are tools he gives people to help them do the most important thing to make changes possible, namely see problems from a variety of perspectives and generate solutions on a variety of levels. Burns empowers the reader-listener, and in so doing makes it possible to see the wisdom inherent in even the most routine life experiences.

The use of metaphors in psychotherapy, particularly among practitioners of clinical hypnosis, has become a core component of treatment. There is still much to learn about why one person hears a story and is inspired to transform some aspect of his or her life, yet another person hears the same story and all but ignores it. What factors influence the potential value of others' experiences as teaching tools? Burns considers these and other important questions and offers us some valuable ideas and guidelines for how to make the art of storytelling a more focused and effective means of intervention.

Burns has sent us some metaphorical rowboats and a helicopter, and for the opportunities he provides us, we can be grateful.

Michael D. Yapko, PhD
Solana Beach, California.

Introduction

Once upon a time . . . As my mother sat on the side of my bed at the end of each day and spoke these words, I was entranced. Four simple and oft-expressed words captured my attention and heightened a sense of anticipation about what may follow. Where would they lead? Would they take me on a journey into a fantasy or along a voyage of imagination? Would they guide me through lands I had yet to explore? Would they open my mind to experiences I had not yet discovered? Would they evoke emotions of fear, sadness, joy, or excitement? I snuggled into the bedclothes, closed my eyes, and enjoyed the anticipation of venturing on an unknown journey.

Those times were special. There was something very intimate about the undisturbed temporal space of sharing a story. There was a bond that linked listener and teller like two arctic explorers somehow isolated in a world of their own, yet intimately roped together in their uniquely shared experiences.

Though the contents of the stories that my mother read to me back then have now been lost in the recesses of memory, the experience lingers with recollections of happiness, closeness, and a feeling of being special. My mother loved literature. She read the children's classics to my sister and myself—tales that spanned the continents, from America to Europe to Australia. As we grew older she took us to pantomimes and plays where we experienced stories enacted in ways that were visual as well as auditory.

My father's tales were different. They were ones from life. His hands were meant for holding tools, not books. Born before the Wright brothers had felt their feet lift from the ground for the first time, he sailed half way around the world at an age when most adolescents, nowadays, are still in school. He labored on farms in outback Australia, worked on road-gangs, skinned snakes to turn their hides into belts, and lost his meager assets in a raging bush fire. He told stories of tragedy and triumph, heartbreak and achievement, challenge and resolve. His tales, in subtle ways I did not understand at the time, taught me about inner resourcefulness and the wondrous capacity of the human spirit.

From both parents I learned much about stories, and part of that learning was that stories are not the exclusive domain of childhood. They have enriched my life as an adult, parent, and social being. They have helped bond the intimacy between me and my partner, children, and grandchild. They play a rich, important, and potent role in my life as a therapist. We would all be poorer without them, for without stories it is hard to imagine how we would develop the skills and knowledge to survive. They are an integral element of our evolution, both as a species and as an individual. And, if they are such a core part of life, is it not logical and natural that they can also be a core element of therapy?

In Salman Rushdie's novel *The Moors Last Sigh,* one of his characters comments that when we are dead, all that remains is the stories. We are born with stories. As our mother holds us in her arms for the very first time, rocks us gently, and speaks to us softly, we are learning a story of love. As we grow, we are read stories that teach us values, morals, and social expectations. Those stories we hear start to shape our life, and the stories that we begin to tell, in turn, define who we are. We come home from school at the end of the day and relate tales about our classroom or playground experiences. We do not give up on stories as we leave childhood behind and take on the responsibilities of young adulthood. Much like we did as school pupils, we bring home the stories of our day at work.

Those tales serve several functions. They not only relate the facts about what happened, but communicate something about us, our experiences, our perceptions, and our view of the world. For just as stories shape the way we perceive and interact with the world, and reveal essential aspects of ourselves, in the later years of life they help us recall the journey of our life, with all its trepidations and triumphs. Even when we are gone, our stories remain behind.

WHAT THIS BOOK OFFERS

Developing the effective use of metaphors in therapy involves two prime components. The first is skill. Like an artist who needs to know the laws of perspective, color, and tone, so the storyteller needs to know the principles for constructing a therapeutic tale that will engage listeners, facilitate their identification with the problem, and have them join in the search for a solution.

The second component is art. Art makes a painting stand out from the crowd and create a lasting impression. Similarly, stories that will be most helpful to the client are those that are crafted specifically to the client's needs and communicated in a way that offers both involvement and meaning.

This book is the product of requests from trainees in the workshops I have presented on metaphors. These requests have been about learning both the skills and art of effective therapeutic communication. Two of the most common questions I encounter in workshop training are "How do you tell stories in a way that effectively engages the client?" and "Where do you find the materials or sources to create appropriate stories?"

The following chapters offer practical steps for answering these questions. They show you how to tell stories effectively, how to make them metaphoric, and where to find sources for therapeutic tales. There are guidelines for communicating stories and using the storyteller's voice most effectively to engage the client and commence the journey of healing. The book gently guides you through these pragmatic processes and on to methods for creating metaphoric stories from your own experiences and other sources.

Trainees and colleagues have encouraged me to include a number of stories that I have used in therapy. In some ways I think of myself as a collector of stories, for they have long intrigued me with their powerful yet subtle ability to teach and heal. As a result, I have gathered them in my travels through Asia, Europe, Africa, Australia, and America. I have listened to the many tragic and triumphant stories of my clients and learned from their life experiences. I have heard the creative and imaginative tales of my children and grandson who know none of the restrictions and structures of adulthood. I have sat with storytellers in tiny villages from sea-level islands in the Pacific to the heights of the Himalayas, observing their art and absorbing their message. I have discovered stories with salient metaphor content in anthologies, folktales, children's books, and on my e-mail. I hope, like any collector, I have learned to discard those that are not so valuable and nurtured those of intrinsic merit—a process I encourage you to follow, not only with the stories you read here but any you encounter in the future.

For experienced therapists this volume introduces a variety of new story ideas on which to construct meaningful therapeutic metaphors. It provides techniques for honing skills, enhancing communication, and making the effectiveness of what we do more empowering and more enjoyable.

For novice metaphor therapists just discovering the potency of therapeutic metaphors, this book offers step-by-step procedures, case examples, and a rich source of therapeutic stories that enable you to apply them immediately into your work, no matter what your theoretical background. The book will help you cultivate competence in the art of therapeutic communication, processes of change, and the rewards of facilitating outcome as well as learn about the methods of applying metaphors.

A WORD OR TWO ABOUT THE TITLE

In calling these metaphoric tales *healing stories,* I am defining *healing* in a broad perspective. Although healing in our western culture is perhaps most commonly used in the context of treating a physical illness or healing a physical problem, I do not wish to limit it to such a reductionistic definition. In terms of what we know about psychobiology (Pert, 1985, 1987; Rossi, 1993; Rossi & Cheek, 1998.), it may be hypothesized that stories, which alter the way we think or feel about something, may also alter something in our mind-body processing. If we observe listeners entranced in a tale we see some very observable signs of mind-body adjustments such as alterations in respiration, muscle tone, and heart rate. Story 2 retells a tale that, for generations of select Fijians, has been used to empower listeners in the psychophysiological abilities necessary to engage in the mind-body feat of firewalking.

Inherent in the title and the content of this book, *healing* also means restoring, establishing, or enhancing mental and emotional well-being. The stories in this collection are primarily about adjusting or modifying attitudes, emotions, and behavioral patterns that facilitate our adaptation to life's circumstances, and consequently ensure our well-being. As such, the stories are not just about fixing what's broken or curing symptoms, but are—as traditional storytelling has always been—about a way of living, a philosophy of life, and an existence that is in harmony with the dynamic relationships existing between mind, body, soul, and environment.

The stories, therefore, are more than problem-fixers. They speak to the listener about health and healing in a way that is preventative. Stories can be enhancing, enriching, and empowering. They can introduce listeners to experiences or challenges they may not yet have encountered and offer suggestions or means for handling that situation if and when it does occur.

Metaphor therapy is not for everyone—either client or clinician—and I do not want to give the impression that it is the *only* way to do therapy. Though stories have a universal appeal and their effectiveness as a teaching tool has long been demonstrated, there are clients who do not appreciate or benefit from such indirect approaches to treatment, perhaps seeing them as evasive, condescending, or irrelevant to their requests. There are those who respond better to direct interventions and may even become angry that they are paying hard-earned money to hear a therapist ramble on with some abstract tale. Watch carefully for such responses as they communicate vital information that either your particular stories are not applicable to that person's needs or that the metaphor approach is not relevant.

The more strings you have on your therapeutic bow, the more you can adapt to such individual clients and their individual needs. Metaphor therapy is just one of those strings—and may not be the best or only one necessary to ensure the target is struck.

ORAL VERSUS WRITTEN STORIES

As both the tradition and truth of the story are in the telling, I have long hesitated to put many of these stories into print. Once they are written, stories tend to take on an immutable quality, as though that is the way they always have been and always should be. The reality is that stories are dynamic. They evolve, they change, and they adapt from teller to teller as well as from listener to listener. Indeed, the power of the story is often in its flexibility and adaptability to the needs of the listener and the circumstances.

I cannot guarantee that the stories in this book are as I originally heard them. Nor can I guarantee that the way you read them is the way I told them to my last client or will tell them to the next. What is important here is that they are not seen for their words so much as their theme or meaning. Look for the therapeutic message in each story rather than trying to memorize or relate it to your client verbatim. These stories are not meant to be told and retold, in the way that an actor may memorize, word for word, the lines of a play, or a trainee hypnotherapist may recite precisely a particularly hypnotic script.

Allow the tales to evolve and, along with them, your own story. Stories emerge from within us, they communicate about our own experiences, and help define us as people. Through stories it is possible for us, and our clients, to find happiness and well-being, as well as the means for creating and maintaining positive emotional states.

THE STRUCTURE OF THE BOOK

The book is divided into four parts to allow quick referencing of the sections you may want to revisit for story ideas when working with a client in therapy. Part 1, **Metaphor Therapy,** examines the power of stories to discipline, evoke emotions, inspire, change behavior, create mind-body feats, and heal. Following this section are guidelines for effective storytelling and the use of the storyteller's voice. The last chapter of this section looks at the application of stories in therapy.

Part 2, **Healing Stories,** is divided into ten chapters, each containing ten stories relevant to the therapeutic outcome theme of that chapter. Each chapter is prefaced with a brief description of the nature of the outcome theme and concludes with an exercise for that particular outcome goal.

The topics around which the stories of each chapter are woven represent a common therapeutic goal. These topics were selected from an unpublished study I conducted of what conference attendants regarded as the ten most common therapeutic goals. I combined the results of this study with my own experience as a therapist to derive a list of ten common therapeutic themes that provide a basis around which you can develop metaphors of your own. However, they are not the only possible therapeutic outcomes and are best used as a guide for finding ideas rather than as a definitive and comprehensive set of goals.

Part 3, **Creating Your Own Metaphors,** guides you through the processes for developing your own outcome-oriented stories. It tells you what to avoid and gives examples of how different types of healing stories in this book were constructed. Following this are how-to-do-it procedures for creating, structuring, and offering effective therapeutic metaphors.

The emphasis of this book is on how to tell stories, how to find metaphor ideas, and how to structure therapeutic tales, rather than on presenting the research underlying metaphor therapy. As both the art and science of metaphor therapy are important, I have provided detailed **Resources** in Part 4 so that interested readers can further explore the nature of metaphors as a language form, the research behind their efficacy, and the variety of their therapeutic applications. It is also a source for locating other therapeutic stories—from traditional folktales to Internet websites.

HOW TO USE THIS BOOK AS A FUTURE REFERENCE SOURCE

An additional reference feature of the book is that the major sections have been shaded on the pages' leading edges to enable rapid accessing of the outcome-oriented chapters and other information you may wish to revisit. I hope that structuring the book in this way will provide a source of readily available ideas for working with particular clients.

Writing this book posed a dilemma, for I wanted it to be clear, practical, and accessible without being too prescriptive. The shaded reference system is thus presented as a possible direction for finding ideas, and not as a directive to use the particular stories mentioned. For a metaphor to be relevant it needs to be personal; it needs to be developed collaboratively with the client; and it needs to take into account the client, as well as his or her problem, resources, and desired outcome. The following are some suggested steps for achieving that goal.

I. Use the client's presenting problem as a guide or pointer to start looking for appropriate outcome-oriented goals

First, see the problem as a means to an end, drawing on the research and clinical evidence about that condition and its treatment as a basis for defining the areas in which to search collaboratively with your client for the relevant therapeutic goals. Understanding the nature of the client's problem helps you formulate an appropriate metaphor in accord with the PRO-approach (see Chapter 15).

Do not use this reference system like the formula that says, "Think depression, conclude Prozac," or, "Think relationship issues, conclude Story X." It may be more helpful to see the presenting problem as a signpost that gives a pointer to the sort of *ideas* that might stimulate the *processes* you go through in formulating metaphors.

2. Clearly define your individual client's specific therapeutic goals by following the steps outlined for an Outcome-Oriented Assessment in Chapter 15.

Once those goals have been defined it is easier to select the therapeutic characteristics of a metaphor that will most facilitate the client's movement toward his or her desired outcome.

3. Choose a relevant metaphor.

The preferable choice is to pick a metaphor on the basis of your own ideas, client cases, or personal experiences. If you are struggling for ideas, then use the shaded sections of Chapters 4 through 13 to find a therapeutic goal that matches most closely to your client's, then check out the Exercise at the end of the chapter for the ideas that you have generated. If all else fails, then revisit the stories I have presented, remembering that they are offered only as ideas and examples. They hold no magic within themselves or in the particular way that they may have been told here in print. If they are helpful, they should stimulate your own ideas that can be creatively adapted to working with each client's set of individual goals.

The Importance of Stories

Because stories are such an important means of communicating wisdom, morals, and philosophies for life, some cultures even have stories about telling stories. The following example is based on a folktale from Nepal. It tells us that some stories are so important that they *must* be heard. Not to listen can be a matter of life or death.

Using the king as a main character highlights that everyone, even the most powerful and esteemed, needs to hear the message of stories. They are so essential to our happiness, well-being, and purpose in life that the Nepalese have entrusted them to the care of a specific deity of stories.

This tale begins in the reign of a king who loved stories with such passion that he brought the most famous storytellers from all over the world to his kingdom. Each night they would tell their tales, both familiar and new, to the king and his court. As you might imagine, dealing with affairs of the state all day long was a tedious activity and listening to an evening tale helped the king unwind, but therein lay a problem. He would relax too much and inevitably fall asleep before the tale was completed. As everyone knows, this is a sign of disrespect and the source of bad omens.

The king's habit angered the Goddess of Stories who felt humiliated and insulted that the king, of all people, regularly breached the etiquette of listening to stories. How could he or his people live happily without completed stories?

Deciding to warn the king, the goddess appeared in a dream to his prime minister, cautioning that the king should listen to stories in their totality, or not listen at all. The prime minister told the king about his dream, and the king vowed to stay awake. Nonetheless, during the story that very night, his mind began to drift, his eyelids started to droop, and soon he was asleep.

The prime minister, anticipating wrath from the Goddess of Stories, asked the storytellers to change the pace of their tales, raise the volume of their voices, or increase the level of excitement at any sign of the king drifting off to sleep, but, again, all failed. The Goddess of Stories was furious for the king had ignored her warning. She had been generous and tolerant, but this added insult to injury.

Once again she manifested herself in the prime minister's dreams. "The king continues to disrespect stories," she said. "He does not hear their messages and, consequently, cannot incorporate their teachings into his life or set a good example for his people. If he persists in insulting stories, he will have to die, and, as the deity of stories, it is my role to punish him. I will add poison to his breakfast the morning after he next falls asleep during a story. If that does not work, I will cause a tree branch to fall on him and strike him dead. If, for any reason, that doesn't work, then I will send a venomous snake to attack him."

But the Goddess' caution did not end there. As the king had already had sufficient warnings, if the prime minister told the king of his impending fate, then he, the faithful servant, would be turned into stone.

What a conflict! His death or his beloved king's! Hopefully he could prevent both. He tried every tactic to keep his sovereign awake, but that night, the king once again fell asleep before the story ended.

The next morning the prime minister subtly swapped his own breakfast for the king's and saved his ruler's life. That evening he again tried to prevent the king from slumbering, but to no avail. The next day, as the king seated himself on a bench in his garden, the prime minister carefully studied the overhanging tree. As soon as the branch above began to creak and fall, he dived on the monarch, pulling him to safety and once more saved his life. The king was grateful, but the prime minister could not explain his actions or advise the king of the fate still to befall him.

That night, as the unreformed king began to nod off during the story, the prime minister crept into the royal bed chamber and hid behind a curtain. The faithful servant maintained his vigil after the king and queen had retired. Just as the Goddess of Stories had predicted, a lethal snake slid into the room and up onto the regal bed. It raised itself, about to strike, but the prime minister struck first. With a clean swing of his sword, he cut off its head.

At that moment the king awoke, saw the prime minister with his sword drawn, and interpreted it as an assassination attempt. The minister was sentenced to death and, while sitting in his cell awaiting execution, realized that he would die no matter what he did. So, wishing to do so with his reputation of loyalty intact, the prime minister told the king the true story behind his actions. He had barely completed the last word before he turned into stone.

The king was struck with grief and guilt. He made a vow that he would never again fall asleep, or stop listening, during the telling of a story. He encouraged his people to show respect for stories, storytellers, and, in turn, the Goddess of Stories. They were to listen, not just to the words, but to the message, and, just as they were to respect the telling of the tale, so they were to use the messages, respectfully, in their lives.

PART ONE

Metaphor Therapy

CHAPTER 1

The Power of Stories

In 1794 a small boy underwent surgery for the removal of a tumor. I shudder to think what thoughts would have been going through my mind as a 9-year-old child facing the prospect of a surgeon's knife more than 200 years ago. Antibiotics had not been discovered. Louis Pasteur had not yet enlightened the medical world about the need for sterilization, and chemical anesthetics for controlling pain would not be discovered for another century and a half. All that could be offered to the boy was a story. To help distract his attention from the procedure, he was told a tale so intriguing that he later avowed he had felt no discomfort whatsoever.

Could a story be that powerful, and could its power linger? For that child it certainly did. Eighteen years later the very same boy handed one of his own stories to a publisher. His name was Jacob Grimm. What was his story? Snow White. He went on to become one of the world's most famous tellers of fairy stories—stories that continue to be retold in words, in print, in plays, and on movie screens two centuries later.

Yet, is this experience of Jacob Grimm's so unique? Is not the empowerment encased in, and offered by, stories available to us all? Do you remember what it was like as a young child to have a parent or grandparent sit on the side of your bed at night and read a story that gave you permission to journey into your own fantasies? Or, more recently, have you shared in dinner party tales that have evoked emotions of laughter or sadness? Perhaps you have experienced being so absorbed in a story related by stage or movie actors that you forgot the hassles of a stressful day, the pain of a headache, or the argument with a spouse.

The *content* of those childhood stories of mine has been lost over the passing years, but it is hard to forget the experience and intimacy of the *process* that takes place between a bedside narrator and entranced child. For, while stories themselves have a special power to communicate, there is also a uniqueness and affinity in the relationship that bonds storyteller and listener.

This bond is one whose origins are shrouded deeply in our human history. At some indefinable time in the past, someone, somewhere, started to tell stories. Since then stories have become an integral part of human society. Regardless of our language, religion, culture, sex, or age, stories are a part of our lives. It is because of stories that our language, religion, science, and culture exist. Stories may fulfill our dreams and, indeed, our dreams themselves are stories.

Over time and across all cultures stories have been told in words, music, and movement. Narrators, holy men, actors, puppeteers, dancers, parents, musicians, and many others have communicated them. They have been printed in books, recorded on tapes, filmed on celluloid, and played on musical instruments. Stories have the power to bond relationships, entertain, and teach. In the past people used to feed and shelter the village storyteller for the pleasure of listening to his or her tales. Today we turn movie stars, our modern-day storytellers, into folk heroes and millionaires.

In Nepal, mothers use frightening stories instead of corporal punishment to control their children. Across the Himalayan range, in Tibet, people seek out stories and storytellers with the power to stimulate strong emotional responses. In times of war stories have inspired soldiers to bravery. From the islands of Fiji a generations-old story empowers prescribed people with the authority to control mind-body processes such as healing and firewalking. In the helping professions we use stories as metaphors to help clients achieve their desired goals and promote healing.

THE POWER OF STORIES TO DISCIPLINE

In Nepal, children are not disciplined by physical means, as mothers do not like to see them unhappy or tearful. Yelling or screaming at errant children is frowned upon. Instead they control children's behavior by telling stories. To keep children quiet or to reprimand them, they tell fearful stories of terrifying characters who may be humans, animals, ghosts, or evil deities. Although we may find it cruel or even emotionally abusive to tell children tales of terror, I describe this practice, not to debate whether it is right or wrong (depending on our cultural view), but to illustrate two points. The first is to portray the way that stories are traditionally used in cultures other than our own. The second is to highlight the power they may have in the control of behavior—a factor relevant to their therapeutic use.

THE POWER OF STORIES TO INVOKE EMOTIONS

Mr. Volk was my high school English teacher, a man whom I thank for his passionate love of Australian literature. Forever recorded in my memory bank is the recollection of him reading Dad and Dave stories to our class from Steele Rudd's *On Our Selection*. He could barely complete each tale due to his convulsions of laughter and the tears that streamed down his cheeks. Even the least literature-oriented of my classmates could not hold back their laughter. Many rocked back and forth in their desks, arms folded across their stomachs as though about to burst with an explosion of humor. Mr. Volk had no solitary claim to tears of merriment. They spread like an infection through the classroom, with the result that students raced from classroom to library, clamoring for limited copies of the stories his laughter prohibited him from finishing in class.

Perhaps we have all experienced the power that stories have to invoke certain emotions. We may recall sitting around a campfire in the woods and listening to the ghost stories of fireside tellers. As Nepalese mothers know, such stories often elicit fear in a child. These campfire tales can also frighten listeners and inhibit sleep for the rest of the night.

Nestled high on the leeward side of the Himalayan mountains, the country of Tibet enjoyed a relatively undisturbed geographical isolation for many centuries. Combined with a deliberate political and religious policy of isolation, it remained (and, to a large degree, still remains) apart from the technological developments of the rest of the world. This permitted the Tibetans a unique freedom to focus on their spiritual development. Storytelling became a means for communicating religious wisdom, but it also served an important secular function as a major recreational pastime. Grandparents held the customary role of sitting around the fire in the evening relating folktales to the rest of the family. In this way they passed on an understanding of the country's history and the values of their society to the younger generation.

In addition to these familial narrators, professional Tibetan storytellers were offered gifts of food in return for the stories they presented. These *lama-manis,* as they were called, told epic legends of battles and bravery as well as stories that evoked the emotions. Norbu Chophel (1983), who has sought to preserve some of the folktales of Tibet, says that people would sit for hours at a time listening to a *lama-mani,* wiping away the tears, then unashamedly head home with red eyes.

THE POWER OF STORIES TO INSPIRE

One example of how stories have the power to inspire and motivate is the real-life account of Captain Robert Falcon Scott, naval officer and Antarctic explorer. In 1900, at the age of 32, he was chosen to command Britain's first national Antarctic expedition. After returning from his four-year pioneering journey, he was promoted from lieutenant to captain. Like most other explorers of the Great Southern Land, he was both enchanted and addicted, planning to return at the first opportunity. Terra incognita called him back just five years later, and in 1909 he joined the race to the South Pole. It became a fight for national pride and colonial supremacy. Britain, which ruled the waves, also sought sovereignty of this vast and barren continent of frozen water.

After sailing halfway around the globe through some of the world's most treacherous seas in a converted wooden whaling boat, he set out across the continent with Siberian ponies as his means of transport. Even these tough, cold-climate equines could not cope with the conditions and either died or had to be shot. Forced to journey most of the way with hand-drawn sleds, he and four companions reached the South Pole on January 18, 1912. It is impossible to imagine, after his years of arduousness, how he must have felt (even the entry in his diary, "The worst has happened," could not truly convey his emotions) when he saw the cold Antarctic wind fluttering a Norwegian flag at the site of the Pole. Robbed of being the first to arrive at 90° south by just one month, Scott lost to an expedition lead by Roald Amundsen.

Unfortunately this was not the only tragedy to beset them, for physical fatigue and inclement polar weather dogged the long haul back across the icy continent. One member of the party died on the homeward march and another, Captain Oates, who was suffering severe frostbite, walked from the shelter of their tent to his death in an Antarctic storm rather than delay the party and thus threaten the lives of his comrades. His act of self-sacrifice was of little avail. Two and a half months after departing the Pole, Scott and the other two members of the party were trapped in a blizzard. They died just 10 miles short of a preestablished depot that offered food and shelter. Later that year a search party found their bodies, with their records and diaries intact.

Scott was soon promoted to the status of a national hero who had laid down his life serving his country. The story of Scott and Oates, illustrated by the moving picture film of the expedition's photographer, inspired thousands of troops and their officers in the muddied trenches of Europe during the Great War. They could identify with the hardships, be motivated by the patriotism, and find consolation in their ultimate self-sacrifice. Dozens of letters made their way from the front lines to Scott's widow, assuring her that her husband's story had empowered them to handle the hardships of battle.

THE POWER OF STORIES TO CHANGE

Jessica was just six years old when her mother brought her to see me, but she was to teach me something about the power of stories. Diagnosed as an elective mute, she chose to whom she spoke and, in all her short years, she had never spoken to an adult outside of her immediate family, and spoke only rarely to other children. She would not talk when in a group of her peers, so other children only heard her speak, ever so softly, when playing with her one-on-one.

To her parents it was not a concern. She spoke freely at home, and her vocabulary, sentence structure, and fluency of speech seemed, to them, comparable to those of her peers. Her mother said Jessica was so chatty that at times they wished she would shut up.

For her teachers it was a different matter. They were deeply concerned. Because she had remained steadfastly mute for a whole year—just as she had done in her preschool year twelve months before—they had no way of assessing her reading abilities or verbal skills. Their system demanded measurement and accountability that could not be provided while Jessica was not playing by the rules.

She saw a school psychologist who could not get her to talk or measure her progress on standard verbally oriented tests. He recommended a behavioral schedule for her classroom teacher to employ. Whether the problem lay in the behavioral schedule or its inappropriate application was not clear. What was clear was that Jessica remained an elective mute.

I greeted Jessica and her mother in the waiting room and chatted pleasantly for a while before asking to see her mother alone. If Jessica did not talk to adults there was no point in my seeing her first and creating a situation that validated my alignment with every other adult outside of the family. In addition, when seeing children I like to speak to the accompanying parent or parents alone so that they do not speak in front of the child in ways that may put down the child, reinforce the problem, or be negative in terms of the appropriate therapeutic approach.

I gave Jessica some paper and colored pens and asked her to draw while I spoke with her mother. It was not long before there was a gentle knock on my consulting room door. Jessica entered with two drawings, one of her mother and one of me. She handed them to me silently and I thanked her, requesting she do some more while her mother and I kept talking. She sat on the floor with paper and pens, and though seemingly absorbed in her task, I knew she was listening to our every word.

This gave me the opportunity to speak to her indirectly by talking to her mother. My therapeutic intent was twofold: first, to communicate to both Jessica and her mother that selective speech was normal and, second, that they may have an expectation of change. At this stage I did not anticipate that six years of resolute muteness would change in a matter of moments.

Addressing my first objective, I spoke with her mother about how we all choose with whom we want to speak and with whom we do not. Some people we like, and so talk openly and easily with them. Other people we may not want to talk to at all. Of those we speak to, some we talk to a lot and others only a little. I wanted to reassure Jessica indirectly that she had the power to be selective, as well as to let her know her choices were normal. This seemed important, as other adults (teachers, the school psychologist, her family physician, and her grandmother) had all been treating her as though her behaviors were abnormal, and it was apparent that that approach had not worked.

To set an expectancy of change, I told her mother a true story, drawn from my own recollections as a primary school student. In my class there was a boy named Billy whom nobody at school had ever heard speak, either to teachers or fellow students. Somehow the rumor spread that he could talk and that he spoke at home, yet he remained silent at school. Billy was teased, but still he did not talk. Classmates and teachers eventually accepted his silence; that was the way it remained for several years. Then things changed.

At this point of the story, Jessica stopped drawing to look up at me. I continued to keep her mother's gaze and progressed with the story.

It was a Monday morning and we were all filing into class after assembly. The cleaners had been in over the weekend and must have left a little hurriedly because the door of the cupboard at the back of the classroom was ajar and the feathery end of a duster protruded out. As Billy walked down the aisle to his desk, his eye caught the protruding feathers, and, before stopping to check himself, he cried out, "Sir, there's a hen in the cupboard!" Everyone laughed and after that Billy talked in school.

Jessica had stopped her drawing and was listening to the story. When I finished she put aside the paper on which she had been sketching and started afresh. I continued to speak with her mother. In a few moments she handed me a drawing of a bird.

"What's this?" I asked.

"Tweetie," she answered.

"Who's Tweetie?" I inquired.

"My canary," she responded.

Her mother looked astonished. I was the first adult Jessica had spoken to outside of the family in her whole six years. As Jessica taught me, the power to change had come not just through a story, but through one told so indirectly that I had ostensibly been relating it to someone else.

THE POWER OF STORIES TO CREATE MIND-BODY FEATS

As well as changing behavior, stories have the power to elicit amazing physical feats. My anthropologist daughter studied the growing impact of tourism on a small island in the Pacific nation of Fiji over a period of three years (Burns, 1996). Beqa is the home of the original firewalkers, and, knowing my interest in such topics, she considerately reserved her interview with the high priest of firewalking, until I was able to visit. The *beti,* as he is called in Fiji, allowed me to sit through the ritual preparation for a firewalk. I was intrigued and excited with anticipation at the thought of watching the rituals. Having spent 30 years of my career studying and working with hypnosis, I expected to observe hypnotic inductions that would facilitate their ability to control pain as the use of trance-like rituals such as hypnosis and meditation have been observed in other practices that seem to defy the usual experiences of pain.

Firewalking preparations involved drinking a mildly anesthetic local drink, *kava,* a talk by the high priest about the reason for the firewalk, and recounting the story that empowered this particular tribe with the ability to firewalk. A pit was then dug, filled with rocks, and covered with logs. The logs were ignited and allowed to rage until the rocks turned white hot. The logs were then dragged clear to form a path over the rocks.

I had no doubt about the heat as one rock exploded in the fire, throwing a fragment of stone at my feet. Involved in conversation, and without thinking about my action, I bent down to pick up this fragment and throw it back in to the fire, much as one would a spark that landed on the carpet from a log fire at home. In just a fraction of a second, the rock seared my fingers.

The walkers slowly trod across these same stones, paused, stood, and grinned as if with a fresh delight at their power over fire. Some of the more experienced walkers stood for 5 to 6 seconds on each stone. I checked their feet when they stepped off, and I could see no signs of burning or blistering, and, indeed, their feet felt relatively cool.

The story that the *beti* related to his disciples prior to the walk, the story that has for generation after generation empowered such feats of mind-body control, is retold in Story 2, "A Tradition of Mind-Body Empowerment."

THE POWER OF STORIES TO HEAL

Phillipa was one of the most phobic people I have ever encountered in my 30 years as a clinical psychologist. She was terrified of being at home alone, yet she was unable to leave because she was scared of people, noises, open spaces, and what unfamiliar experiences may await her. When her husband left for work, panic crashed over her like a tidal wave. The only safe place on the whole planet for Phillipa was her front lawn. For hours each day she would stand there, sheltered between the tall brick wall that screened their home from the street and the incarcerating wooden walls of her house, too scared to go inside and too scared to go out. A story told in therapy empowered Phillipa to alter the balance of her life and get on living.

Her husband initially asked if I would make a home visit. "No," I replied, concerned that if Phillipa were not encouraged to leave her safety zone there would be no incentive for her to change or move away from her inappropriate and narrowly secure boundaries. "If she wishes to do something about overcoming this," I explained, "she must come to see me." He doubted she would, unable to recall the last time she had left home, but soon after she arrived for her first appointment.

At first Phillipa was too scared to consult me without her husband being present, and, for the first few consultations, I did not even know what she looked like. She sat with her head hung low, her long hair falling mop-like over her face, covering it as effectively as a veil. Her responses to my questions were minimal and monosyllabic, guarded by the uncertainty of fear rather than the resistance of anger or disinterest of depression.

With little response from her and a fear of me, perhaps not too dissimilar to any other stranger who may invade her life and have certain expectations of her, I decided to tell her a story. My reasoning was motivated by several factors. First, if I was putting any perceived pressure on her to communicate when she was reluctant to do so it was likely to make the situation uncomfortable for both of us and even more fearful for her. Storytelling made no demand for any verbal or overt responses from her in any way whatsoever. She was free not to communicate if she wished.

Second, in the roles of teller and listener we were forming a relationship. It became an activity we were sharing and experiencing together. No longer were we separate individuals with disparate goals because the process of participating in this experience together altered the relationship and facilitated a common bonding.

Third, it was my therapeutic objective that the story should relate my understanding of her problem and express a realistic goal for its resolution. These processes are also discussed later in Chapters 14 and 15.

At that stage I knew little about her. I was not aware that she loved animals though it was obvious she was fearful of, or perhaps even terrified by, her fellow humans. An animal story seemed to be less threatening than a tale about unfamiliar human characters. What is more, the animal needed to know fear and ambivalence, just as she did when she stood on the front lawn, frightened to go in or out. It needed to be clingy, hanging on to something like the front lawn that offered a somewhat inappropriate and dysfunctional sense of security. The story character also needed to be able to let go of fears and insecurity, while finding new and more appropriate ways to manage life.

An octopus came to mind. Its numerous tentacles meant it could cling tenaciously to inappropriate objects. Its experiences could closely replicate her own. So, around this character, a tale emerged over several consultations. The story's slow evolution was in part due to the fact that I was then just beginning to work with therapeutic metaphors. I would run out of story and need time between consultations to think about where the tale would go next. This, in fact, proved to be a distinct therapeutic advantage and enhanced my confidence about using metaphors by knowing that I did not magically have to produce some wonderful, creative story right on the tip of my tongue at the very moment I expected I should. It also taught me about developing metaphors collaboratively with the client—a fact that I only later discovered facilitated therapeutic outcome (Martin, Cummings, & Hallberg, 1992).

As the story developed from session to session, Phillipa started to lift her head and feel more comfortable seeing me without her husband being present. She began arriving more enthusiastically at her consultations, and commenced conversation by saying, "I know what happened to the octopus next," keenly wanting to discuss the continuing adventures of our mutual friend. She was not being told how to solve her problems but was creatively designing her own outcome. The tale of a little octopus became *our* story, not just mine.

Some weeks after we began the story, she spontaneously produced a series of felt-pen drawings depicting the theme of our tale that reflected a hidden artistic talent. I encouraged her to develop this ability, and, though still frightened to venture out alone, she arranged to attend art classes with her daughter. The teacher was impressed with her skills, and, out of all the students in the course, she selected Phillipa to display her work in a solo exhibition.

Phillipa sent me an invitation to the opening, and her husband phoned to ensure I would be there. When I arrived she ran over to me, took me by the hand, and led me around the gallery, en-

EXERCISE 1.1

Pause to reflect for a while on what stories have had a significant impact on your life:
    What was the story? What impact did it have on you? What was its power?
    Did it teach you something?

- influence your behavior?
- evoke certain emotions?
- facilitate mind–body changes?
- promote some aspect of healing?
- enhance feelings of empowerment?

Understanding the impact of stories on yourself will help you understand and appreciate their influence in therapy.

thusiastically describing each painting in turn. She held her head high, her face beamed with delight, and, although to the trained eye she displayed subtle (and perhaps normal) signs of anxiety, she seemed comparatively comfortable away from home, among a crowd of people.

Phillipa has used her artistic talents to win wider acclaim. I have since seen her and her works photographed in the newspapers, and I have watched her being interviewed on television about how she has generously used her gifts to support children's institutes. The story we shared was a fulcrum. It permitted her to alter the balance of her life and empowered to her to initiate such powerful healing, but that was not the complete picture. The conclusion may have been different without Phillipa's talents and application to change.

Our story, "Soaring to New Heights," which was a part of that process, is retold in Chapter 4, Story 11. More details of Phillipa's case and the way we constructed our metaphor are provided in Chapter 14.

CHAPTER 2

Effective Storytelling

On the shuttle bus from my hotel to the Phoenix airport, I could not help overhearing the conversation between two people seated immediately behind me. We were all returning home after attending a conference on Ericksonian psychotherapy and hypnotherapy. The couple behind me were obviously meeting for the first time, which was not surprising since more than 1,000 people from 25 countries had attended the meeting.

She asked him what had brought him to the conference, and his answer was one I have heard expressed many times in the workshops that I have conducted on metaphors. He replied, "I wanted to learn more about telling metaphors. I watch the experts." He continued, "They tell them so effortlessly. Somehow they seem to pick up on just the right story for that particular client. Their ideas are so creative. They weave them into imaginative stories and tell them in a way that entrances the client. I struggle to begin. I do not know where to get the material for metaphors, or how to tell them effectively."

In the previous chapter we examined the power of stories as forms of communication and instruments of change. Because much of this power is in the telling of the tale, as well as the relevance of the story, this chapter focuses on how to tell stories effectively. The emphasis is on stories in general rather than therapeutic tales specifically. If you can communicate meaningfully with stories— whether they are accounts of the day's happenings, party jokes, bedtime tales, or whatever —you will have the necessary storytelling skills to use metaphors in therapy.

Effective storytelling includes three variables: the teller, the listener (or listeners), and the process of communication. In this chapter the focus is on the first variable, the storyteller, and the tools that he or she can use to communicate a tale effectively and metaphorically. We examine the basic steps for effectively telling stories and how to use your predominant communicative tool: the voice.

In guiding you through this process we begin at the beginning. The conversation on the shuttle bus to the Phoenix airport reminded me that it is good to watch the masters at work, but to replicate that work we need to develop the skills at which they have had years and years of practice. Although these skills are readily learnable, there is also something of an art to their practice.

TEN GUIDELINES FOR EFFECTIVE STORYTELLING

1. We are all storytellers.

We all tell stories. We tell others about our day and ask them to tell us their stories. We inquire, "What did you do at school today?" "How was work?" "How did you spend your day?" Our stories are a way of reconnecting with the people we know and love. They are a way of filling in the gaps and making the links that span the time we were apart.

Just as stories are a way of reconnecting with the people we know, they are also a way to connect with new people. When we meet people for the first time, we may ask what sort of work they do or what sort of interests they have. We listen to the stories they tell about themselves, and we assess whether those stories connect or relate to the stories that we have about ourselves. If their stories attract us, we listen and reply with stories of our own. The purpose of these is to find the common theme of the stories that links us together. We tell and listen to such stories to discover a mutual interest or activity. If our stories do not match, we do not connect.

Take the example of the couple meeting for the first time at a social event. If they both tell stories about enjoying romantic picnics, liking similar movies, or sharing similar activities, there may be a chance that they exchange telephone numbers, meet again, and develop a relationship. If he starts to tell stories about drunken weekends with the guys and she tells stories about attending the opera, they may not make the same connection.

The point here is that we *all* have the skill to tell stories. In communicating with others we are constantly alternating between the role of teller and role of listener as part of our everyday process of interpersonal interaction. Admittedly, some do it more effectively than others. Some seem to be natural raconteurs, but each of us uses stories to connect and reconnect with other people.

Storytelling is also the basis for many of our social interactions. We go to a football game, attend a concert, accept an invitation to a party, or see a movie, and later tell stories about it. I once attended a workshop on humor conducted by a psychologist and two stand-up comedians. At one stage during the workshop one of the comedians asked, "Where do people get their most laughs?" I was expecting that he would say at his weekly show and suggest where we may purchase tickets. He did not. He said that people get their most laughs over a dinner party table, where people share stories and retell experiences of life.

As I reflected on the comment, I could appreciate what he was saying. In such social events someone will often initiate conversation with a story of something amusing, meaningful, or significant that has happened recently. Others begin to bounce their stories off the first one, and the result is a snowball effect. Once one person has told a story, somebody else will comment, "That reminds me of . . .", or "I remember a time when I . . ."

We share the joy and sadness of our life through stories. We tell tales of our frustrations and

> **EXERCISE 2.1**
>
> ■ Relate a story of your day to a friend or family member. Pay attention to what it is you want to communicate, whether it is a point of humor or an experience from which you have learned. Observe how natural it feels to tell a story from your experience.
>
> ■ Listen to the stories other people relate about their day-to-day experiences. Observe how people use stories and do so easily and naturally.
>
> ■ At a party or social gathering, make a point of listening to the stories that other people tell. Note how they trigger ideas, images, or stories of your own.

achievements. We relate anecdotes about our journey through life that may resonate with other people and the experiences of their journey. Hearing their tales may help us on our own journey.

In these ways we are all constantly telling stories. In one way or another we already do it, and, for the most part, do it effectively. We ensure our message is heard, but having others hear it is only part of the story. We also listen to our own stories. We use stories as a method to redefine our experiences and give them meaning. Stories are a tool for interpretation and definition in that they give structure to our world and make sense of what, at times, may be a chaotic situation.

Because we are all storytellers, the skill of communicating in metaphors is not something that we have to learn from scratch. It is that something that you are already doing, and doing on a daily basis. Acknowledging that fact may give you some of the confidence necessary to experiment with storytelling in therapy.

2. Use your own enthusiasm, reality, and experience rather than focus on techniques.

Make the process enjoyable for both you and your listener, and be sure that the story you tell is one that you enjoy or that the telling of it challenges you.

Begin by telling friends and family the day-to-day tales you want to relate. Do not try to make them metaphoric (the next chapter provides plenty of examples for doing this). Although there are some skills, techniques, and strategies that make storytelling more effective, one of the most important ingredients is your own enthusiasm. This is what adds the emotion or mood to the story and what gives it spontaneity and life.

I have a friend who is a well-known artist. I am intrigued by the parallel of principles in our professions. He says that the basic techniques in art, such as perspective, color and tone, are important, but they simply serve as a vehicle for the artist's creativity. Storytelling is also about both creativity and techniques, and how you balance these will result in a style that is uniquely yours. The steps I offer are a guide to help you develop that style.

Story 92, "The Secret that Will Never Be Known," is not a story that I have ever told therapeutically, but is one I love to tell. I have frequently used it in workshops because it illustrates a number of points in the process of telling stories. First, it is a tale that I can tell with enthusiasm and enjoy-

EXERCISE 2.2

- Practice telling stories with enthusiasm. Use those that allow you to express your feelings of involvement without concern for techniques.
- As an experiment and task of possible contrast, try relating a story about an event that you found boring and uninteresting. Observe your experiences as you tell it. Also observe the verbal and nonverbal feedback cues from your listener.

ment. For me it is fun, and, because of this, I communicate my affect through the story in a way that attracts the listener's attention. Second, the story allows the teller to use and develop the senses. Bringing sensory experiences into a story (as I shall discuss later in this chapter) helps make it more real and more enchanting. Third, "The Secret that Will Never Be Known" is a story that enables the teller to watch the processes of engagement and entrancement in the listeners.

3. Use your intelligence, integrity, and ethics.

Storytelling needs to be done with a sense of responsibility just as metaphor therapy—along with all other therapeutic practices—needs to be offered within the guidelines of appropriate ethics.

In this sense I consider that a story needs to tell *a* truth and not necessarily *the* truth. What I mean is that the story needs to be ethical, moral, and responsible. In a therapeutic sense it needs to provide the listener with something that is helpful, constructive, and practical. It needs to address appropriate ways for resolving a problem, enhancing an experience, or improving a quality of life. If drawing on a case example, I would not include the client's name or, if a name seems relevant to the tale, I would create something completely fictional—as I have done in the case stories included in Part Three. If telling a case story of a client who had successfully resolved a phobia to another client who is also phobic, I may change the gender, age, occupation, context, or circumstances of the account to better match the circumstances of the listener. In other words the story may not tell *the* truth of the actual case, but *a* truth about how someone may overcome a phobia.

Once we have assumed the responsibility of accountable storytelling, the therapist can take some risks. By that what I mean is to use the story boldly. When we use stories therapeutically, they are about change, about doing something differently. As a general rule clients come to therapy because they are seeking change. What they have done before has not worked, and maybe what they are doing at that moment is not working. Therapy is thus about helping a client to do something differently so he or she can achieve a different result. To achieve this result, therapeutic stories may need to be challenging. They may confront the client's belief systems or attitudes to life. They may challenge patterns of cognition or behavior. They may question assumptions about emotional responsiveness. The client may need to take some risks, venture into new and unfamiliar territory, or experiment with new ways of behaving to attain the desired result. Therapeutic metaphors may offer the challenges that help facilitate the client's experiment with risk.

Some years back a client taught me an important lesson in taking such therapeutic risks. He came from a remote mining town and was in the city for just one week, allowing us only three consulta-

EFFECTIVE STORYTELLING

> **EXERCISE 2.3**
>
> Experiment with being responsible and bold in your storytelling.
>
> - Take the risk to speak up in supervision groups or tutorials where your voice has not been heard or your story has not been told.
> - Observe the effects on both you and your listener or listeners.

tions. He took control of the first consultation from the moment he sat down, launching into a lengthy, uninterruptible, obsessive waffle. I tried being indirect and I tried being direct. I attempted to offer cognitive behavioral strategies, metaphors, and hypnosis, but nothing seemed to deflect him from his ruminative reiteration of detail upon detail of his problems.

The second session went exactly the same way. I drew on every string of my therapeutic bow, only to find that, again, nothing worked. When he arrived for the third session, he began to reiterate what he had already expounded on for two full sessions. I did not know what else I could do. As he prattled on over the same boring details, I again asked myself how this pattern of behavior might be interrupted, but nothing had worked so far. What was left?

I thought to myself, "This guy's conversation is nothing but repetitive and boring rubbish." In my internal conversation I debated whether it was responsible for me to tell him that, then asked, "Why not?" As nothing else had worked perhaps it was time to take a risk.

When I confronted him with my observation, he stopped in mid-sentence, burst into tears and said, "That's what everyone thinks of me." For the first time someone had confronted him honestly, and for the first time he was challenged to examine his own patterns of behavior. That was the point of change.

4. Make the story fit.

First, the story needs to fit your listener or client. We discuss in the next chapter how to make a story metaphoric and how to structure it in a way that best fits your client's problem and desired outcome. However, the easiest way to do this is to bear in mind the listener's goals or objectives.

If the client's goals match the story's theme, then some of the peripheral details of the story may not be so significant. Nonetheless it is helpful if the story matches the struggle, conflict, or problems the client is experiencing. The facts do not need to be identical, but they must be a metaphoric replication of the principles and processes involved.

Jeff was a client who belonged to a particular Indian religious sect. Jeff was not his religious name, or even his former name. He told a story of rejection by a senior guru with whom he had previously felt he had a good relationship. In his words the rejection "unbalanced" him, led him into a state of depression, and, a few months later (in an event he saw as causally related), he was diagnosed with cancer. Fortunately, surgery was successful and he was given a clean bill of health. However, he wondered whether the emotional stresses of his rejection had contributed to the illness, and he felt that he needed to clear what he described as the "blockage" of this incident to let his energy flow again and maintain good health.

He used a metaphor about walking through an Indian village with large, open monsoon drains
down the sides of each street. One day as he walked through the village he realized that his sandal-
clad feet were treading in water and mud. He had never experienced that before and was curious to
find its source. As he turned a corner he found one of the gutters was blocked with debris, forming
a dam that had burst its banks and caused the water to flood onto the streets.

We spent most of the session talking about the gutter and what needed to be done to clear out
the blockage. We spoke about who was responsible for taking the action to do so. We talked about
what differences there would be when the energy started to flow again and could be channeled in
the proper directions. In discussing a blocked gutter we did not mention a rejecting guru. We simply
engaged in a metaphoric conversation that matched the problem of the client and helped develop the
resources and course of action necessary for him to move on.

The story of this case and the metaphor Jeff brought into therapy have been woven into a teaching tale similar but not identical to that used collaboratively with Jeff. It is Story 3, "Owning Responsibility."

The second level of fit is for the teller. There is no point in attempting to tell a story in which
you cannot be involved or with which you cannot relate. This is where it is helpful to draw on your
experiences as a person and therapist rather than rely on other people's tales in a script-like manner.
I love *The Teaching Tales of Milton H. Erickson* (Rosen, 1982) for it is a pleasant bedside book that provides me with ideas and stimulates recollections of my own experiences, but they are not *my* stories.
I cannot tell, nor would I try to tell, the stories Erickson told, and he could not have told my stories
in the way I do. As mentioned in point 2, effective storytelling needs to include your enthusiasm, reality, and experience—and the best way to ensure it does is for it to be *your* story.

5. Make the story real.

The more real the story is for you, the more real it is going to be for the listener. Do not focus so
much on the words, at least initially. At this point the language is not as important as the tone, the
mood, and the feeling. To create these, use your senses, envisaging and communicating to your listener the subtleties of light, color, shades, and shapes that help define and enhance awareness of the
visual sense. Describe the sounds and all the varieties of auditory experience. Be aware of the smells,
aromas, and fragrances that are part of the tale. Experience and talk about the tactile sensations. Include not only what the characters of the story touch, but how they are *touched* by the breath of a

breeze or the warmth of the sun. Where appropriate, bring into the story sensations of taste, for all of these senses add to its reality, aiding your visualization of the story and, consequently, your ability to communicate those images that best involve your listener.

During my supervision of a colleague, he got married and went with his wife on their honeymoon to Bali. When he returned he told me a story, saying, "One day we were out walking. We heard a gamelan orchestra. We walked to it, listened for a while, and had a beautiful time."

I asked him to close his eyes for a while to visualize the experience, then tell me the story again, including the sense-awareness that he visualized.

"One day we were out walking," he began. "The sky was clear blue and warm. We were strolling along beside a green rice paddy when we heard the hollow bamboo sounds of a gamelan orchestra. We followed the music until we came to an open-sided hut where the orchestra was playing. The people were dressed in traditional clothes. One gestured for us to come inside. We sat down and listened to the orchestra. It was a beautiful experience."

I asked him to visualize the scene once more, paying closer attention to his senses. This time he was to include not only the awareness of his senses, but the emotions or feelings that he was experiencing.

He retold the tale like this: "My wife and I were out walking. We were holding hands, feeling close and enjoying the clear blue, tropical sky. As we strolled along beside a rice paddy we noticed the gentle breeze wafting the lush, green stalks almost as though waves were washing over the fields. We felt its gentle coolness on our skin while experiencing the inner warmth of our love for each other. It felt like heaven. It was hard to imagine life could get any better. Then, simultaneously, we heard the hollow, melodic sounds of a gamelan orchestra riding the waves of air that drifted across the fields. We were both enjoying the tempting tastes of the music so much that we decided we wanted to discover more. Like children following the Pied Piper, we set off to explore what might be happening.

"Behind the rice fields was a tall wall of dark green jungle. Though we could not see them, we could hear monkeys chattering away, high in the branches. The gentle breath of the breeze through the rice paddies, the chatter of the monkeys in the jungle, and the sounds of bamboo instruments blended into a natural symphony.

"In a carved, open-sided hut sat the gamelan orchestra. The wooden instruments were intricately carved and brightly painted. The players were dressed in matching sarongs, loose, white shirts and glistening, sequined head bands. First one, and then several people, welcomed us warmly, treating us like honored guests. We sat cross-legged on a grass mat that had the smell of a fresh-mown lawn. The plunking music was rhythmic and hypnotic; it lulled us into a sense of well-being. Entranced, we sat through the whole performance. We reluctantly left the warm and welcoming environment when the orchestra finished playing. What started out as a casual stroll turned into a wonderful experience."

The three stories that he told all had the same theme: He and his wife had walked across a rice field and listened to an orchestra. But each story was very different. In fact, you may ask yourself which seemed the most real? Which engaged you the most? Which most held your attention? With which did you most identify? The last account of the story was very different from the first. Instead of just giving the *facts* of the story, it communicated much more about the *experience* of the story. By visualizing and reexperiencing it, my colleague allowed me, as the listener, to participate more meaningfully in his experience.

EXERCISE 2.5

- Tell a story of something that has happened recently to you, to a friend, or to a family member. Concentrate on the experience rather than thinking about the "correct" words.
- Retell the same story but bring in the senses and your experiences of them.
- Then tell it for a third time. Expand on it, including the emotions or feelings that describe how you felt.
- Observe the response from your listener. Observe the differences in his or her attention to each of the three stories that you told.

6. Make an outline of the story.

Do not write it out verbatim. The emphasis now is on organizing the idea, theme, or structure of your story.

There are three steps to making a story outline. First, begin at the end, for this is the way most stories we tell actually happen. A story becomes a story because of its ending. For example, one weekend we visited a coastal town. We dined at a restaurant and as we left, two men from the adjoining motel waved us to stop, asking for a lift into town. They were a little merry from a drink or two, and as they got into the backseat, I noticed they did not buckle their seat belts, thus violating the law. Thinking they were adults capable of making their own choices, and because we only had a short distance to travel, I did not point it out to them, though it was probably my legal responsibility as the driver. As we drove one asked, "How fast can this car go?" I hedged in answering, pointing out the speed limit, but he insisted on knowing how fast I had pushed the car. Male pride got the better of me and I confessed to pushing the speedometer over 100 miles per hour on an open country road once just to see what it would do. This episode might not have been memorable enough to repeat were it not for the next sentence from my passenger. "I'm interested in how fast cars go," he said. "You see, we're cops." I later discovered they were in town to put on a road safety display at the local fair!

Because stories naturally start at the end, it is helpful to structure them backward. Look for the message you want to communicate or the point you want to make and use that ending as the beginning of your outline. The first question in preparing a story should ask about the finish or punch line: "What is the outcome? What is the moral? What is the point I wish to communicate?" In this way it is like planning a vacation. It is first helpful to have a clear idea of the destination. Once you know where you want to go, you can look at the challenges you may meet or the obstacles you need to overcome to get there: for example, negotiating with the boss for time off, saving up the money, making the relevant booking, and packing the clothes you need to take with you. This is the second stage, the middle of the story. Once you've sketched out these stages, you can go back to the beginning—the third stage.

In planning these aspects of your story, do not write it out as a script. Do not memorize it and do not feel confined by it. Telling a story is not like reciting a Shakespearean play where the words

EXERCISE 2.6

- Make an outline of a story that you would like to tell.
- First make a note of the desired outcome or ending to the story.
- Second, note the obstacles that the character needs to overcome or the challenges he or she encounters before reaching the goal.
- Third, outline the steps or processes that the character needs to go through to reach the end and the resources or skills that he or she needs to acquire along the way.

are permanently recorded in history and repeated identically, century after century, by each subsequent actor. An outline allows you to use your own spontaneous phraseology and to incorporate the language and gestures of your listener into the story.

7. Rehearse the story in your mind. Tell it to yourself. Play with it. Alter it. Vary it. Adapt it.

Most of the stories recorded in Part 3 of this book are very different from how I originally told them. Of those that come from sources other than my own experiences or case examples, all are different from how I originally heard them. They are still in a process of evolution. The printed pages of this book have captured them at one particular moment of their telling. If I had been writing this two years ago, or two years hence, the tales would probably be very different. The next client to hear any one of these story ideas will hear it differently. The story will change (a) in accord with the needs and goals of the client, and (b) with me. As I rehearse or retell any story it will evolve, change, adapt, and alter.

At high school our debating master encouraged us to rehearse in preparation for debates. "Stand in front of a mirror," he would say. "Watch yourself, listen to yourself, observe your gestures and mannerisms, think about how your audience will respond, hear the things that you say, listen to what you

EXERCISE 2.7

- Find a new story that you enjoy. There may be one (or hopefully more) that you like in this book. It may be a story from your own experience or possibly one that somebody has told you.
- Rehearse the story in your mind. Speak it out loud if it's helpful. Choose a quiet time when you have a moment to yourself, such as driving to and from work or taking a walk by yourself.
- In rehearsing it, attempt to incorporate the things that you have acquired in the preceding steps. Bring in your senses, incorporate the emotions, take the story from the problem that needs to be addressed to the development of skills and resources necessary for a successful conclusion.

are telling that is too much, hear the things that need to be expanded or clarified." I still follow his advice though I do not stand in front of a mirror these days. If I have a conference presentation coming up, or a talk-back radio program on which I am to appear, I will rehearse in my mind the things I may want to communicate as I am driving to and from work. In those moments of commuting, I may also pick up on a new story that I have heard and plan how it may be adapted into a therapeutic context, particularly if it is relevant for any current clients. The principle behind this is simple: The more familiar you are with any material, the easier it is to be flexible, spontaneous, and adaptive in using that material.

8. Tell the story to someone else.

The object of this guideline is to gain practice in storytelling with a listener. Do not ask for criticism of your story, although helpful feedback about your style of narration and how it did or did not engage the listener may be useful. The most important objectives are simply to have a listener, to practice your storytelling skills, and to observe the impact on your listener. Follow the same procedures as in the last step of rehearsing it to yourself, but this time do it with an audience, even if only one.

EXERCISE 2.8

- Ask someone to be a listener. If this is a social or fun story, use a friend or family member. If it is a story that you want to use metaphorically in therapy, it may be helpful to invite a colleague to be a listener or to tell it in supervision.
- Do not ask for criticism of the story or your telling of it. It may, however, be helpful to get feedback from the listener so as to learn what his or her experience was of hearing the story.

---

9. Observe your listener.

Listen to their verbal feedback. "Yes, I know what you mean" is the sort of comment that gives you information about how the story is connecting at some level for the listener. If this happens, it may be worth developing the story along the lines that you are going.

"No, that's not the way I feel" is a clear indication that your story is not matching the experience of your listener and may need to be adapted or changed. Ask yourself or your listener how you may adapt the story to make it more relevant or contextual. Remember that research (such as Martin, Cummings, & Hallberg, 1992). shows that developing metaphors collaboratively with clients gives them more therapeutic impact and makes them more memorable.

Watch for your listener's nonverbal feedback as well. A person engaged in the listening process often appears to be entranced. He or she displays phenomena similar to what they may experience in hypnosis. The gaze is likely to be one of fixed, unbroken attention on the storyteller. Respiration is likely to match the emotion of the tale or to have slowed. His or her body is probably still and immobile. The listener is likely to fidget less and display less movement than before the tale began.

EXERCISE 2.9

- Observe your listener. After all, the story is for your listener. His or her response is what is important.
- Make a mental note of your listener's behavior, his or her posture, level of attention, rate of respiration, and amount of muscular activity.
- What does this observation tell you? What feedback does it give you about the content of your story or the way it is being told?
- If appropriate, adjust the content of the story or the style of your telling. Observe what difference this makes for your listener.

Conversely, if a person is not absorbed in the storytelling process, his or her attention wanders, and so does the gaze. He or she is likely to be more restless or fidgety. The same focus of attention is not present. Such nonverbal feedback poses several questions for the storyteller. Am I telling too much? Am I not communicating enough? Does the story need more or less involvement of senses and emotions? What is most relevant for my listener? What needs to be expanded and what needs to be deleted?

In offering you 101 written stories, I do not have the benefits of receiving those verbal and nonverbal cues as to how relevant or irrelevant my stories are. I cannot observe your words, facial expressions, or body language. Without this feedback I cannot develop the stories collaboratively with you and, consequently, some stories may strike an accord, and some may not. Some may seem poignant and some meaningless. These problems can be avoided by telling oral tales in a person-to-person context and astutely observing the messages from your listener.

As you work through these steps of effective storytelling, your skills will develop and your own style will evolve. Learning to tell stories effectively is like any other learning process. When you first learn to drive a car, you need to focus on many things such as depressing pedals, putting on turn signals, and turning the steering wheel. There is an art and skill of coordinating the different combination of activities between the arms and legs, but once these skills are acquired, most drivers find that they can drive successfully while thinking about something else all together. A person may successfully drive from home to work without consciously paying a lot of attention to how he or she drives the car, thinking instead about work, home, or another topic altogether.

As you become more comfortable and skilled in telling stories, it becomes easier to do other activities at the same time. Soon you will be able to observe your client, ask questions about the processes that are going on for your listener, and adapt the story to the needs of the situation, while still telling an interesting and meaningful tale.

10. Be flexible.

There is no correct way to tell a story. There are guidelines, but they are just guidelines. For every listener or client, the tale needs to be different and the style of telling it needs to be different, because no listener or client is the same.

In addition, each storyteller is different, and the circumstances in which the story is told vary. As

EXERCISE 2.10

- Let your stories evolve. Do not be confined or restricted to them. Do not feel that they need to be repeated the same way each time. Because it worked once for one client does not mean that it will work again for another client.
- Take a theme or story line. Tell it to different people. Tell it in different ways, observe, and adapt it to your different listeners.

a result, every telling of a story needs to be flexible and adaptive. Only by being so can it maximize the power of the story to communicate and cause change.

Never think of a story as finished. Let it evolve for you and your client over time. Allow yourself to be surprised at how different a story that you told to one client last week is from a story you told to another client this week. Keep experimenting so that you allow the opportunity to see what works best for you and your client at that particular time.

In Chapter 1 I described the case of Phillipa. It illustrates how a story may evolve in a reciprocal way with the teller listening to the feedback of the listener and incorporating that information into the story. "Soaring To New Heights," Story 11, is not the same as the story that Phillipa and I shared. If and when I tell it to another client it will alter and adapt again. The truth is that when communicating in metaphors the story is never ending.

SIX GUIDELINES FOR THE STORYTELLER'S VOICE

The storyteller's voice is his or her primary professional tool, akin to what a stethoscope is to a physician or a wrench to a plumber. The more we learn to use it effectively and maximize its power, the more effective we will be as agents of change.

There are skills and techniques that can enhance our ability to narrate a tale and engage the listener. But techniques are not the whole story. Again, there is an art to using your voice effectively. Part of that art is in being natural, or in using the skills you already have and experimenting with the following suggestions to develop them further. In telling a therapeutic tale to a client it is important to bring those qualities of yourself and your experience into that situation. As mentioned earlier, use both your integrity and enthusiasm in the narration. Trying to act a role, memorize a script, or put just the right intonation into an expression because a book told you to do so—much as an actor may do with the words of a play—is not necessarily the base for a good therapeutic relationship.

Having said that, there are some pointers that are worth bearing in mind to help increase the effectiveness of communication via stories.

1. Vary your storytelling style.

Several variables can affect the style of our speech. The first variable is the type of activity in the story or theme of our communication. If, for example, the matter is thoughtful or ponderous, our speech

> ## EXERCISE 2.11
>
> - Observe your own different styles of talking and how the content, language, and sound of your speech varies in different circumstances.
> - When telling a story, work at using the relevant talk style. If the story involves a worker or boss relationship, use the style of speech that you would in a similar circumstance.

may be slow, considered, and deliberate. If we are reading from a book or script, our speech may be rhythmic and repetitive, lacking emphasis and intonation. If we have memorized and are reciting either a hypnotic script or a metaphoric story, our speech will reflect that activity.

In spontaneous speech we are more likely to put in the natural emphases and intonations that come with the emotion or the experience of what we are relating. These different styles communicate something to the listener about our involvement (and consequently their involvement) in the subject matter and processes of the story.

Second, the style of our speech can be influenced by our emotions. We speak differently when we are expressing feelings of affection than we do when we are expressing feelings of anger. If we are relaxed our speech tends to be slow, reflecting our emotional state of tranquility. Conversely, if we are anxious our speech can be rapid, perhaps punctuated by the short, shallowness of our breathing. A happy feeling brings with it light, joyful speech. Depression has a sound of sadness that is flat and monotonic. The point is that emotions affect the style of speech, and listeners can detect or make interpretations about the underlying emotions.

Third, our listeners can influence our style of speech. Does your partner know almost as soon as you answer the phone whether you are talking to a man or woman, an adult or child, a friend or sales person? We are likely to talk differently to our boss than to our lover. We address a shop attendant differently than our physician. Both the style and content of our speech vary when we are communicating with persons of our gender or another gender. There is a difference in the way we speak at a professional meeting with colleagues and the way we talk at a social outing with a group of friends.

Know the variety of speech styles you use and explore how they may help maximize the communication of therapeutic messages through metaphors.

2. Choose your rate of utterance.

The rate at which we speak changes with circumstances and emotions. In telling stories you should adjust the rate of utterance to reflect the content on the story. If, for example, the story is a metaphor designed to enhance relaxation or facilitate a hypnotic induction, then the rate of utterance is most effective if it paces the client and begins to lead into slower and more tranquil experiences. The rate of speech may start at a normal speed of communication and gradually slow with the deepening of tranquility experienced by the client and expressed by the story. When a story is focusing on a problem of anxiety or agitation, the rate of utterance may be quicker and more hurried to engage the

EXERCISE 2.12

- Observe the responses of your listener.
- Match the rate of your speech to the emotional and physical state of your listener.
- When you are pacing the story comfortably with your listener, use the rate of utterance to start to guide your listener toward the desired state.

client in experiences of the problem before slowing the rate to help engage them in the experiences of the outcome.

3. Modulate your intonation.

Intonation refers to the tone of voice used and emphasis placed on a word or letter. Intonation distinguishes a statement from a question. It may be used to put accent or weight on a particular word. This adjustment or variation of tone is perhaps more common in languages other than English.

Chinese has four different tones. When I was learning that language prior to traveling in China, I found it difficult to get the right intonations in the right places. Some years later when learning Vietnamese, I found the task even harder as there are six different intonations that can apply to each letter, at times giving several intonations to the one word. A simple word like *ma,* depending upon the intonation, can mean phantom, mother, rice, seedling, tomb or horse. A slight variation and you could embarrassingly be calling your mother a tomb, or horse. *Ga* with similar variations can mean objects as divergent as a railway station or a chicken. Your intonation can pose problems when seeking directions or ordering a meal!

English does not have the same subtlety of intonation but we do nonetheless modulate language by altering the amplitude of our speech, its frequency, or its tone to put greater emphasis or meaning on an expression. Using intonations thoughtfully can enhance the effectiveness of our communication.

4. Adjust the volume of voice.

Volume of voice refers to loudness or softness of voice. Whispering is seen as a way of communicating something private and secretive. Speaking in soft tones to a lover is intimate. Communicating quietly tends to trigger a listener's acuity. Speaking loudly, as in raising one's voice, tends to express

EXERCISE 2.13

- Audiotape yourself telling a story, whether to a friend or to a client.
- Listen to the different characteristics of the storyteller's voice.
- Define the characteristics and observe how you use them in telling the story.

anger or authority. Loud speech or noise is something that people find uncomfortable and want to avoid. If the volume of our speech is too high a listener literally may want to switch off.

Listen to the way the volume of your voice communicates the message of your story. Observe whether it is eliciting an appropriate listening response from your client.

5. Incorporate affective involvement.

In the steps for effective storytelling, we discussed the value of bringing in the emotion of the story. I have already given an example in Guideline 5 of how incorporating affective involvement altered the story of a supervisee who had recently honeymooned in Bali. While it is important to include the emotion in the *content* of the story, it is also important that the emotion be included in the story-teller's voice. If the story is set in summer, allow yourself to feel the heat and let your voice express it. If you are describing an activity that you really loved or felt passionate about doing, bring the passion into your voice. If your story begins with stress and arousal, experiencing the arousal yourself reflects in your voice. As you lead the content of the tale into a state of tranquility, the listener hears and experiences it more if you are also experiencing and expressing it.

EXERCISE 2.14

- Bring the five senses into your story. They will help you feel it. Let your voice reflect the experience of those senses.
- Include your emotions, experience the mood or feeling of the story, then let your voice reflect it.
- Listen to your story on audiotape. Assess how involved you sound in the story.

6. Align your affect with the story's affect.

Aligning affect means that the emotion expressed is the emotion that is most consistent with the story. A person may be emotionally involved in telling a story, but his or her emotion may not be congruent with that story.

EXERCISE 2.15

- Listen to an audiotape of yourself telling a story or several stories.
- Take particular notice of your affective involvement.
- Assess how appropriate and how aligned that emotion is.
- If your emotion is not aligned (for example, if you are telling a relaxing story but can hear tension in your voice), ask what you may do to help align your emotion more effectively with the feeling of the story.

Therapists often witness examples of misalignment of emotions. For instance, a person in marital therapy who clenches his or her fists, raises his or her voice and says, "How many times do I have to tell you, I don't want to argue?" has body language and emotions that are incongruent with his or her spoken words.

Let me illustrate it another way. Clench your jaws, clamp your teeth tightly together, tense the muscles around your mouth, and try to say, "I love you." With such tension it becomes very difficult, if not impossible, to express the relaxed emotional intimacy of a message of love.

In any communication people see the body language and read the affect long before they hear the words. In fact, if the emotion is strong, a person may miss the words altogether—one of the core problems at the basis of many relationship difficulties. So, in telling stories we need to be sure that we not only have affective involvement in the story, but that the involvement is appropriate, and the tone aligns with the story content.

CHAPTER 3

Stories in Therapy

Once you know the guidelines for effective storytelling and the skills of the storyteller's voice, you can begin to address how best to create and employ metaphoric stories to facilitate the attainment of a therapeutic goal. The survival of our species and the enjoyment of our individual lives depend on our adaptability to experience. Experience is what facilitates learning, broadens our understanding, and deepens our knowledge.

One person can share his or her learning experiences with another through storytelling. This process short-circuits the laborious and long-term activity of each individual having to learn something anew. Those who have had the experience are able to communicate to others, through their stories, how to face a similar challenge, what tools are needed to deal with the situation, and how they can enjoy the rewards of achievement.

When my father told tales about applying for his first job as a farmhand after migrating to Australia at seventeen years of age, he was doing more than just reliving a memory. The farmer wanted to check my father's honesty and willingness to work so he told him to stand out in the sun all day opening and closing a gate. Dad thought, "If he's prepared to part with his money for such a menial task, I'm prepared to receive it," and stood swinging the gate for a whole day. In relating the tale he was teaching me something about developing work ethics, applying yourself, getting what you want, and having a positive attitude. Likewise, when I share with my grandson tales of adventure, such as climbing Africa's Mt Kilimanjaro, trekking the mountainous jungles of Irian Jaya, or exploring the icy continent of Antarctica, I am giving him experiences about setting goals, facing challenges, dealing with the unexpected, and having fun.

Stories—and metaphors—are thus an efficient and meaningful method for communicating about experience and sharing what we have learned with others to help make their journey easier and more enjoyable. A therapeutic metaphor is a story designed to help clients reach their goals in the most effective and efficient way. It is about filling the experiential gap between what is and what can be.

Every culture throughout history has used stories to communicate values, morals, and standards. Buddha, Jesus, Muhammad, and Lao-tzu did not lecture, but told stories. They did not quote facts, statistics, or evidence-based data, but instead related tales of life. Instead of teaching the rhythmic rote learning of times tables, Lord's prayers, or chants, they offered parables that opened the range of experiences and interpretations available to their followers.

Their stories have lived on for as long as two and a half thousand years, are still retold by their followers, and the principles of their tales may be found in some of the metaphors throughout this book. Many examples of timeless, classic tales, such as Aesop's fables are still valued for the simple and profound wisdom they impart fifteen centuries after first being penned.

What is surprising is that teaching tales took so long to be recognized for their usefulness in modern-day psychotherapy and counseling, while, what is not surprising, is the popularity with which they have been incorporated. Carl Jung spoke of symbols rather than metaphors, but his work, like stories that bridge the history of humanity and cross the bounds of culture, forms links between the ancient Eastern masters and the psychological thinking of his day. His definition of the symbolic comes close to the essential elements of the way therapeutic metaphor is often defined.

A word or an image is symbolic when it implies something more than its obvious and immediate meaning. It has a wider "unconscious" aspect that is never precisely defined or fully explained. Nor can one hope to define or explain it. As the mind explores the symbol, it is led to ideas that lie beyond the grasp of reason. (Jung, 1964, pp. 20–21)

STORIES, TALES, ANECDOTES, AND METAPHORS

So far I have used terms like stories, tales, and metaphors without any clear definition of what they all have in common and how they differ. Usually they refer to the oral, but sometimes written, communication that takes place between one person and another. They may be drawn from one's experience, grounded in a perception of reality, or created out of the richness of one's imagination. Whether entertaining or educating, all make a point, carry a message, or express a moral.

Differences do exist among these terms. *Stories* are the accounts that we give of an event or series of events such as telling our partner or family about a humorous or frustrating event that occurred in the workplace. Stories are the framework we use to relate what we did on vacation, over the weekend, or out for the evening.

Stories describe fictitious as well as actual events and may be in the form of a legend, myth, anecdote, novel, or news item. Long or short, they may be recounted orally or in writing. Even the shortest synopsis of an event and the longest novel share similar characteristics. There is a beginning, designed to capture the attention of the listener or reader. From there the tale weaves its way through a descriptive relation of events, either elaborately, as in a novel, or succinctly, as in a poem. Eventually the story reaches a conclusion that is usually designed to entertain, instruct, or educate.

Tales mostly follow the same format as a story and, though they may be true, are more often fictitious. We tend to associate tales with an imaginative theme, and they are often interpreted as untruths. We may say things like, "don't tell tales," or, "that's just a tale," as though what is being communicated is questionable, or perhaps even malicious.

Tales provide a format that allows us a relatively free rein on our imagination and creativity. They tell stories that break the boundaries of reality, defy the laws of logic, and transport us into a land where the sky can be green, the trees purple, and the people perfect. They can fly us into the rule-bending realms of science fiction or send us into improbable lands, such as those in *Alice in Wonderland* or *Gulliver's Travels.*

The word *anecdote* has its origins in the Greek *anekdota,* which literally means "things unpublished." It is an account not endorsed by the rigors of the scientific community and has not gone through the review process of a journal article. It is both personal and experiential. It has an essence of subjectivity, relating the narrative of an amusing or interesting incident.

A *metaphor* is yet another communication form in the story genre. A metaphor takes an expression from one field of experience and uses it to say something about another field of experience. It implies a comparison between things that are not literally alike and, as such, can be used in the application of a description, phrase, or story about an object or action to which it bears an imaginative, but not literal, resemblance. It is this imaginative or symbolic association that gives metaphors their literary and therapeutic potency.

Metaphors in therapy are designed to be a form of indirect, imaginative, and implied communication with clients about experiences, processes, or outcome that may help them solve their literal problems. Therapeutic metaphors may include stories, tales, anecdotes, jokes, proverbs, analogies, or other communications. What distinguishes them from other tales, stories, or anecdotes is the combination of (a) their purposefully designed, symbolic communication and (b) their specific healing or therapeutic intention.

In this book I use most terms synonymously. I use the words *metaphor* or *therapeutic story,* though, to emphasize that a particular story is not just a casual, anecdotal account nor an inconsequential tale such as we may relate at a party. By metaphor or therapeutic tale I refer specifically to a deliberately crafted story that has a clear, rational, and ethical therapeutic goal. It is, in other words, a tale that is based on our long human history of storytelling, that is grounded in the science of effective communication, that has specific therapeutic relevance to the needs of the client, and that is told with the art of good storytelling.

METAPHORS IN THERAPY

Milton Erickson originated the use of systematic, structured, and intentional metaphor stories for therapeutic gain. His work has already been extensively documented by others such as Rosen (1982), Rossi, Ryan, & Sharp (1984), and Zeig,(1980). Stephen and Carol Lankton have also written extensively about the complex yet powerful, multiple embedded metaphor (Lankton & Lankton, 1983, 1986, 1989). They, like Erickson, have strongly emphasized the importance of listening to clients, hearing their language, and incorporating their experiences into therapy. On this basis, the therapist usually constructs appropriate metaphors to facilitate the desired change. Mills and Crowley (1986) have made the very natural, yet creative, adaptation of using stories in the context of childhood therapy, whereas Kopp (1995) has focused on using those metaphors generated by the client.

Kopp illustrates that metaphors do not just come from teachers and that all of us picture our world metaphorically. Individuals, families, social groups, cultures, and indeed the whole of humanity use stories to explain their reality, give meaning to life, and provide standards by which we live. Some metaphors are helpful and constructive. To think in a theatrical metaphor—that life is not a rehearsal—may help a person enjoy each moment to its fullest. Conversely, some metaphors are not constructive and do not facilitate a functional perspective of life. To think the forces of the universe are against me may lead to experiences of depression or paranoia. What this means from a therapeutic perspective is that helping clients alter a dysfunctional metaphor alters the way they construct their experience and, consequently, modifies the experience itself.

Pat was a middle-aged woman who was referred by her physician because of insomnia that began after she had been admitted to the hospital for minor surgery a year earlier. She had since received counseling and taken medication without benefit.

Pat was born in China and raised by a Chinese family in Malaysia before moving to the West in her early adult life. She said that, according to Chinese folklore, when a person goes to sleep the soul leaves the body. If the person is awakened during sleep, especially if away from the home to which the soul is familiar with returning, the person must be addressed by name for the soul to reunite with the body. If this reunion of body and soul does not happen properly then problems including sleeplessness occur.

In the hospital, she believed that she must have been awakened from the anesthetic without anyone's speaking her name, and thus her soul had not fully returned. She believed the only way to cure her insomnia was to undergo again anesthesia in the same operating room and be awakened by a staff member calling her by name.

To me, her solution seemed too complex—and maybe even embarrassing—to organize. My Western skepticism regarding her beliefs also inhibited me from taking her suggestion seriously. Instead I taught her self-hypnosis and applied it unsuccessfully to improve her sleep pattern.

Again Pat reiterated what she saw as the cause of her insomnia and the necessary steps for resolution. This time I listened more attentively to my client's metaphor. Using hypnosis I guided her through the steps of going to the hospital, being anaesthetized, and being awakened by the nurse using her Chinese name, as she said her soul was most familiar with this name. Smugly confident that I had learned my lesson about listening to the client, I was dismayed when her sleep patterns remained unimproved.

A third time Pat told me she knew the answer. "I need to go back to the hospital, be put to sleep, and be awakened by name in the theatre," she said. "That's where my soul left my body; that's where it needs to be reunited."

I spoke to Chinese friends and also her physician, who was Chinese. None of them were aware of the particular belief that she held, but what mattered was that her metaphor held the explanation and the solution. Ultimately, her story was heard and we arranged with the hospital for her to return to the operating room.

When I arrived Pat was already in bed in a surgical gown. I asked her to initiate the self-hypnosis with which she was now familiar and she was wheeled into the operating room. I then spoke to her by her Chinese name and invited her to come out of the hypnosis. She was wheeled into the recovery room where I again addressed her by name and asked that she only open her eyes when she had gained everything she wanted from the experience. She brought her attention back to the room, smiling with peace and contentment. When I saw her a week later, she reported having slept successfully every night since her visit back to the hospital. At a six-month follow-up she had maintained a stable sleep pattern.

Fortunately listening to client-generated metaphors does not usually lead one into such elaborate procedures for attaining an outcome. Yet, Pat reminded me of the need to listen carefully to the self-generated stories clients may have for their symptoms and possible solutions. She also reminded me not to assume that my professional, scientific, university-degreed metaphor was any more valid than hers.

WHY TELL METAPHORS?

There are many advantages for communicating metaphorically in therapy. Because metaphors quickly and effectively tap into a long historical means of communication, they are, in a sense, *atheoretical*. Before we had theories, our forebearers would sit around the campfire in the evening roasting the catch of the day and talk about their experiences. In the same way, we reconnect with others around the dinner table or water cooler at work. These communications bring us together, share the learning of our experiences, and confirm the connections of our reunion. Given this historically grounded base, we can use metaphors in therapy regardless of the particular orientation or model from which we operate.

Just as stories help us reconnect, they also help us make new connections and form new relationships. Storytelling is not just about the verbal *content* of the tale. More importantly, it is about the connection *processes* that unify existing bonds and help create new interactions.

In addition to enhancing relationships, both teacher and pupil often prefer stories as a teaching mode. Stories relate information about experience more than about fact, and it is primarily through experience that we learn. What makes stories such a wonderful teaching medium is that we do not need to have the experience ourselves to be able to learn from it. Stories told by our parents about being burned by a fire, bitten by a snake, or attacked by a stranger are sufficient for us to learn that such things are dangerous. We know to avoid them through the tales we are told about them and thus do not need to personally suffer the pain for ourselves.

The learning gained from personal experiences is essential for survival and maturation, but we may be able to short-circuit the pitfalls and enhance the pleasures by listening to the stories we hear. The childhood stories that my mother read at my bedside were not simply about entertainment or hastening youthful slumber. They taught me about being human, about coping with adversity, and about seeing humor. The stories that passed around as we spent summer vacations camped at the beachside with relatives taught me about family relationships and values. Similarly, metaphors can provide the means to teach our clients the necessary abilities to learn from a problem and enhance the quality of their lives.

Evidenced-based research confirms the experiential aspects of metaphors and metaphor telling that communicate therapeutic values. As this book is about the art of storytelling, the sources for finding metaphor ideas, and the processes for structuring effective therapeutic tales, it is not within its scope to provide a comprehensive, critical review of the literature. It is essential, nonetheless, that any therapeutic interventions we use have a sound basis of empirical support and are cognizant of both

FIGURE 3.1   A GUIDE TO FURTHER READING ON METAPHORS

(a) **Metaphors as a language form.** (Bettelheim, 1976; Black, 1962; Haskell, 1987; Honeck & Hoffman, 1980; Lakoff & Johnson, 1980; Ortony, 1979; Radman, 1995; Sommer & Weiss, 1996; Sternberg, 1990; Turbayne, 1991; White, 1996)

(b) **Research data about metaphors.** (Angus & Rennie, 1988, 1989; Donnelly & Dumas, 1997; Evans, 1988; Harris, Lakey, & Marselek, 1980; Kingsbury, 1994; Kohen & Wynne, 1997; Martin, Cummings, & Hallberg, 1992)

(c) **Variety and types of metaphor therapy.** (Burns, 1998; Hammond, 1990; Hersley & Hersley, 1998; Kopp, 1995; Lankton & Lankton, 1983, 1986, 1989)

(d) **Sources of metaphor stories.** (Barker, 1985; Close, 1998; Groth-Marnat, 1992; Lankton & Lankton, 1986; Mills & Crowley, 1986; Rosen, 1982)

(e) **Some of the therapeutic models in which metaphors have been applied:**
cognitive therapy (Gonclaves & Craine, 1990; Kopp & Craw, 1998; Muran & DiGiuseppi, 1990)
counseling (Matthews & Dardeck, 1985)
couples therapy (Hoffman, 1983)
ecopsychology (Burns, 1998)
education (Kohen & Wynne, 1997)
Ericksonian psychotherapy (Rosen, 1982; Zeig, 1980; Zeig & Gilligan, 1990)
family therapy (Combs & Freedman, 1991; Dolan, 1986; Lankton & Lankton, 1986)
hypnotherapy (Hammond, 1990; Kuttner, 1988; Lankton & Lankton, 1983; Stevens-Guille & Boersma, 1992)
Jungian psychotherapy (Kopp, 1995; Siegelman, 1990)
psychoanalytic psychotherapy (Bettelheim, 1984; Kopp, 1995)
solution-focused therapy (McNeilly, 2000; O'Hanlon, 1986)
strategic therapy (Haley, 1973)
systems thinking (Duhl, 1983)
transactional analysis (Campos, 1972)

(f) **Clinical populations and problems to which metaphors have been applied include, but are not limited to:**
asthma education (Kohen & Wynne, 1997)
bulimerexia (Thiessen, 1983)
cancer (Chelf, Dreschler, Hillman, & Durazo-Arvisu, 2000; Remen, 1996)
children (Ingal, 1997; Sommers-Flanagan & Sommers-Flanagan, 1996)
family relationships (Combs & Freedman, 1990; Dolan, 1983; Hoffman, 1983)
pain-reduction (Kuttner, 1988)
post trauma stress disorders (Burns, 1998; Kopp, 1995)
somatic complaints (O'Hanlon, 1986)
traumatic memories (Grove & Panzer, 1989; Kopp, 1995).

the art and the science of that approach. To that end I have included a detailed bibliography in Part 4 of further reading and information across the spectrum of literature on metaphors. As a guide for your continuing exploration of metaphors as a language form, means of communication, subject of research, and therapeutic tool, a list of suggested readings is given in Figure 3.1.

With a growing interest in postmodern thinking and alternate ways of learning, the world of science has been rediscovering the value of traditional stories in codifying experiences, sharing knowledge, and communicating wisdom. There are many resources where such stories can be found, including cultures, religions, and traditions different from our own. Groth-Marnat (1992) has compared metaphors from "archaic cultures," biblical parables, Sufi stories, Zen teachings, and fairytales. He claims, "Since the use of metaphoric stories as a means of creating change seems to occur in most cultures throughout history (and pre-history), there must be some advantage to them" (p. 7). He encourages practitioners of therapy to search such traditional stories for their wealth of therapeutic content and variety of change strategies.

My aim in this book is to illustrate examples of those older traditions and current conceptualizations. I have included and developed story ideas from Tibet, Vietnam, East Africa, China, the Middle East, Nepal, North America, and other areas. There are tales that have originated from Sufism, Buddhism, Christianity, Zen, and Judaism. Some are created from client vignettes or the evidence-based data of psychological research, whereas others originate from everyday life experiences. In doing this, I hope to illustrate ways you can effectively synthesize these various sources into practical and effective therapeutic interventions.

Some of the stories that follow may resonate for you, strike a chord of personal understanding, or highlight a useful message, whereas some may seem pointless or even evoke a rejection. This is a risk when stories are written for a generic market and not told to an individual at a personal level with particular attention to that person's unique requirements in the therapeutic process. You should note these reactions in yourself for they are the sort of responses you may expect from your clients.

Even if you do not "like" a particular story, think about how it may be heard and perceived by a client. Put yourself in the position of your client and try to assess whether it may have appeal, meaning, or relevance for someone distressed, anxious, depressed, or struggling to come to grips with a certain issue. As each of these stories is designed with a particular therapeutic outcome in mind, that goal, and the problem the story addresses, may not be applicable for you as a therapist but may hold value or merit for one of your clients. While reading them, be aware of the necessity of matching your therapeutic tales to the problems presented by your clients, the resources they need to develop, and the outcome they seek to achieve. That way your stories will hold the most personal relevance and the greatest potential for change.

STORIES IN THERAPY

PART TWO

Healing Stories

CHAPTER 4

Enhancing Empowerment

As feelings of powerlessness, helplessness, and lack of control have been identified as major features of a number of psychological disorders, enhancing empowerment is often a primary and major therapeutic intervention in any form of psychotherapy. For example, feelings of helplessness and hopelessness can be major characteristics, if not causes, of depression. People often suffer with anxiety or phobias when they do not have control, or perceived control, over events in their lives. Power struggles can be a basic cause of relationship difficulties when couples are fighting for individual power rather than seeking to discover how they can mutually empower the relationship. Most forms of substance abuse involve a client's perception that the drug, alcohol, food, or cigarette controls the person rather than the person having control over the management of that substance. In cases of people suffering with chronic illnesses, patients who can give meaning to their diseases and feel that they can master their condition make a healthier adaptation to the diagnosis and are in a much better position to heal.

The stories in this chapter are about enhancing empowerment in a variety of areas from psychobiological issues to illness management, to stress and anxiety, and to loss. They give examples of how to count on oneself and learn the importance of accepting compliments.

STORY 2
A TRADITION OF MIND-BODY EMPOWERMENT

Therapeutic Characteristics

Problems Addressed

- Limited abilities
- Inadequacy
- Inferiority
- Fear and apprehension

Resources Developed

- Learning through stories
- Sharing talents and gifts
- Negotiating results
- Discovering new abilities

Outcomes Offered

- Empower the mind-body.
- Conquer fear.
- Share power and knowledge.
- Model empowerment.

In times gone by, the tribes of Fiji were often at war and, consequently, built their villages high on easily defensible, fortified mountain sites. They displayed a very human reaction: When we are threatened, we seek ways of protecting ourselves, building walls to shut others out and ourselves in, both physically and emotionally.

In one such mountain village lived a famed storyteller who, as was the custom of the time, received offerings of food or gifts by his listeners. One was an eel catcher who loved stories but had little to give, save for a fresh catch of eels. It seemed so inadequate compared to what some of the other villagers gave, but he set out to find, and give, what he could.

Following a fresh mountain stream up a narrow gully, through the deeply dappled jungle, accompanied by the melodies of insects and birds, the eel catcher came to a picturesque spring where fresh water bubbled from the earth. This, he thought eagerly, was surely a place for him to find an appropriate catch for the storyteller.

Burying the length of his arm into a promising hole, he hoped to grab a deliciously plump prey. He was experienced at his work and, without seeing his first catch, he knew it was going to be good. But the eel catcher was in for a big surprise.

He pulled from the hole not an eel, but a small, human-shaped spirit god. "This is wonderful," thought the eel catcher. "A deity is surely a far better gift than an ordinary eel." Now he would not be embarrassed by his gift. The storyteller was sure to be delighted and would continue spinning beautiful tales.

The little deity, however, didn't share the same enthusiasm. Uncertain of his fate, he began to plead for his life, offering the eel catcher power over fire in exchange for his freedom. "With the power of fire," said the little god, "you can offer the storyteller and the rest of your village a gift so unique and irreplaceable that you will be honored and respected forever."

The eel catcher had to admit he did not have power over fire, nor did anyone else in his village. This would undoubtedly impress the storyteller. He could see power over fire had many advantages such as cooking foods, warming huts, clearing jungles to grow crops, and hardening the spearheads. It was something the surrounding villages of hostile neighbors did not possess, and empowered with the gift of fire, he and his fellow villagers would no longer need to fear their attacks. They could all live in peace—and listen to stories in peace.

The eel catcher accepted, whereupon the god directed his captor to dig a pit as a means of demonstrating the eel catcher's new power. He was to fill the hole with rocks, and a fierce log fire was lit on top. The eel catcher watched as the rocks warmed from an inert gray through the intense red of a cooking fire, to a heat of pure whiteness. At this point the spirit god began a slow walk across the stones, beckoning the eel catcher, "Follow me."

Imagine the eel catcher's hesitation at being asked to do something he had never done before. He was scared as he had never walked on white-hot rocks before, nor seen anyone else do so. Reason told him he could be seriously burned. He struggled between trust and doubt, want and fear. Fear stopped him from stepping forward.

"Come," encouraged the little god, "you have the power. You hesitate out of doubt rather than ability. The fact is you have the ability to do more than you ever thought possible. Don't let your fears limit you. Step beyond what you see as your limitations. Permit yourself to discover what you are capable of achieving."

With a deep breath he took his first, hesitant step forward. His doubts had not completely faded, but he was courageous enough to try. He followed in the little deity's footsteps and discovered something he could never have found while still shrinking back from the perimeter of the fire. He could do it! His feet were unscathed. His flesh did not burn. He knew he had gained power over fire—and with it the power over fear.

The eel catcher cherished his personal discovery even more than the gift from the god. It was something he would not forget, something he would not let go of, and he wondered how he might be able to replicate the feat again for the benefit of his fellow villagers. We only need to do something once, he thought, to know we are capable of doing it. The more we do it, the better we become. Each time I do it, I can become more confident, more capable, and less fearful.

Despite his joy, he was not possessive about his new discovery. Having acquired the ability, he shared his talents with the storyteller and the rest of the village, bringing immense rewards to others and deeply enriching their lives.

And the eel catcher himself became a storyteller—of at least one very special tale. Through the story of his experience, he passed the power on to his son, and he, in turn, to his son. It has continued to be inherited in a direct unbroken lineage to this very day.

EMPOWERMENT

STORY 3
OWNING RESPONSIBILITY

Therapeutic Characteristics

Problems Addressed

- Situations of conflict
- Loss of control
- Helplessness
- Feelings of being blocked or stuck
- Need to blame others

Resources Developed

- Awareness and understanding
- Owning responsibility
- Being rational and practical
- Making choices

Outcomes Offered

- Empower yourself.
- Use personal responsibility.
- Seek practical solutions.

Barry was a disciple of an Eastern religion and wore the robes that gave public testimony to his beliefs. He held his allegiance seriously, renounced worldly possessions, and spent a decade in an Indian ashram studying the philosophy of his religion and its associated devotional practices.

During his time at the ashram something occurred that caused him great physical and emotional pain. His religion taught love, compassion, selflessness, and tolerance, but this incident seemed to betray all those principles.

When a division occurred in the sect after a conflict between his master and a senior disciple, Barry's loyalty was also divided. He respected his master but felt a personal closeness to the breakaway guru who established his own sect. At times Barry would visit the breakaway guru on the other side of the village to listen to his teachings, but the master did not approve, saying those who visited the renegade disciple would not be allowed back into his ashram. Although Barry did not like or agree with the directive, he obeyed it.

After ten years he returned to life in the West, where he established a branch of his master's sect, but the dilemma he felt between his master and the other guru continued to gnaw at him. The struggle was constantly in his mind, and he could have no peace until it was settled. There was only one solution. He had to return to India to see the breakaway guru.

The reception was not what he had expected, especially after years of inner anguish. The guru refused him an audience and Barry returned home in a state of total despair. He felt depressed, stuck, powerless, and without direction. Within six months he was diagnosed with cancer, and feared he might die before the conflict was resolved.

Barry complained about this blockage in therapy. He illustrated his metaphor with an example of how, one day, while walking through the town adjacent to the ashram, he found himself ankle deep in water and mud. It slopped through his sandals and soiled his feet.

Turning a corner he found that one of the gutters was blocked with debris, causing the water to well up, burst its banks, and flow onto the streets. Although water ran across the road and spilled into houses from which people were bucketing it out, the dam of debris remained. As much as they tried to clear out the water, it kept flooding back in. Everyone, he noted, seemed to be addressing the effect, but not the cause.

But how could the drain be cleared and the normal flow of energy restored? At first Barry thought about who was to blame. Surely there must be an official who was responsible for looking after the drains. Why hadn't the people turned to him or her?

Then he thought about responsibility. Would he let his own house get flooded while waiting for someone else to take responsibility? Would he blame someone else for the failure while what was valuable to him was being lost or destroyed? If he wanted the problem fixed would the question be one of practicality and action rather than blame?

Seeing that those being affected were the most involved and had the most urgent need to see something resolved, Barry realized blaming others would not solve the problem. Waiting for *them* to fix *our* issues could result in a long and unproductive wait—and is something over which we have no control. "If you know," he concluded, "that the blockage is destroying *you* and *you* can do something to unblock it, then you'd be foolish not to."

Then he thought about what he would need to do if his house were being flooded and his possessions destroyed. What could he do to clear the blockage? Once the blockage was cleared, how would his life be different? What changes might he expect to experience in the ways he thought and felt? What emotions might he feel, and would those emotions be ones of achievement, confidence, relief, or empowerment?

Finally Barry applied the lessons from his story to his current situation. When he took responsibility and removed the debris that formed the blockage in his life, he felt both happier and healthier. He again began to manage his own life, rather than feel someone else was controlling his destiny.

STORY 4
COUNTING ON YOURSELF

Therapeutic Characteristics

Problems Addressed

- Change
- Difficult challenges
- Low self-esteem

Resources Developed

- Learning acceptance
- Adjusting to change

- Finding ways around problems or obstacles
- Learning to value yourself

Outcomes Offered

- Solutions are possible.
- Weigh the facts.
- Value—and count on—yourself.

Sometimes life fits comfortably into a routine. We grow accustomed to the familiar, and in it feel a sense of security. For generation upon generation this is how it had been for the residents of a small mountain village. They had followed a tradition that adapted life to the rhythmic patterns of nature. Potato crops were grown in season. Stock migrated with seasonal pastures, up and down the mountainsides. Everyone expected this pattern to continue forever.

But just as patterns are familiar, so changes are inevitable. Nothing is the same forever. And that is just what these particular villagers were experiencing now. Many felt things were out of their control. For the last few seasons the climate had not been kind, and now there was less food to go around and more mouths to feed.

The village elder consulted with his council. "We may not be able to control many of the things happening at the moment," he advised, "so we need to adjust to them. It is the only way to ensure the survival and happiness of our people." The council decided to send ten young men on a journey to the capital, where they could find employment and, hopefully, send money back to help support the community.

Once selected, the ten young men began their long and arduous journey. They had many mountain ridges to traverse, steep ravines to negotiate, and raging rivers to cross. They encountered many new and challenging experiences on their journey, each of which they faced successfully until it appeared they finally would be thwarted. In front of them lay a seemingly impassable object, a wide, fast-flowing river full of treacherous currents and swirling eddies. For a while they explored its boulder-strewn bank, seeking out the shallowest and safest crossing. There was just one possibility—a section dotted with wet and slippery rocks that might serve as stepping stones. Sheltered by a cliff and partly hidden by trees, the route was not fully visible to those remaining on the bank. There was little they could do to support each other. It was every man for himself.

In turn, each made the hazardous journey. When it appeared they had all reached the opposite bank, someone suggested they should count the group to ensure that everyone had arrived safely. One of the young men counted. There were only nine. Who could be missing? What could have happened to him? Uneasiness fell on the group as they pondered which of their peers might have slipped into the raging waters, been washed downstream and, possibly, even drowned. They searched the banks but could not see anyone in the water or washed up on the shores. What were they to do?

When they regrouped a second young man decided to count again. The result was the same. The concern grew serious and they resumed the search, scouring the riverbanks more carefully but still without the slightest trace of their missing friend.

Another count confirmed it. In fact, each young man took his turn at counting, and each came up with the same result: Only nine had made the crossing safely. They were sure one of their friends had been swept to his death in the murky waters of the wild and turbulent torrent. A sense of sadness and grief fell upon them, and they sat huddled in a group crying for their lost friend.

At that point, a stranger wandered by and paused to inquire about the reason for their unhappiness. They told him how ten of them had set out from their village. They had foolishly crossed this dangerous river and one of their friends had been lost in the process, for when they got to this bank they could only count nine. He was sure to have drowned. There was no other explanation as they had searched diligently for him. What else could they do now but grieve?

The traveler, seeing the problem, asked the name of the friend who was missing. The young men became puzzled. Eyes searched from face to face but nobody could name the friend who was missing. The stranger requested that they count again. Again, each young man took a turn, and each came to the same conclusion. There were definitely only nine.

Bursting into laughter, the stranger sought to reassure them. "No one is missing," he said. "It is good, and indeed important, that we care for and value each other. But not valuing ourselves has its complications as well. The problem is that each of you has been so modest you have failed to count yourself."

STORY 5
THE IMPORTANCE OF ACCEPTING COMPLIMENTS

Therapeutic Characteristics

Problems Addressed

- Low self-esteem
- Rejection of compliments
- The complications of false modesty

Resources Developed

- Learning to value yourself
- Accepting compliments

Outcomes Offered

- Develop self-worth.

One day a pretty young snake bathed by the edge of a lake. Having washed, she stretched out on a warm rock to dry, and began to preen herself. A fly buzzing by looked down, saw her, and commented, "My, your scales are gleaming so attractively in the sunlight. You look sleek and clean. You are such a beautiful snake."

The snake, shy and embarrassed, slithered off to hide. Seeing a hut nearby, she disappeared through the thatched grass walls. She did not realize it was the home of the village sorcerer. Frightened, he grabbed his drum and started beating it loudly to frighten away this evil intruder.

A tortoise who was slowly journeying across an adjoining field heard the rhythmic beat of the drum and began to dance. An elephant, seeing this unseemly display from such a sedate creature, stood on the tortoise's back. The tortoise excreted fire, and the fire ignited the sorcerer's tinder-dry grass hut. Black clouds billowed up into the sky, darkening the land. A deluge of rain fell from the heavens but quickly abated, allowing the sun to spread its warm and drying light. A mother ant, seizing the opportunity to dry her eggs following the flood of rain, spread them in the sun. An anteater, quick to see an opportunity for a meal, gobbled down the ant's eggs.

The ant took the anteater to court. Seeking redress under the laws of the land, she approached the judge of the jungle, the king of beasts, and described her problem. The lion convened a court, calling together all the parties involved.

First he addressed the anteater. "Anteater, why did you eat the ant's eggs?"

"Well," the anteater replied, "I am an anteater. That is my role or destiny. I was only doing what came naturally. What other alternative was there for me when the ant spread her eggs so temptingly in front of me?"

Turning to the ant, the lion asked, "Ant, why did you spread your eggs where they might tempt the anteater?"

"It was not my intent to tempt the anteater. Surely you can see I am a better mother than that, but what else could I do to care for my young?" replied the ant. "They got wet in the heavy deluge of rain. They needed to dry out and the sun shone so warmly."

Looking to the sun, the lion continued his investigation, "Sun, why did you shine?"

"What else could I do?" asked the sun. "It is my job. The rain had poured and, as everyone knows, the sun must follow the rain."

"Rain, why did you pour?" asked the lion in his search to unravel the truth.

"What else could I do?" responded the rain. "The sorcerer's hut was on fire, the whole village was under threat. I only wanted to help."

"Hut, why did you catch on fire?"

"I couldn't do anything else once the tortoise excreted fire on me," answered the charred remnants of the sorcerer's hut. "I was made of grass. I had stood there for years. I was very dry and had no resistance."

"Tortoise," inquired the king of beasts, "why did you excrete fire?"

"It was the only thing I could do. The elephant stood on me. With her weight, my life was threatened. I had to do something to try to escape."

The lion looked up at the elephant. "Tell me Elephant, why did you tread on the tortoise?"

"What else was there to do?" asked the elephant. "She danced so wildly. Her behavior was most unbecoming and inappropriate for a tortoise. I thought she had gone crazy or something. I didn't intend to hurt her. I just wanted to help settle her wild mood."

The lion turned back to the tortoise. "Why was it you were dancing so wildly?"

"What else could I do?" responded the tortoise. "The sorcerer was beating out such rhythmic and compelling dance music on his drum, I had no choice. I just had to dance."

"Sorcerer, why were you beating your drum?"

The sorcerer answered, "What else was there for me to do when the snake entered my hut? She frightened me. She was dangerous. Serpents are the representations of evil forces and bad omens. I had to chase its evil presence out of my home."

"Snake," inquired the king of beasts, patiently working his way through the line of witnesses, "why did you enter the sorcerer's hut?"

"What else could I do?" answered the snake. "The fly embarrassed me with its words of praise. Somehow, somewhere I had to hide my face, and the grass hut of the sorcerer was the closest refuge."

Finally the lion turned to the fly. "Fly, why did you praise the snake?"

The fly did not address the king of beasts but instead turned to look at the snake and asked, "What? Don't you know how to take a compliment?"

STORY 6
JIM AND THE JOKE BOOK: A STORY OF SELF-EMPOWERMENT

Therapeutic Characteristics

Problems Addressed

- Uncontrollable circumstances
- Problems with health, marriage, family relationships, and work
- Feelings of powerlessness

Resources Developed

- Learning to accept
- Creating abilities to change what can be changed
- Developing creative resolutions
- Finding the means for empowerment

Outcomes Offered

- Accept the unchangeable.
- Learn strategies for change.
- Do something different.
- Feel good about what you can do.

Jim was a senior university lecturer who had climbed the ranks of academia. He was frequently invited as a conference lecturer, a visiting professor, or a specialist consultant. In spite of his accomplishments, he maintained a gentle sense of warm humanity and depth of care for his staff and family. Although his life wasn't perfect, the caring had not ceased. He could blend a gentle union of knowledge, wisdom, and a caring heart to meet life's challenges.

Unfortunately, there was much of Jim's life in the last few years over which he felt that he was increasingly losing control—and that was the objective reality. He suffered from a chronic illness since childhood and, though generally stable, it occasionally flared up, leaving him physically and emotionally fatigued. There was nothing he could do to alter his condition.

He and his wife had not been happy for a long time. It was not that home was a battlefield, but more that they had just grown apart, leaving little joy, excitement, or feeling of mutuality. Jim had tried to talk with her, discussed developing mutual interests, and even suggested marital counseling, but all met with negativity—and he felt powerless to make a difference.

His one child, a daughter to whom he felt extremely close, had met and fallen in love with a young man whose company was about to transfer him to the other side of the continent. Again Jim felt powerless over "losing" his daughter.

EMPOWERMENT

Events at work added to his loss of empowerment. His university had implemented a new program of economic rationalization, employing a business consultant who had no feeling for the traditions of academic life, as Jim had grown to know and love them throughout his career.

Jim's planned career path was blocked. His colleagues with whom he'd worked for years, and who looked up to him for leadership, were being retrenched. Feeling as powerless as an automobile stripped of its engine, he became depressed and grew to dislike going to work in the mornings.

In therapy we explored how he could start to reestablish, even in small ways, the sense of control or feelings of empowerment that Jim required for his well-being. After considering the question, he said, "There are many things that are outside of my power to change at the moment: my illness, my marriage, my daughter's move, the policies being implemented at work. I have been hoping, wanting, and battling to change them, but the reality is they won't and I can't do anything about them. My efforts to change what can't be changed have left me feeling helpless and inadequate. It's like I've been trying to take the world and spin it in a different direction. It can't be done, and my efforts, no matter how intense or well-intentioned, only leave me feeling like a failure.

"I realize," he continued, "if what I have been doing wasn't working, I need to change direction. I needed to find what I *can* alter rather than fight what I can't. If I had to live with situations as they are for the time being, I need to find how I can do so more comfortably and enjoyably."

One lunchtime, while idly perusing the shelves of the university bookshop, his eye fell on a book he would not normally have contemplated reading. Jim pulled a book of jokes from the shelf and purchased it.

He read several jokes each morning over breakfast. It was a fun way to start the day, and different from his past pattern of worrying about what new uncontrollable dramas may unfold at work. He chose a joke that he liked and committed it to memory. He rehearsed it in his mind on the drive to work.

When he arrived he retold the joke to colleagues. Soon they were bringing along jokes, too, commencing the day in the staff room over coffee and sharing humor instead of misery.

By this one simple action Jim changed not only his own feelings about going to work but also the atmosphere among his fellow staff. Instead of feeling powerless and miserable about what they had previously seen as unchangeable and inevitable, they became more positive and energized. The camaraderie built on joke-telling developed into action, and his colleagues became proactive about representing their cause, all because Jim found something changeable in circumstances that seemed so unchangeable.

STORY 7
EMPOWERMENT THROUGH SELF-ASSERTION

Therapeutic Characteristics

Problems Addressed

- Lack of assertion
- Dependency
- Compliance to others wishes

Resources Developed

- Learning to say no
- Communicating your wants and needs
- Building effective self-assertion skills

Outcomes Offered

- Stand up for yourself.
- Find and develop inner strength.
- Asking may get you what you want, but it doesn't guarantee it.

Some years ago I met a woman who almost invariably said yes to things when she really wanted to say no. As a result she was always doing what other people wanted rather than what she wanted. If her friends wanted to go to a movie when she would have prefered to listen to a band, she would go to the movie and spend her time wishing she had gone to see the band. She wanted to learn how to make choices for herself more often, but she needed skills to assert herself.

In the first consultation she asked if she could smoke. Here, I thought, was a good opportunity to model the self-assertive skills she sought. I wanted to give her an example of how to make an assertive response with explanations or reasons. I wanted to offer a model of how to say no in a way that made it understandable, and possibly even palatable. I explained that smoking could serve as a distraction from the things that she wished to discuss, and she may benefit from having an hour without a cigarette. From my perspective, I explained that if I were focused on the unpleasant experience of inhaling somebody else's smoke, I may not concentrate as well on her therapy. She seemed to accept this and refrained from smoking.

We discussed the benefits and methods of saying no. We explored strategies by which she could begin to assert herself in nonthreatening ways. How could she start to ask for what she wanted? What could she do that was most likely to ensure her success? What things could she ask for that wouldn't result in World War III erupting? Who were the people with whom she felt safest asserting herself?

We examined ways she could start to say no in safe situations and the people with whom it was safe to do so. Together we talked about how she could politely reject the offer of coffee, an invitation to go out, or how she might firmly, yet courteously, say no if her boss asked her to work late when she had arranged to go out.

We discussed how she might voice her opinions clearly to let others know what she wanted. How might she be clear in her own mind about what she wanted? When she was, how could she communicate it in a way that let others know, but did not raise their resistance by being too aggressive? How could she judge that balance between what was assertive and what was aggressive?

Just as asking for something does not always mean getting, so *not* asking makes the possibility for receiving nonexistent. Thus, we explored the skills, not just of asking, but of being prepared for rejection. How would she manage the situation when others said "no" to her self-assertive requests?

On the second consultation she sat down and said, "Last time you recommended some means for me to assert myself more."

"That's right," I agreed, hoping this acknowledgement would bring forth some examples of how she had put them into practice.

EMPOWERMENT

"You suggested that instead of always tending to others' needs I should take time to request and do the things I want."

"Yes," I concurred, pleased that she seemed to understand the message so quickly.

"You said," she continued, "that I should start to assert myself in gentle ways and be prepared for the fact that others might not always like the changes I start to initiate."

Again I agreed.

"Well," she said, "I've decided to put what you have taught me it into practice. I'm going to have a cigarette while we talk today!"

STORY 8
THANKING YOUR SYMPTOMS

Therapeutic Characteristics

Problems Addressed

- Serious illness
- Significantly altered lifestyles
- Dealing with bad news
- Shattered ambitions

Resources Developed

- Learning to accept reality
- Learning how to alter the way we perceive things
- Learning to look for the positive

Outcomes Offered

- Look at adversity differently.
- Explore how your symptoms can benefit you.
- Find and develop your inner strengths.

Something that Denise said reminded me of something that Marlene had said. And what Marlene said reminded me of something Selina said. That was a few years ago but it is still clear in my mind.

At 35, Denise was a senior manager in a large corporation. Both she and her husband lived the high life, devoting themselves to their careers rather than having children. Both had climbed the executive ladder in different companies, drove prestigious cars, and owned a house in the "right" suburb.

Everything had gone according to the grand plan they had mapped out. Then something strange happened to Denise. She had pains and burning sensations in her left leg. Initially her physician said not to worry about it, but weeks went by and the symptoms did not change. Denise soon learned she had multiple sclerosis.

The symptoms spread into other parts of her body. She had difficulty walking and could no longer go to work. As work had been such a large part of her existence, identity, and life, she fell into a state of grief and despair. She enjoyed the corporate life with all its challenges, excitement, and feelings of riding life on the edge. Her illness ripped the carpet from under her feet. She could no longer walk in the directions that she wished to go and was forced to reexamine her very singular lifelong goals and ambitions.

In conversing with Denise, she said something to remind me of Marlene.

Marlene was a fellow therapist, a woman in her fifties who had always had a deep and genuine concern for other people. Just as Denise's career had been her life, other people had been Marlene's. She had spent her life caring for others, but recently the tables had turned.

Marlene had been diagnosed with breast cancer and had a mastectomy. Her illness and subsequent treatment had forced her to stop working, but she had not lost heart like Denise had. She was eager, almost driven, to facilitate her own rehabilitation and prevent any recurrence of cancer. Her goal in coming to therapy was to gain assistance in restoring her sense of empowerment over what had been happening both physically and emotionally in her life.

While talking about the changes that had taken place in her life, Marlene said something to remind me of Selina, a retired school teacher. Selina had not had an easy life. She had been born a Jew in Germany before World War II. She and her husband fled to Shanghai and later migrated to Australia where she found herself caring for a young family in a foreign country. She did not speak English, her marriage was under strain, her husband had an affair, and then he left her.

I learned that one of the characteristics that defined Selina so clearly was her resolve not to be beaten by her circumstances. She continued to raise her young family while studying for a degree in education. She became a teacher and eventually a school principal. She was devoted to her work and the children that she taught. Teaching became both her love and her life, especially after her own children had grown and left home.

When the law said it was time to retire, she did so reluctantly. Within six months she was diagnosed with abdominal cancer and attended one of the top oncology units in the country where, according to her account, a leading specialist advised her that she had only three months to live. At first she was stunned and depressed by the doctor's words, but then she decided she didn't want just to sit back and wait to die. Selina was the first patient with cancer to consult me and, as I recall, was the first patient I ever saw with a potentially terminal illness. As a result, I think I learned more from her than she did from me.

I remembered Selina when I worked with Marlene and Denise. Denise had long held a desire to write. She attended a few writers' courses and felt there was a creative part of her that was unexpressed. She never had time to write due to her busy corporate lifestyle.

At first she felt the grief and emptiness of losing her job and her lifelong goal. She could not go back to work; that style of life had come to an end. But as one door closed, she saw another door open. She said, "At least I've got something for which to thank my multiple sclerosis. Now that I can't do what I was doing, I've got the time to write. I've got the time to express my creativity and to do something I was not able to do before."

Likewise, Marlene had said, "My cancer has led to an unexpected change in my life. Previously, I used to get up to the alarm every morning. I'd rush around getting breakfast, getting ready to race off to work. I'd water the potted plants in a hurried, last-minute rush to dive for the car keys and battle my way through rush hour traffic. Now I have the time to water the potted plants . . . and watch them grow."

EMPOWERMENT

Both Marlene and Denise discovered something new and beneficial from their illnesses, and this fact reminded me of what Selina had said in therapy: "Now that I know I am going to die, I am free to live." And she did.

STORY 9
A MODEL OF EMPOWERMENT

Therapeutic Characteristics

Problems Addressed

- Mind-body healing
- Lack of self-confidence
- Dependence upon others for answers

Resources Developed

- Learning from others—even paradoxically
- Finding and using your own resources
- Building the skills to care for yourself

Outcomes Offered

- Use the mind to facilitate healing.
- Feel good about being self-assertive.
- Take care of number one.
- Learn from experience more than words.

A healer once wandered from village to village laying hands on her followers. People came from far and wide to seek her assistance. It was said that as you knelt before her and she rested her hands on the crown of your head, you were empowered by the spirit. In this act of faith your soul was strengthened, your resilience enhanced, and you attained the fortitude to ward off both evil and illness.

Some people questioned whether it was the power of some spiritual force that came from outside, or whether the belief and ritual surrounding it triggered inner healing abilities the person already had. Either way, people felt different after the healer touched them.

This healer did not accept money for her services. Instead, followers made an offering at the end of a healing session. Mindful of this, a poor, elderly, and ailing woman attended a healing meeting. She expected to gain a lot and so brought (what was for her) a large offering. It was her last loaf of bread.

The gathering was large. The healer looked at all the people. She was tired. She had had a number of meetings through a number of villages over the last few days and, by this stage, was also feeling a little lazy. She didn't want to go through the effort of laying hands on so many people. Instead she thought of a creative solution. She asked her followers to close their eyes, meditate tranquilly, and imagine that she was personally laying her hands on each and every member's head. The experience, she said, would be as vivid and real as if she had actually done it.

The elderly woman did as the healer asked. She felt the power of the spirit. She started to sense a new confidence about her life. There was something definitely healing in the experience. Her body felt better—more energized and less pained. Though she may not have put it in such words, she experienced a mind–body empowerment.

The healer too was pleased. She had gotten the afternoon over with quickly. People seemed contented and, at the end of the meeting, they filed passed offering their gifts in the customary way.

When it came to the elderly woman's turn, she knelt humbly before the teacher with her only loaf of bread in her hands, and said, "From my heart, I thank you. Today you have given me great help. I could imagine your hands on my head and the healing energy through my body. I feel recuperated.

"Now, if you close your eyes and meditate for a while, you will be able to imagine that you are receiving this, my last loaf of bread. You will be able to see it, smell it, and taste it in your imagination just as vividly as if you were actually eating it."

Putting her loaf back into her basket she said, "For that, I thank you." And the woman hurried home, feeling stronger, happier, and healthier.

STORY 10
EMPOWERING JOE

Therapeutic Characteristics

Problems Addressed

- Divorce
- Loss and grief
- Depression
- Disempowerment
- Anger
- Suicidal thoughts

Resources Developed

- Standing on your own two feet
- Rediscovering capabilities
- Creating situations for change
- Doing rather than knowing
- Appreciating challenges

Outcomes Offered

- There is life beyond loss and grief.
- Feelings are changeable.
- There are options other than suicide.
- In loss there may be gain.
- We are capable.

Jeff was Joe's therapist. "You are feeling emasculated," he said. "You have been disempowered. What you need is to rediscover your own sense of empowerment."

Pete was Joe's best friend. He might have thought something similar but he would not have used those words. It was not so much what Pete thought or said, but rather what he helped Joe *do* that mattered.

Joe felt like he was at the bottom of the biggest and deepest hole that he had ever fallen into—and saw no way out. All his plans, hopes, and dreams had crashed as heavily as Goliath when slain by the stone from David's slingshot.

He had been a devoted family man who saw it as his duty to work long hours to meet his family's needs. He needed to pay the mortgage, meet school fees, buy sporting equipment, cover car payments, and purchase a new refrigerator. He *had* to work hard.

The stone that shattered his dream was his wife's unexpected request for a separation. He tried to work things out with her, but one night he came home to find himself locked out and never allowed to return.

Jeff asked about Joe's relationship with his mother. They talked about the past, and Joe saw patterns in all his relationships with women.

Pete, on the other hand, arranged to go jogging with Joe at six each morning. He would knock on the door to awaken him, if necessary, and they would spend the first hour of every morning running around the suburb where Joe had rented an apartment.

Despite Jeff's guidance and Pete's jogging, Joe still hurt. He had lost his wife, children, and dreams of a happy family life. To see the kids meant constant court battles, big legal fees, and considerable heartache. Nothing seemed worth it any more. He felt suicidal, but he told neither Jeff nor Pete, for there was something embarrassing about his self-perceived weakness and lack of control.

Jeff said, "Because your disempowerment is associated with women, I suggest you see a female therapist." Joe felt rejected—again. Even his therapist was dumping him.

As they jogged, Pete invited Joe to join him on his trip to the Himalayas. Joe found all the reasons why he couldn't: He couldn't afford it, couldn't take the time off work, and didn't want to be away from the kids, even though he couldn't see them often.

He had nothing to look forward to, and one day he contemplated killing himself by crashing his speeding car into a large tree. At the last moment he swerved away. Two thoughts stopped him. The first was that he would never ever see his kids again and he did not want them going through life knowing their father had committed suicide. The other was that the way everything was going in his life, he was likely to screw up his suicide attempt. It would be just his luck to end up in a wheelchair—and be worse off.

His new therapist asked when he had felt most confident and empowered in the past. He knew it was when he had felt in control of his destiny, but the knowledge did not supply the motivation to change his misery.

Pete insisted that Joe accompany him to Nepal: He organized the itinerary, scheduled a fitness program, and dragged Joe backpacking through the woods on weekends. Together they flew to Kathmandu and were on the trail for just two days when the unexpected happened—Pete became ill and had to turn back. Although Joe understood, and ensured Pete a safe escort back to Kathmandu, inwardly he felt hurt and angry, seeing it as another rejection, as someone close leaving him on his own, yet again.

The parallels between this trip, his marriage, and the therapy with Jeff did not escape him. He had planned to begin a journey with someone for whom he cared, but each and every other one turned his or her back on him. Joe had a choice: He could turn around and go back with Pete, or he could go on by himself.

If you were to know Joe, you would know he is frugal and persistent. He had spent a lot of money to get to Nepal, and he had spent months preparing for the trip and was not going to waste it all. The choice was clear: He would go on by himself.

While the journey was not easy, he was exploring new territory, going places he had never been before, and facing challenges he had never anticipated. In some ways he was out of his depths, but somehow he felt that his feet were firmly on the ground. He was *doing* and *achieving* what he would not have thought possible to achieve by himself—so much so that by the time he got back home, he felt like a different person. He had rediscovered his empowerment, not through talking about it, but through *experiencing* his own capabilities. He felt no need to return to a therapist.

His gratitude was to Pete, not just for taking him to Nepal, but also for leaving him there alone. It had been the separation that gave Joe the chance to stand on his own two feet—and do so at the top of the world. It created experiences he would not otherwise have had.

If one separation can do that, thought Joe, maybe there is the potential to gain from others. Maybe in even the most traumatic losses and most shattering disasters are opportunities for new discoveries. Maybe it is *because* of such events that we grow and find our empowerment. If life is without challenge, there is no need for us to develop our capabilities. Perhaps the biggest challenges present us with our greatest opportunities for growth.

Joe discovered that tragedy can house some surprising treasures. From loss we can gain. Knowledge may help us, but, ultimately, the *experience* of discovering our inner strengths and capabilities is what leaves us feeling empowered.

STORY 11
SOARING TO NEW HEIGHTS

Therapeutic Characteristics

Problems Addressed

- Fear
- Anxiety
- Depression
- Indecision
- Dependency
- Uneasiness in unfamiliar territory

Resources Developed

- Letting go of a burden
- Accepting advice
- Following directives

EMPOWERMENT

- Finding independence
- Rediscovering old means of attaining happiness
- Discovering new resources and abilities
- Being in the moment
- Gaining empowerment

Outcomes Offered

- Let go of the past.
- Conquer fear.
- Become self-sufficient.
- Focus on new heights of achievement.
- Look ahead.

Once upon a time a young octopus lived in the warm, shallow, and clear waters close to a sandy shore. Life was carefree. She swam over reefs, mingled with colorful fish, and relaxed in the gentle wash of the waves. But there was something a little different about this octopus. She liked to hang onto things. Sometimes, to gain a sense of exhilaration, she would wrap her tentacles around a fish and go for a joy ride. Sometimes she would wrap her tentacles around a firm and solid rock where she could feel comfortable and secure.

As the little octopus grew, she ventured further and further afield, exploring deeper waters. One day as she was swimming somewhat hesitantly through these new territories, she encountered a strange and unusual object. The hull of a large ship cast its gloomy shadow over the waters. Dangling from its bow was a strong, sturdy anchor, around which the little octopus, seeking some source of security, wrapped her tentacles.

As she clung to the anchor, it began to drop, plunging down through waters that grew darker and colder. The little octopus could feel the pressure of the water squashing in as strongly as her apprehensions wanted to burst out. She didn't know whether to hang on or let go. While the anchor itself felt safe and strong, its descent into the gloom and pressure of the ocean was very frightening.

The octopus was afraid to let go of what security the anchor offered in this unexpected change of events, and she was frightened of the depths into which she was being plunged. At last, the anchor struck the sea floor with a thump. The little octopus grasped tighter, uncertain whether to maintain her grip on the thing that plunged it into such unfamiliar depths. Somehow it seemed like a false security, but, in the dark and gloom of that uncertainty, the little octopus was reluctant to let go.

Frightened, scared, and indecisive, the little octopus felt both reassured and apprehensive when a fish emerged from the gloom. The octopus called out for help. The fish listened to her tale then said, "I am sorry. I cannot help you, but there is a bigger fish following me. He may be able to provide the help you need."

It wasn't long before the bigger fish swam by, moving with a gentle, relaxed motion. His eyes seemed kindly and caring. "I can help you," said the fish in reply to her request for help, "but first you need to do something to help yourself. You need to let go of that anchor to which you have been holding. Then I can show you a way out."

I don't know how the little octopus let go of the anchor. I don't know whether it was gradually and hesitantly, by peeling off one tentacle at a time, or whether she was willing to let go of her grip completely and totally, all at once. She might have kept hanging on with one or two tentacles, feeling the freedom of the other limbs before finally choosing to venture into a more complete freedom. Maybe she needed to hold on just a little longer before building up the courage set herself free.

The kindly fish waited, encouraging and congratulating the octopus with each step forward. Then, when the little octopus had relinquished her tenacious grip, the fish said gently, "Follow me."

The fish began to swim back and forth, gradually making his way upward. The ascent wasn't as quick and as rapid as the octopus anticipated, but the fish seemed to know what he was doing, aware of the problems of ascending too quickly. He guided in such a way that the little octopus was learning how to manage by herself if ever she was caught out of her depth. She began to feel stronger and more competent. The unfamiliar surroundings no longer frightened her. In fact, the journey began to feel like it had been a real adventure.

As they continued to ascend, the waters started to grow warmer and brighter. The little octopus began to feel lighter and happier. The oppression and despair of being in the gloom of those unfamiliar depths lifted, and the octopus felt the joy of freedom returning. She caught up with the fish and, for a while, they swam side by side. The octopus no longer needed to follow. At times she began to swim ahead, taking the lead and forging her own way forward. It did not seem like a long time had passed before the fish said, "From here you are ready to go on by yourself. You no longer need me to accompany you. You have learned the way back to where you want to be."

The little octopus thanked the fish and swam upward, as she had learned from the fish's kindly mentoring. The waters continued to grow brighter and warmer. Light rippled off the surface and shone into the sea, highlighting the yellows, reds, and blues of the tiny fish that darted in and out of the naturally sculptured coral reefs.

Something had changed, not just the events that had occurred, but within the octopus. The octopus no longer felt contented just to be where she previously had been. She felt different. She made her way out of the water, crawled onto the beach, and stretched out on the sand. For a while she basked on the warm sand, enjoying the soporific comfort of the sunlight on her body, hearing the sounds of the sea birds overhead and the gentle swish of the wind in the palm trees. There was something nice about taking time out to recuperate.

The octopus's rest was also a time for consolidation and validation. Gently resting there in the pleasant warmth of the day, the little octopus reflected on the things that had happened, affirming what she learned and validating the message of that experience. The clingy little octopus seemed like a distant dream, a foggy image from the depths of the ocean. Feeling a new sense of strength, the octopus began to think that it was time to move on.

Feeling warm, comfortable, and confident, she raised herself up on her tentacles. She studied the beach and the backdrop of limestone cliffs that rose abruptly toward the sky. Making her way across the sand, the octopus ventured toward the cliff. She began to climb toward the cliff top using her tentacles wisely and carefully. The going was not always easy, but the octopus felt challenged by the unfamiliar. At times she really struggled, but, not once did she lose sight of her destination. She climbed higher and was rewarded with the triumphant feeling of success.

At the top of the cliff, a cool, refreshing breeze blew in from the ocean. The octopus spread her tentacles out like wings and began to lift on the breeze as though she had been doing this her entire life. Like an eagle she soared into the air, riding the gentle currents, gliding on the thermals, and experiencing the pure enjoyment of flying to new heights.

EMPOWERMENT

Looking down, the octopus watched the undulating waves of the ocean from whence she had traveled. Looking up, she viewed the open expanse of a clear, blue sky, an expanse that seemed to represent a new sense of anticipation, and held the hope of a new set of aspirations. At last the octopus knew her new ability to fly free, to let go of the past, to enjoy the experience of the moment, and to anticipate the delights of what lay ahead.

EXERCISE

Now record your own story ideas. As we listen to stories, they often remind us of our own experiences, trigger memories of similar stories we have heard in the past, or elicit creative ideas for a metaphoric tale that fits for a particular client.

Use a notebook to record your ideas for stories of empowerment. There is no need to write out the whole story; just a simple note of the theme will do. Perhaps you may want to brainstorm and let the ideas flow without censure. It may help you to refer to them in the future when you are looking for story ideas about empowerment.

CHAPTER 5

 Acquiring Acceptance

Clients often come to us because they cannot accept that some things in life cannot be changed: "I wish I hadn't had an abusive childhood"; "I wish my spouse was different"; "I wish these things weren't happening to me." When we desire to control the uncontrollable, we set ourselves up for disappointment and possible depression. The illusion that we can control the uncontrollable (and therapy sometimes supports this illusion by emphasizing personal power or control over *every* life situation) is a surefire formula for unhappiness and leads to problematic consequences. Thus, the art of acceptance is not only necessary for our emotional survival, but also desirable for our happiness.

While we may not be able to change what happens, we can choose how we see it—and acceptance is one of those choices. For a person who battles to control the uncontrollable, acceptance *is* a change. When life is not going well, we need to acknowledge what we cannot alter *and* look at how to change what we can. Both are legitimate and essential therapeutic goals. The following stories are about accepting who we are, what we have, what life brings our way, and what cannot be changed.

STORY 12
ACCEPTING LIFE AS IT IS

Therapeutic Characteristics

Problems Addressed

- Lifestyle choices
- Conflicts between money and leisure; work and pleasure; security and freedom
- Challenges to your choices

Resources Developed

- Learning to accept life as it is
- Developing tolerance of others
- Enjoying what you have

Outcomes Offered

- Be happy with what life brings.
- Take time to enjoy.
- Be contented with simple pleasures.

A fisherman sat on the rough, rock sea wall and cast a line into the water. He lay back against the supportive trunk of a palm tree. The fronds, strummed by a gentle breeze, hummed a soothing lullaby. The late afternoon light danced in tiny golden mirrors on the rippling sea. The fisherman didn't need to stop and think, "This is paradise." Out of familiarity, he accepted this was the way it was most of the time.

This particular morning, as he did almost every morning, he awoke and plucked fresh mangoes from the tree at the front door of his modest home. He walked into the jungle to gather coconuts and tropical fruits. He tilled his garden for a while, cultivating a staple crop of sweet potatoes. He walked the short distance to his home when his stomach told him it was time for lunch with his family, for he didn't own a watch. Following a meal, he stretched out in a hammock for his usual afternoon siesta.

He didn't need to worry about his possessions or children. Nobody in the village owned much, most house doors were always open to visitors, and there were no security systems. His children wandered the neighborhood safely, and the island had never even been visited by a police officer.

Now, as the sun dropped calmly and colorfully toward the horizon and the sea breeze caressed the warmth from the day, he sat on the rocky wall that had been constructed gradually by generations of his forebearers.

A holiday resort that attracted wealthy foreign tourists had been constructed recently not far from his traditional fishing spot. A businessman on vacation became restless with nothing to do apart from sitting by the pool. He stepped out of the confines of the resort to take an evening stroll along the beach and met the fisherman sitting on the sea wall.

Approaching the man, the businessman asked, "What are you doing?"

"Just catching a fish or two for my family's dinner," came the reply.

"Why restrict your catch to just one or two?" asked the businessman, who had already pigeon-holed the fisherman as lazy. "There seem to be plenty of fish in the ocean. If you spent a little more time here, you could catch three or four fish."

"Why would I want to do that?" asked the puzzled fisherman.

"Well," replied the businessman, surprised by the fisherman's lack of financial logic, "you could keep one or two for your family and sell the others. If you save the money, you could buy an extra fishing rod and double your catch."

Still puzzled, the fisherman again inquired, "Why would I want to do that?"

"Well," answered the tourist, "with the extra money you made you could buy a net. That way you would catch even more—and earn more money."

"What value would there be in that?" asked the humble fisherman, preferring the solitude of his fishing spot to the interrogation of a stranger.

"Then," said the wealthy tourist a little frustrated by the fisherman's business naiveté, "you could buy a boat, maybe borrow some money, buy several boats, set up a whole fishing fleet, manage your own company, invest your returns on the international stock market, and become very wealthy."

The simple fisherman looked up quizzically at the man with such weird ideas. The sea and land provided for him plentifully. Why should he want to deplete it? Why should he want to take the bounty from his family and friends only to sell it back to them?

"If you follow my advice," continued the tourist, "you could become rich and have anything you want."

"What would I do with all the money, if I had it?" asked the fisherman.

"You could do what I do," answered the businessman proudly. "Each year you could take two weeks vacation to do what ever you wanted. Why, you could even visit a tropical island, just as I've done, where you could sit on the sea wall and fish at your leisure."

STORY 13
LEARNING TO ACCEPT OUR CIRCUMSTANCES

Therapeutic Characteristics

Problems Addressed

- Seeking the impossible
- A need for what you can't have
- Unbridled greed and desire
- Nonacceptance
- Thinking "the grass is greener on the other side"

Resources Developed

- Learning to assess reality
- Accepting what life offers
- Discovering and appreciating what you have

Outcomes Offered

- Feel good about who you are.
- Accept your own qualities and attributes.

Once, a stonecutter worked at the hard rock face of the quarry, chip, chip, chipping away at the tough surface. The sound of the mallet and chisel constantly rung in his ears: chip, chip, chip.

His job was slow and arduous. In summer, the heat of the sun reflected off the rocks, making his workplace as hot as a furnace. In winter, there was no shelter from the rain or cold that turned the quarry as frigid as an icebox. As he chipped away, he spent his time wishing for a better life, yearning for the power to change his circumstances. He would fantasize himself in places of which he could only dream, for he knew that his fantasies would never be—or so he thought.

Late one day, as he was dragging his tired body home, he passed the lavish mansion of a nobleman. Peering inside, he saw the affluent dress of the rich man, the beauty of his wife, the plentiful
food on their table, and thought to himself, "If only I could be that nobleman, I would be rich and
powerful. I could escape all the problems and discomforts of life as a stonecutter. Oh, how I wish I
were a nobleman."

The stonecutter was shocked and surprised, for no sooner had he made the wish than he found
himself seated at the head of the table. He became the very nobleman he had been observing: richly
clad, with a beautiful wife at his side and all the food he could imagine set out on the table. He enjoyed his new life, the affluence, and power. He was able to order around his servants, his employ-
ees, and his wife. He relished his authority and flaunted it haughtily, but things were to change.

One day the king came to visit the nobleman's town. Because of his noble status, he was obliged
to participate in a guard of honor. He had to humble himself before his ruler. As he bowed in sub-
servience, he again started to wish for something more. He thought to himself, "The king has more
influence and power than a nobleman. I wish I were the king."

Hardly had the thought crossed his mind before he found himself mounted on the king's horse,
clothed in regal robes and flanked by loyal troops. His route was lined by prostrating people, including the nobleman he had so recently been.

Returning to his palace, he seated himself on the high, autocratic throne while the subjects of
his realm presented themselves to him, bowing, and bringing gifts. This was the life. Being a ruler
was great. He thought he could really take to this kind of lifestyle. It sure beat being a stonecutter.

He made the most of his position. He traveled to the farthest reaches of his domain. He loved
the power that forced everyone—peasants, priests, academics, and nobility—to prostrate themselves
before him. On one such summer journey, an intense and relentless sun beat down on the king. He
sweltered in his regal robes. His royal personage was forced to perspire. He had no control over it and
had to abandon his power quest to seek shade. There in the shadows his envious thoughts again
emerged. "The sun," he mused, "has great power. It is even more powerful than a king. I wish I were
the sun."

The magic that had transformed him previously worked instantly once again. He found himself
high in the sky, shedding light on the world, beaming down upon kings and emperors, burning sun-
bathers, and causing cancers. He could force people to seek shelter from his heat, retreat from their
fields, or take a reluctant afternoon siesta. This was the greatest. He relished the power . . . until one
day a cloud floated across the sky and blocked off his light. At first he was annoyed, then he began to
think, "The cloud is strong enough to stop the heat and light of the sun. The cloud is therefore more
powerful than the sun. I wish I were a cloud."

Instantly he was again transformed. He floated around the sky as a tall, puffy, cumulous cloud.
He could rain down on earthlings and watch them run for cover or search for umbrellas. He could
rob the heat from the sun and create a cool chill. He could make rivers breach their banks and dams
burst their walls. He could cause floods that demolished houses and ruined people's lives. Yes, the
cloud definitely had power. This was the way he always wanted life to be . . . until one day a sudden
wind howled through the heavens, blowing the cloud away. The cloud was powerless. It had neither
strength nor direction. "The wind," thought the cloud, "that's where the power lies. The wind is
more powerful than a cloud. I wish I were the wind."

In another act of magical transformation, the cloud instantly became wind. Howling through the trees, rushing across the land, tearing topsoil from paddocks, blowing umbrellas inside out, taking roofs off houses, and flattening haystacks, the stonecutter had great fun as the wind. "This is the life," he thought. "As the wind I have unlimited power." He blew ferociously around the globe. He whipped up seas. He sunk boats. He caused huge waves to crash on tiny islands. He had never enjoyed himself more . . . until one day. He huffed out one almighty blow that just came to a sudden halt. In front of him stood a tall cliff that remained unmoved. He tried again, unable to bend or shake the mighty cliff. "The cliff," thought the wind, "can stop my wildest gales. Obviously the cliff is more powerful than the wind. I wish I were the cliff."

Instantly he became the cliff. Tall and strong, he could hold out against the worst hurricanes the wind could hurl at it. People came to admire his grandeur and worship his natural beauty. They picnicked at his base or tried to match their strength against his by climbing his face. He was a dominating presence over the entire countryside. "Yes! This is it," he thought. "At last I have found it. At last I am powerful. I am the cliff."

The thought had barely entered his mind when, down at his base, he heard a steady, "chip, chip, chip."

STORY 14
REMEMBERING WHAT NOT TO FORGET

Therapeutic Characteristics

Problems Addressed

- Issues of responsibility management
- Meeting the demands of work
- Issues of time management
- Health and well-being
- Neglect of past resources

Resources Developed

- Taking time to remember what worked in the past
- Accessing past coping skills
- Accessing past pleasures
- Developing skills for self-caring

Outcomes Offered

- Accept your abilities.
- Rediscover useful resources.
- Develop strategies for stress and time management.
- Remember the need for self-nurturing.

A woman once told me how she rediscovered something so important that it seemed hard to imagine she could have ever forgotten it. Unfortunately, there are times in all of our lives when the simple truths get overlooked, or when the wisdom we hold within is brushed aside by all the necessities of life and living. That is exactly what happened for Samantha.

She had been raised in a tiny coastal town. From what she told me about it, it was hard to imagine a more idyllic environment in which to spend a childhood. She would walk home from school along the beach, combing the shores for beautiful shells, soft-backed cuttlefish for her bird aviary, and other mystical surprises that might be washed up in the ocean's flotsam.

She loved the freedom she felt as the refreshingly cool sea breeze blew through the long strands of her hair. She ran with the joy of the world, her feet sinking softly into the sand and cool waters lapping over her toes. Seagulls called above, and terns dropped from the air like darts as they targeted a hidden meal. When dolphins frolicked in the bay she leaped up and down with excitement, but the thing she loved most was sitting on her favorite rock on a craggy headland, watching the pastel hues of a sunset as a warm ball of light dropped into the arms of the sea.

The older she grew the less time she had to stroll the shores. Time became important in a way it never had been in childhood. She was an adolescent. She was learning to take on the responsibilities of impending adulthood, and with adulthood came the implication that it was time to forget the playful pleasures of childhood. Now it was time to prepare herself for the future and forget the joy of being in the present. There was homework to do, exams to study for, and a career to think about.

Samantha adapted well. She passed her exams with brilliance, gained entry to a good law school, and left her seaside town to follow a career in the city. In the first few years she always found time to return to her seaside home for the vacations, but these faded quickly. The growing pressures of a new career meant that there was little time to visit home—and even less time to walk her formerly much-loved shore.

Success led to affluence and a beautiful apartment in the "right" suburb but, unfortunately, not to happiness. Samantha felt a growing sense of despondency. She missed the freedom and joy of her childhood. Hoping to recapture it, she commissioned an artist to paint a large picture of a sunset across her hometown bay. She sat in front of the painting trying to recapture the memories.

It was beautiful, but it didn't work. Her despondency increased and her health decreased. She found herself becoming more and more susceptible to colds and flus—those annoying illnesses that remind you of your vulnerability and let you know that something is not quite right.

She searched out new age music, hoping to bring the sounds of waves, seagulls, and whales into her living room. She forced herself to sit in front of the painting and listen to the artificial sounds of the ocean. But her mind wasn't there. She had deadlines to meet, financial goals to achieve, and business issues to address.

One day she had to visit a client who lived by the sea. As she left his office late in the evening, the sun was setting. Following her heart, rather than the dictate of her mind (which reminded her of the urgent report she had to complete by tomorrow), she pulled her car into a seaside park. Samantha kicked off her shoes, slipped out of her stockings, and waded in the waters at the ocean's edge. The cool, moist sands massaged the soles of her feet, the fresh ocean breeze soothed her soul, and she felt herself lifting, as on the wings of a gull.

She felt rejuvenated. The time had been restorative and enjoyable. Her heart lifted, her body relaxed, and her mind focused in the present. As a child she had learned something about the source of her health and happiness. All along a part of her had known how to access it. She wondered how she could ever have forgotten something so important, and how she could ensure she never forgot it again.

STORY 15
WE ARE ALL DIFFERENT

Therapeutic Characteristics

Problems Addressed

- Our own narrow perspective on issues
- Nonacceptance of differing attitudes
- Being intolerant of others

Resources Developed

- Developing greater understanding
- Seeing the other person's perspective
- Learning to accept individual differences

Outcomes Offered

- Tolerate differences.
- Accept others' attitudes and actions.
- Maybe there is no "right"—just differences.
- Caring for others can have many diverse expressions.

A horseman rode into a clearing, wondering where he could tether his horse. Looking around, he found a pole, dug a hole, and tramped it firmly into the ground. He walked down to a nearby river to take a drink, then, before leaving, thought to himself, "I will leave the pole in the ground. Another horseman who comes along this way will also have somewhere to tie his horse."

The next visitor was not a horseman, but a traveler who happened to be walking through the same area. Coming to the clearing where the pole was stuck in the middle of the trail, she thought to herself, "If people come by here in the night, they could walk straight into this pole and hurt themselves." Acting out of concern for others, she pulled the pole out of the ground and threw it aside.

A day or two later, a fisherman was walking down to the river to cast his line when he saw the pole lying to the side of the clearing. He picked it up and carried it down to the riverbank. There he used it as a seat to raise his body above the muddy soil. When he was about to leave, he too acted out of consideration. "I will leave this pole here," he thought. "Any other fisherman coming down to the bank will also have a dry place on which to sit and cast his line."

A short while later a boatman rowed down the river looking for somewhere to hitch his boat. He saw the pole on the embankment, nosed his bow into the shore and, like the horseman, dug a hole, and inserted the pole so that he could safely hitch his vessel. On departing, he displayed consideration for other boaters. "I will leave the pole embedded in the bank. That way, any other boatsman coming down the river can also use it as a convenient mooring spot."

The next by-passer was a lumber cutter. He had been out felling green trees all day when he saw the pole inserted in the embankment. He thought to himself, "What a nice dry piece of wood. It will burn well and keep my aging mother warm during the coming winter." He heaved it onto his shoulder, carried it to his mother's home, and chopped it up.

Each traveler had treated the pole with good intent and in consideration of his or her fellow travelers. Each had done so in a way that was both rational and practical. Each used the pole well.

Each traveler was different. Each perceived the pole differently, and, because of these perceptions, each took a different course of action.

Who can say which traveler was right, or even whether there is a right?

STORY 16
THE ULTIMATE WISH

Therapeutic Characteristics

Problems Addressed

- Holding unrealistic dreams or wants
- Making happiness conditional
- Wanting perfection

Resources Developed

- Accepting the simple things
- Discovering that pain and suffering can be experiences for growth
- Accepting what life brings

Outcomes Offered

- Want what you can have.
- Learn from life's experience.
- Pain and pleasure are all part of the journey.

A university professor had a dream. She was driven by a passion to find and possess her ultimate wish. Already a world-renowned scholar of Mayan archeology, she had authored several books, published her research in the most prestigious journals, and spoke often as the keynote lecturer at international conferences. But this wasn't enough. She had discovered many treasured artifacts that were now safely locked away in museums. She had unearthed much knowledge about Mayan culture, but this, too, was not enough. What she coveted most was, according to her colleagues, a myth, a rumor, a mere hint of something that might, or might not, be.

Her studies had made her familiar with the cuneiform Mayan language, and she searched for meanings in this once-spoken language that was now as dead as the stones on which it was inscribed. Over the years something had intrigued her and given rise to her passionate mission. The cuneiforms hinted that the possessor of a particular vessel would have his or her ultimate wish granted. This was what she desired with such burning passion. It was this message that made her declare, "I never will be happy until I find the sacred vessel that grants a person's ultimate wish."

She was not one to spend time analyzing her own self-talk. She never stopped to think how hanging happiness on something so intangible might destine her to a life of disillusion. If life's enjoyment was contingent on finding just one object that may not even exist, she was severely restricting her chances of happiness. What if she never found it? What if it didn't exist? What if it did exist, but didn't have the power to grant the ultimate wish? Did this mean she would never be happy?

For now, she wasn't happy. The Mayan tablets gave no reference to the whereabouts of her obsession, save that it was stored in a special, unidentified temple. Then one day something happened that changed the course of her career—and life itself. While flying in a light aircraft over the jungles of Central America, strong winds blew her plane off its course. Looking down in an attempt to fix a bearing, her trained archaeological eye detected a solitary conical hill rising from the jungle. Her heart skipped a beat. To any other it may have been no more than a beautifully symmetrical hillock. To the professor, it was a strangely isolated, and previously unrecorded, temple.

Full of anticipation, she quickly organized an overland expedition. She made sure she hired her usual assistant, a man native to the area. He was reliable, hard working, and loyal, but had a weakness for alcohol. To guarantee his loyalty and honest labor, the archeologist went to elaborate efforts to ensure no intoxicating beverages found their way into the expedition supplies.

Hacking their way through the dense jungle and excavating the centuries-neglected temple was arduous. The temperature was hot. The humidity was high, and her assistant made it only too clear that he longed for a drink. Indeed he could think of little else at the end of a hard day's labor.

Per chance, he was the first to burst into the inner chamber of the temple. His nose quickly detected the smell of the sweetest bourbon. He followed the aroma across the chamber to an altar on which sat a single vessel. He pulled the plunger from the bottle's neck and swigged a deep draft of the best bourbon he had ever tasted.

The professor was not far behind. She smelled the bourbon on his breath and, thinking he had secreted some into their supplies, cursed herself for not having checked more thoroughly before departing. Even this failed to distract her for long. Her eyes quickly fell on the vessel sitting on the altar—exactly where her assistant had replaced it.

It looked no different from any other Mayan work: a creamy-colored ceramic vessel with painted depictions of the sacred jaguar as well as both the sun and moon gods. Nonetheless, she knew *this* was the vessel.

Like her assistant, she pulled the plunger from the neck of the bottle but, unlike her assistant, she smelled no bourbon. When she shook it, the vessel was empty.

She carefully packed it for the return trek, and they began the difficult journey home through the jungle. She could not wait to tell her skeptical colleagues. Now that she had found it she certainly felt happy.

The professor may not have been so elated if she had known what was going on behind her back. Whenever her assistant felt the urge for a drink, he would secretly unpack the vessel and drink from its endless supply. Then he would carefully repack it and return it to its box. This time, he thought, the professor had really discovered something worthwhile.

After two or three days of walking and thinking, the professor's curiosity had risen to a level that overwhelmed her. Could this vessel indeed grant her ultimate wish? Could it provide what she wanted most of all? Did it really have the power and magic that had been alluded to on those stone tablets?

One night under a full moon, she took the box and sat back to lean against a tree. She unpacked her precious possession and decided to test the sacred vessel's fabled ability to grant the ultimate wish. She pulled the cork on the empty vessel. There was no aroma. Holding it in the moonlight, she wished her ultimate wish. "I wish for freedom from hurt, pain, tragedy, and sadness. I wish for total happiness."

Again, she had not stopped to think about what she said. Pain, hurt, and unhappiness are part of everyone's experiences. As unpleasant as they may be, they are essential elements of everyone's journey through life. From them we learn the lessons of survival. They contribute to our experience and our growth. Life cannot nor will not be *totally* happy. Without pain, tragedy, hurt, or sadness, there is no life.

Barely had she made her wish than she got what she requested. She fell lifeless beside the bottle, free of hurt, pain, and sadness. The next morning her assistant arose from his tent. He made breakfast and took it to the professor's tent. Surprised to find her missing, he began searching. It was not long before he discovered his lifeless employer sitting under the tree with the sacred vessel at her side. "If ever I needed a drink," he exclaimed, "it is now." He picked up the bottle, pulled the plunger, and sipped on the bountiful supply of bourbon.

STORY 17
ACCEPTING WHAT LIFE BRINGS

Therapeutic Characteristics

Problems Addressed

- Desire for control of the uncontrollable
- Expectation that life should adjust to you
- Intolerance of inconveniences

Resources Developed

- Accepting that some things are unchangeable
- Learning to adjust to the unchangeable
- Asking for the achievable

Outcomes Offered

- Accept what life brings.
- Tolerate inconveniences.
- Realize that things could be worse.
- Make sure that what you ask for is what you want.

When I was a child I had a teacher named Mr. Farmer. I think one of the reasons I remember him so well is because of the way he taught. He taught in stories, parables, and proverbs. He used to say things like, "Every privilege has its responsibilities." I don't think that meant much to me as a child, but now that I'm an adult I've come to appreciate his message. Stories and sayings have a tendency to stick in our memory banks and may come back at some later date.

Mr. Farmer once told a story about a frail and elderly widow who lived alone in a humble abode some miles from the nearest village. Each Friday she made the slow and laborious journey into the local markets to buy her provisions for the week. She planned carefully so as to make just the one journey a week. Indeed, it was something that frequently occupied her thoughts. She had wondered about making two or three lighter trips per week, but that would mean having to make the journey even more frequently. No, once a week was enough.

With the passing years the journey had become increasingly arduous, especially the uphill trek home when she was laden with her purchases. No buses went her way. She lived such a solitary existence that there were no friends she could ask to give her a ride. Taxis were too expensive. No, she had to rely on her own resources, as difficult as the task may be.

One particular Friday, as was her ritual, she wrote out her shopping list, dressed for town, and gathered her two baskets. She carried one basket in each hand to distribute the load evenly, give her balance, and make the journey easier.

As she made her way toward town, a strong and bitter wind blew straight in her face, forcing her frail body to struggle against its strength. Being a woman of faith, she began to pray. She asked God to change the direction of the wind. She prayed all the way into town as she struggled against the cold blast, but the wind kept blowing, and it appeared her prayers had gone unanswered. It neither abated nor changed direction.

In the village she did her usual rounds: the bakery for her loaf of bread, the dairy for her milk, the grocer for her vegetables, and the butcher for her meat. Gradually she filled each basket, testing to see if they were evenly weighted. When all items on her list had been ticked off, she turned around to make the uphill journey home—and faced straight into the wind. Sure enough God had heard her prayers and changed the direction of the wind!

STORY 18
ACCEPTING A LOSS

Therapeutic Characteristics

Problems Addressed

- Experience of loss
- When life doesn't go our way
- Facing the unexpected

Resources Developed

- Accepting problems
- Learning to reframe a loss
- Looking for the best possible explanation
- Adjusting your perspective of events

Outcomes Offered

- A loss can be minimized by how you see it.
- Look on the bright side.
- Find the least painful solution.

An unemployed father of four shuffled hopelessly along a lonely road. He had left home at the crack of dawn, as he had done every day for the last few months. His despair was evident in his reluctant gait. He anticipated that his rounds of the town would again fail to produce any paid labor.

The family was struggling. Bills were piling up, the kids sometimes went to bed hungry, and his wife was becoming depressed. As he dragged his feet along the dusty road, his toe kicked something. Curious, he bent down to pick it up. It was an old, battered, and unfamiliar coin. Not enough, he thought, to ease our plight.

Nonetheless, he took it to the bank. "It is not legal currency," the teller said to him. The man shrugged. It was the way his luck was going. The teller suggested he take it to a coin collector down the street. The collector confirmed its antiquity and gave him $30 for his find.

Overjoyed, the poor man began to ponder what he might do with this windfall. As he walked passed a hardware store, he noticed some beautifully grained wood on sale. He could build his wife some shelves, for she had been saying for sometime there was nowhere to put her pots and jars in their modest kitchen.

Exchanging his $30 for the timber, he lifted it on his shoulder and started the journey home. Along the way he happened to pass a furniture maker. The manufacturer's professional eye quickly spotted the attractive grain, the rich color, and the high quality of timber the man carried on his shoulder. He had an order to build a display cabinet, and with that timber he could ask a high price, so he offered the man $100. When the poor man hesitated, the furniture maker tempted him by offering a choice of certain pre-made furniture.

There was a cupboard that would surely please his wife. He swapped the timber and borrowed a wheelbarrow from the furniture manufacturer to carry his cupboard home. On the way he had to pass through a new housing estate. A woman, decorating her new home, looked out of the window and saw the man wheeling the very cupboard she wanted for her laundry. She offered him $200 for it. When he hesitated, she raised the offer to $250. He shook hands on the deal, returned the wheelbarrow to the furniture maker, and again set off home.

He paused at the gate. Pleased with his fortune, he reached into his pocket and pulled out the cash the day had brought his way. He wanted to count it one last time and was eager to show his wife.

That very moment a robber leaped from behind a bush, accosted the man at knife point, stole the $250, and fled. His wife had seen the attack from the kitchen window. She ran from the house. "What happened?" she cried. "Are you all right? What did you lose?"

He shrugged his shoulders and said, "Oh, just a battered old coin I stumbled across this morning."

STORY 19
GOOD LUCK, BAD LUCK. WHO KNOWS?

Therapeutic Characteristics

Problems Addressed

- Facing misfortune
- Experiencing loss
- Management of unexpected events

Resources Developed

- Accepting what happens in life
- Learning to avoid value judgments
- Living in the moment

Outcomes Offered

- Values are what we impose on life events.
- Acceptance is a matter of attitude.

One day a poor farmer's only horse escaped its paddock and fled into the hills. When the neighbors heard of this loss, they saw the gravity of the situation. Without the horse how could the farmer till his small plot of land? And if he couldn't till the land to grow a crop, how could he feed his family? They helped him search for the horse, but their efforts were in vain, and all they could do was express their condolences. "What bad luck," they told the farmer.

"Good luck, bad luck. Who knows?" replied the farmer.

It so happened that some days later his horse returned. The neighbors felt pleased for him and became ecstatic at the news that the horse had brought with it a herd of fit, young, wild horses. "This is great news," said his neighbors. "You will be able to break in the new horses and sell them all at a good price. What good luck."

The farmer was philosophical. "Good luck, bad luck. Who knows?"

However, he did as the neighbors suggested. He and his son started to break in the new horses. The task was not easy. In the process, one horse bucked violently, throwing the farmer's son from the saddle. His son fractured his leg in the fall. They had to seek medical aid they could ill afford. The son's leg was cast in plaster, and he could no longer help with breaking in the horses or tackling the many essential jobs around the farm.

The story soon spread around the neighborhood. The poor farmer's family was certainly having its ups and downs. Once again neighbors gathered to offer their condolences. "What bad luck," they told the father.

The farmer only shrugged his shoulders and again replied, "Good luck, bad luck. Who knows?"

Well, as the course of events go, the country fell into war while the son was still convalescing. Military officers came to the village to conscript all the able-bodied young men. Seeing the farmer's son in bed with his leg in plaster, they granted him an exemption from duty.

Once more the neighbors gathered. "Our sons have been conscripted," they complained. "They have been taken off to war. They could be injured or even killed. Your son has escaped. What good luck you have."

The farmer explained that for him good and bad were just the judgements that we put on life's events. Life was experiences and that was it. The laws of nature had no intention of creating good for one person and ill for another. If it rains heavily on two adjoining properties, one's crops may benefit from the moisture, the other's dam may burst and wash away the crops. The rain itself is neither good nor bad, though the adjoining farmers may attribute to it their respective judgements. For example, the next season comes around and the first farmer now curses the heavy rains of the previous season because the bumper crop it helped produce depleted the soil this season. The crop is not nearly as good. The second farmer is now jubilant. The burst dam moistened and enriched the soil. He may have lost his crop last season, but now he has a bumper harvest. The event itself has not changed but the attitudes of the farmers about it have. Therefore, it is not so much *what* has happened, explained the poor and patient farmer, but rather *how* we interpret it. Good and bad are the values we place on experiences that have no values in and of themselves.

"That is why," he said, "when you offer condolences or congratulations on my fortune, I reply, 'Good luck, bad luck. Who knows?'"

STORY 20
SEEKING PERFECTION

Therapeutic Characteristics

Problems Addressed

- Being perfectionistic
- Holding unrealistically high standards
- A need to see perceived imperfections rather than qualities

Resources Developed

- Tolerating differences
- Learning to accept imperfections
- Judging others as we want to be judged

Outcomes Offered

- What you give is what you get.
- Waiting may mean missing something.
- See others for the qualities they have.

A group of women had gathered to celebrate the forthcoming marriage of a friend. During the evening the bride-to-be asked one of her older and still single friends, "How is it that you have never married? Have you never found the right guy?"

"Oh, yes," she said. "I found the right man all right."

"Then what happened? Why didn't you marry him?" inquired the betrothed.

"It was like this," said the friend. "I knew exactly who I was looking for. He had to be the perfect man. I had a checklist of all the qualities I wanted in a guy and I set out to travel the world to find him. He had to be just right, and he was."

"Tell me, then," asked the curious bride-to-be. "What happened?"

"Well, I started searching in New York," said the friend. "There I found a very wealthy man. He was generous with his money, but he was withdrawn, introverted, and unsociable. That knocked him off the list right away.

"I traveled on to Los Angeles, searching everyplace in between New York and the West Coast. In LA I found a man who was not only rich but also fun-loving, happy, and outgoing. He had the affluence and all the social qualities I could ever expect from a guy. The unfortunate thing was that he wasn't very handsome. I kept thinking, 'if we marry I will have to wake up beside that unhandsome face every morning.' No, he wasn't Mr. Right, either.

"In Sydney I felt I was starting to get close. There I came across a guy who had his own independent means. He was friendly and outgoing—and stunningly handsome. He was tall, blonde, and muscular. He was a surfer, worked out at the gym regularly, and had the body of a pin-up model. But with all the men I met, there always seemed to be an unacceptable down side. With him, it was his arrogant male attitude. He was a chauvinist.

"So I traveled on to Europe. In London I met a man who was rich, outgoing, handsome, and liberated in his ideas about women. This was getting really close. At first I thought I had finally found him, but he lacked the romance and sensuality that I was seeking. It's nice to have a guy who will cook and do the dishes, but I guess I want the red rose and moonlight picnic treatment as well.

"Journeying across the channel to Paris I found him. You know what they say about the French. Well, he had it all. He was wealthy, friendly, handsome, liberated, and *very* sensual. He got top rating on every item on my checklist. There was no question. He was my perfect man."

"Then," exclaimed the curious bride-to-be, "why didn't you marry him?"

"Oh," responded the friend, "The reason was simple. He was looking for the perfect woman."

STORY 21
LIFE IS NOT WHAT IT SHOULD BE

Therapeutic Characteristics

Problems Addressed

- Feelings of frustration
- Intolerance of others' wants
- Expectations of perfection
- Desire to have everything right

Resources Developed

- Accepting unexpected events
- Tolerating others
- Allowing for imperfections
- Reframing rigid ideas

Outcomes Offered

- Life is not what it should be.
- Life is not perfect.
- Acceptance helps us manage frustrations.

Recently, I organized a conference in my city. If you have ever done anything like this I am sure you can appreciate what a hair-tearing and nail-biting experience it can be. The more pressure we put on ourselves to ensure that everything is just right, the more stressful it can be.

Many of my friends consider me to be an adventurer. Certainly I have traveled to many exotic places, but I never travel without being well prepared. I go with a planned itinerary, having read as broadly as I can about the remote areas into which I might adventure. I prepare myself physically, climbing every hill I can find, carrying a backpack over backcountry trails, and swimming. I weigh up the probabilities of all the things that could go wrong and try to be prepared if and when they do. I take a medical kit that is good enough to see an army through a war.

It is not that I'm afraid of the unexpected; indeed I relish it. Part of the joy of adventure travel is coming across the unexpected, discovering new places, meeting new people, journeying into unique cultures, tasting different foods, and pitting one's wits against the challenges of unfamiliar environments. Yes, I relish the unexpected, but I like to be prepared for it when it happens.

I take with me that same desire for preparedness into other aspects of my life—like organizing a meeting. For a year or two I had been mulling over the idea of the conference until I got it right. I approached potential keynote presenters and confirmed their attendance. I booked the venue and finalized the menu months beforehand.

The week before the conference, one presenter urgently requested a video camera to tape a consultation for her workshop. I traveled 40 miles to deliver the video camera, only to be advised she had already borrowed one! Then the penny dropped: If she was recording a video, she would also require audio-visual projection. She had not indicated this previously, and it was not available in the room into which she had been scheduled. We had to reshuffle everything at the last minute to accommodate her request. After making an effort to ensure everything was well-planned, I felt *this should not be happening*.

The evening before the meeting, my secretary and I visited the venue to make sure everything had been set up according to our instructions. What we found was a disaster. Together we spent several hours setting up one room and reorganizing another. Again I thought, *this should not be happening*.

When I belatedly arrived home, the phone was ringing. The keynote lecturer who was to launch the meeting the next morning was calling to cancel his keynote address due to a personal tragedy in his family. A hole gaped in the program like a trapdoor opening up beneath the gallows. There was no way it could be filled at such short notice. His reasons were fully understandable, and he had my deepest empathy. Nonetheless, I could not help thinking, *this should not be happening*.

The next morning another presenter announced he was unwilling to accept the upright chairs provided for his demonstration, as he could only work comfortably from a lounge chair. Under my breath I was cursing. He knew what he needed beforehand, so why couldn't he have made his request earlier? Why should I be feeling so responsible? Again my head was ruminatively reminding me, *this should not be happening*.

At the end of the day, I walked from the venue back to my consulting room. One of the street corners I pass has a small stationery store that always displays a white board out front with a hand-written quotation. On this day it caught my eye, just the way something does when you feel as though it is meant especially for you. The message read, "Life is not what it should be. It is what it is."

EXERCISE

Use a notebook to record your own stories and ideas for goal-oriented metaphors of acceptance. Look for examples in your own experiences and in your caseload. Then, once you have jotted down the idea

1. Begin to think about how you might structure the story to retell it.
2. Bear in mind the 10 Guidelines for Effective Storytelling described in Chapter 2.
3. Incorporate not just the story ideas, but also the mood or sensory experiences that are associated with it.
4. Practice telling the story to someone who is willing to do nothing but listen.

ACCEPTANCE

CHAPTER 6

Reframing Negative Attitudes

I am not the first to say that life is an ambiguous stimulus—a three dimensional, surround-sound, multisensory Rorschach inkblot—in which experience is largely determined by how we perceive and conceive it. Our attitude toward life, its specific events, and other people affect how we feel more than the events and people themselves.

How we act on the basis of those perceptions, in turn, reinforces our attitude. If we see the world as a terrible place in which to live, other people as unfair, or life as having stacked its cards against us, we create a formula for unhappiness. Looking for the beauty in the world, seeing the positive qualities in other people, and accepting that life has its ups and downs can lead to a healthier adaptation and a happier disposition.

Elsewhere, I have told the story (Burns, 1998) of leaving home one wild, wet winter's morning with my grandson in the car. He wiggled in his seat with excitement at the rain belting the car, running in rivulets up the windshield, and being swished away by the rapid beat of the windshield wipers. On the radio the announcer described the day as "terrible." I turned off the radio to listen to my grandson, aware of how the same event could be perceived in two totally opposite ways, and aware, too, of how I had a choice about which perception I listened to, and which I adopted as my own.

The outcome-oriented stories in this chapter look at reframing unexpected events, attitudes about ourselves, issues of the past, and current crises.

STORY 22
LOOKING UP

Therapeutic Characteristics

Problems Addressed

- Encountering loss
- Experiencing grief
- Feelings of disappointment
- Facing unexpected changes
- Desire for the unattainable

Resources Developed

- Learning to accept reality
- Developing the use of reason
- Looking for the positive
- Learning to change thoughts and feelings
- Shifting attention to the positive

Outcomes Offered

- Grieve appropriately.
- Accept what life brings.
- Reframe ideas.
- Create positive from the negative.
- Find new options.

A Zen master had been away from home for several days. He had not really enjoyed his trip. It was not that the monastery he visited was any less comfortable than his own humble home (which only provided the basic necessities for survival anyway). What he missed was the familiarity of his own surroundings.

The bed did not feel like his own. He missed the prayerful whisper of the breeze through the eaves of his timber house. The same bird songs did not accompany his morning meditation. When he finally started for home, his heart lifted.

Unfortunately, tragedy had struck in his absence. The Zen master arrived to find that his home had burned to the ground. All that remained was a parched piece of earth, a surprisingly tiny pile of blackened ash, and the smoky smell of his lost abode.

He stood staring at the charred remains. "Why me?" he asked initially. "I've been away teaching, doing good, wishing happiness on all fellow beings. What did I do to deserve this?" But he soon realized that the powers of the universe had not singled him out for any special treatment. It was just one of those unfortunate life events. Such questions could only lead to pain and depression. They would not help him to deal with the loss, find a purposeful direction for the future, or take immediate action like finding a place to sleep for the night.

A wave of sadness washed over him. He had really liked his little home and its comforting familiarity. For years his homecomings had felt like returning to a beloved friend. Then he reminded himself that, as a Zen master, he should not be attached to material possessions. Yet somehow the sadness seemed appropriate. It was, he assured himself, acceptable to grieve for a loss, so he stayed in the moment, mindful of his sadness, until it felt like it was time to move on.

Next he found himself wishing it hadn't happened. He wished he had stayed at home. He wished he had checked to ensure his cooking fire had been extinguished. If only he had done those things, his little home might still be there. "But," he assured himself, "it has been destroyed. That is the reality. No matter what I wish, I can't change that. Wishing for something that can't be changed can only result in more unhappiness and suffering."

As he focused on the charred remains of his house, he continued to be plagued with questions and doubts. Realizing this, he lifted his gaze to the sky. Twinkling stars dotted the dark backdrop of the heavens. A full moon smiled down benevolently. A sudden thought struck him and made him smile. "I may have lost a house but, at last, I have an uninterrupted view of the sky at night."

STORY 23
THE LAW OF NATURE

Therapeutic Characteristics

Problems Addressed

- Feelings of loneliness
- Pessimism
- Facing hardship and adversity
- Dealing with hostile circumstances
- Poor health
- A lack of material resources

Resources Developed

- Accepting our circumstances
- Learning patience
- Developing optimism
- Using your resourcefulness
- Developing a determination to learn and survive
- Letting go of the past
- Using your mind and body to enhance your well-being

Outcomes Offered

- Develop a positive mental attitude.
- Learn self-worth.
- Be strong in adversity.
- Live in peace and harmony.
- Have confidence in using your resources.
- Reframe unwanted attitudes and ideas.

If you are ever fortunate to visit the Linh Son temple in Vietnam, don't limit your exploration to the large open pagoda. The real attraction here is not in the property or edifices. It is worth taking the time to explore beyond the boundaries of the temple to seek out the embodiment of enlightenment.

As you walk, you pass a large, resonant bell. Cast (at least in part) in gold, it has a deep, vibrating tone. But the bell is not the reason you would want to visit, either.

At the side of the temple is an ordinary-looking coffee plantation. Among the coffee bushes is a small yellow hut that is home to an ascetic, Letrung Trang. "Maybe it is the smallest house that anyone in the world lives in," he says. Looking at his hut I could believe that he is right, for it is smaller than my garden shed back home, barely large enough to accommodate a bed, books, and a little cooker.

"I am fortunate," he says gesturing toward the surrounding plantation. "Many people throughout the world drink coffee. Many know how it tastes. Many enjoy its flavor. But how many have the pleasure of simply sitting here and watching it grow? I watch the seasons come and go. I observe the cycle of life. I see times of dormancy and times of growth. I watch new buds spring forth, smell the blossoms, and experience the fruit coming to maturity."

Life for Trang has not been easy. He has not always been able to sit undisturbed in this peaceful retreat. The son of a Japanese father and Vietnamese mother, he is fluent in several languages. As a result, during World War II, the Japanese occupational forces pressed him into service as a translator.

Adversity did not deter him. He was in his thirties when he went to school at a Franciscan convent and attained his secondary education in the French language. He was arrested and detained for his outspoken views against the Communist regime, yet he pressed on with his quest for knowledge and completed a master's degree in American literature. Like the coffee plants he watches daily, he has known both good and bad seasons. Like the beloved bushes, he too matured.

When I spoke with him, his body was very skeletal-like, yet lithe and fluid. He spoke and gestured energetically. His teeth were rotting and he used glasses to read, but he was healthy and mentally alert. "How old do you think I am?" he asked. "Would you believe I am 68 and am very healthy! I eat just once a day. I take no medicines. If our mind is good, our body is healthy. If we think virtuously, we do not get sick. Illness is the product of bad thoughts."

We spoke of the Vietnam War. He and his people had suffered in ways I could not begin to comprehend. Yet he seemed to bear no anger, hostility, or bitterness to any of his oppressors. "After the rain," he said, "there is always sunshine. After the storm there is peace. It is the law of nature."

STORY 24
GOOD FOLLOWS BAD

Therapeutic Characteristics

Problems Addressed

- Depression
- Generalized negative thinking
- Attributions of external control
- Attributions of stability

- Attributions of global thinking
- Feelings of helplessness and hopelessness

Resources Developed

- Developing the ability to alter perceptions
- Learning to question your assumptions
- Finding exceptions to global depressive thoughts
- Discovering the ability to enjoy simple pleasures

Outcomes Offered

- Develop positive affect.
- Own personal power for change.
- Accept life's variability.
- Accept each event as an individual event.
- Choose your preferred perception.

"I am depressed," Maria said the first time we met, expressing her emotional state in more ways than her words. Her body slumped into the chair, her face was forlorn, and she displayed no signs of joy. It seemed as though happiness were as alien to her as a Martian. "Whenever something good happens," she continued, "something bad always follows."

Indeed a lot of "bad" things had been occurring in her life: things she hadn't planned, things she hadn't expected, things she did not choose. Just when circumstances began to improve, and her hopes began to rise, something would happen. Like a beach-bound wave, life circumstances seemed, at least to her, ready to dump her breathless on a barren shore. Maria gave several examples, as if to prove her point and validate her conclusions.

Her marriage had come through some tough times, and things were just beginning to look up. They had paid off their mortgage, and the children thankfully had grown into stable and independent young adults. Money was not as short as it had been previously, and they were able to enjoy a mutual, long-term ambition to travel. Then her husband announced that he was having an affair. He was a bastard. This wasn't fair.

Maria got a job after going back to college. Others valued her for the quality of her work. She took pride in what she did and, because of it, felt a growing sense of self-esteem. She didn't *need* her husband, and, in fact, began to relish the pleasures of her independence. Then there was a downturn in the industry. Her boss fired her. Men were bastards. Life wasn't treating her fairly.

In time Maria met another man who seemed gentle and caring. He came into her life like a knight in shining armor and rescued her from her despair. Her self-worth blossomed once more. She felt she was riding on the crest of an emotional wave, hesitant that it may crash but not wanting to acknowledge that events and circumstances in life are subject to change. No emotion, no experience, no matter how tightly we may want to hold onto it, lasts forever. And it didn't. He left her for a relationship with a man. All men were bastards. Life never gave her a fair chance.

Despite the definitive view of life that she brought into therapy, she was eager to improve her situation, and she progressed well. She did many things to bring about this change, but above all else she was willing to question her own conclusions about men and life. Did the treatment she thought she received at the hands of three men really mean that all men were bastards? If half the world's population fit into this box-like category then it was certainly a difficult place to live. Was there just one man who might be an exception? Yes, her brother was definitely different from the men she had been meeting. By finding exceptions, the "rule" was no longer all-inclusive. By assessing each one and each life event on the basis of its own merits, Maria did not distort them in her perception by the baggage of past experiences.

If we form an attitude that all trees are just green, we may never see the subtle and beautiful differences in the leaves from the light of the rising sun, through the brilliance of midday, to the final hues at dusk. If we continue to cling to this belief, we may miss out on seeing the beauty of other varieties or fail to appreciate the colors of fall.

In spite of all the bad things that had happened to her, had Maria ever experienced pleasure, or had life ever treated her well? What made her happy? Together we discussed the joys of swimming in a summer's sea, of watching spring bulbs herald a new season in golden brilliance, and of seeing newborn birds descend into her garden for their first taste of the delights she left out in her birdfeeder.

The conversation about these pleasures of life was enough to change the expression on her face, bring a twinkle of enjoyment to her eyes, and open up the hope of new possibilities that she may create for herself. By shifting her attention to the ongoing pleasures of life around her and being less focused on the negative issues that had preoccupied her thoughts, she felt better.

Maria changed the way she looked at life's events and circumstances. She could see there were things over which she had control, and thus she didn't always have to be washed back and forth by the tide of life like a helpless jellyfish. She came to discover that bad was not forever, anymore than good was. "Maybe," she said on one occasion, "it is not even a question of good or bad, but just experience. Good and bad are just the interpretations we place on what happens."

The change in her attitude did not escape me, and I could not help inquiring, "Do you remember what you said the first time we met?"

"No," she answered.

"Well, when we first met, you said that whenever something good happened, something bad always followed. Now you seem to be telling me something different."

She smiled at this. "That's life, isn't it?" she replied rhetorically. "If something good happens, something bad may follow it. But if something bad happens, something good may follow. I guess that's the pattern of things. It really depends on how you look at it."

STORY 25
ADJUSTING YOUR SAILS

Therapeutic Characteristics

Problems Addressed

- When life doesn't go your way
- Encountering unexpected, unwanted events
- Onerous tasks

REFRAMING

- Feelings of frustration
- Holding negative attitudes

Resources Developed

- Adapting to unchangeable circumstances
- Learning to look on the bright side
- Finding the positive
- Seeing pleasure rather than pain

Outcomes Offered

- Change what you can.
- Keep the big picture in sight.
- Seek out the pleasurable and positive.
- Look ahead.
- Make choices about how you want to feel.

I have a friend who is a keen sailor. On many occasions I have heard him say, "You may not be able to change the direction or strength of the wind, but you can always adjust your sails."

As I own a small sailboat, I am particularly attuned to nautical sayings and their more general applicability. My boat sits out the winter months on a mooring in an estuary where a variety of marine vegetation and barnacles adopt its hull as their home, causing damage and impairing its sailing performance. With the approach of each sailing season, the boat needs to be hauled out of the water, cleaned down, and prepared for the new season.

For some time, the boat's mast had needed repairs, but the boat repairer had always said the task was not urgent, and he would get to it later. As he never did it, I finally decided to do the job, along with some other repairs, myself. I awoke at 5:00 A.M. each morning, took a break during the heat of the early afternoon, and returned again in the evening.

I laboriously stripped the paint off the keel, cut back some rust spots, and applied both a recommended rust converter and a similarly recommended waterproof sealant, but they were incompatible and bubbled away like a witch's cauldron. My days of hard labor in hot, humid conditions were lost. I had no choice but to completely strip it back and start over again.

One evening as I was working after sunset on what had now become a terribly onerous chore, a guy in his mid-twenties walked by, relaxed after just returning from a pleasant twilight sail. We exchanged a few words before he continued walking.

Next, I turned to the mast. I removed fittings, pressure-hosed as much flaky paint off as possible, applied paint stripper to the remainder, sanded it back to the bare aluminum, and painted it with an etching primer. It was long, hard work in weather that was not conducive to anything but siestas. I cursed the climate, the boat repairer, and the mast for every inch of its interminable length.

"Are you still here?" asked a cheerful voice later that week. It was the young man who greeted me a few nights ago. He wore the white uniform of the boat on which he had just spent his afternoon sailing. He had a relaxed gait and pleasant smile.

"Yes," I grunted, which did nothing to hide the frustration, annoyance, and intolerance that had been building up in me during the day. "There is this myth about boats. You buy them thinking that you will spend your weekends cruising beautiful oceans for relaxation and pleasure. They never tell you that you will be wasting your life away working your butt off to get it in the water in the first place."

"Oh! It is all part of the fun," he said cheerfully.

"It hardly seems like it at times like this," I moaned.

He looked a little surprised at the negativity of my response. "Can you sail your boat without doing all this work?" he asked.

"Yes," I answered, realizing that it was still sailable in its current condition. Certainly the maintenance would help keep it that way for many years to come and so my labors would have their rewards, but perhaps I hadn't needed to make all the repairs at once.

"Then," he said with a big smile before he turned and walked off casually toward the sunset, "It really is for the fun of it, isn't it?"

STORY 26
CHOOSING YOUR MODEL

Therapeutic Characteristics

Problems Addressed

- Being dependent
- Ambivalence and uncertainty
- Adopting a victim role
- Expectation of something for nothing

Resources Developed

- Altering the focus of your attention
- Building competency
- Acquiring the power to select your role models

Outcomes Offered

- Learn ways to step out of the victim role.
- Model competency rather than pathology.
- Take personal responsibility for your well-being.

A hunter had spent the whole day unsuccessfully stalking prey through the jungle. He was feeling frustrated by his lack of success and embarrassed to return to the village empty-handed when he came to a clearing. At the edge of the clearing lay a wild boar with a broken leg.

"At last," thought the hunter, "an easy target." But something made him hesitate. On the one hand, he welcomed the prospect of such an easy prey. Surely he would be well received in the village if he carried home such a prized trophy. On the other hand, he felt sorry for the boar.

While he procrastinated at the edge of the jungle, a lioness entered the clearing. At first he thought she too was stalking the boar. Again he felt ambivalent. Might the lioness smell his presence and attack? He could shoot at her, but what if his arrow fell short or only wounded her? Might he then be more vulnerable to attack? Perhaps, he thought, he should stay motionless and hope she kept her attention on the boar.

As he watched silently he noticed she carried fresh kill in her mouth. What happened next surprised the hunter. The lioness dropped her meat in front of the boar. She ate her fill, nuzzled the rest toward the ailing boar and, as it began to eat, quietly went on her way.

The hunter, fascinated by this generosity, could not kill the boar and returned to his village empty-handed. The next day his curiosity guided him back to the clearing. He witnessed again the unbelievable caring of the lioness who brought food to the injured boar.

He concluded that nature cares for its own. Why should he work so hard trying to feed himself and the members of his extended family? The universe always provides for those in need. So he modeled himself on the creature that could have been his prey.

He sat alone in a jungle clearing. The days went by and nothing happened. No lioness, or other creature, came with sustenance. He grew hungrier and hungrier, but still he waited, firm in his conviction that the universe would provide for him as it had done for the boar.

The longer he waited the weaker he grew, until eventually he was too weak to move. Close to dying, he heard a noise, and thought his salvation had at last arrived. Into the clearing limped a lame boar. The hunter recognized it as the very same animal he had seen the lioness feeding.

"What are you doing sitting here in such a weak and famished state?" asked the boar.

The hunter replied, "I saw the lioness bring you food when you were weak and sick. Like you, I am waiting for the universe to provide."

"You foolish man," the boar burst out in laughter. "You choose the wrong role model by imitating the ailing. Don't expect that the world will come to you. If you want a better role model, you should do as the lioness does."

STORY 27
LETTING GO OF THE PAST

Therapeutic Characteristics

Problems Addressed

- Life challenges
- Emotions of fear
- When principles and practice conflict
- Hanging on to the past
- Rigidity of thought and behavior

Resources Developed

- Developing compassion
- Learning to give of yourself
- Finding ways to let go of the past
- Journeying toward a goal

Outcomes Offered

- Put people before principles.
- Exercise compassion.
- Leave the past in the past.
- There are various paths that lead to your goal.

Two monks set out on a spiritual journey across the mountains. They wanted to know more about themselves and their relationship with the world. To this end, they were traveling to a distant monastery where a famous teacher was giving instruction on spiritual development.

Not all journeys are easy going, and the monks were not sure what lay ahead, but they set out believing the goal was worth whatever challenges they might encounter. Had they grown fearful of what unexpected events may have awaited them, or had their imaginations projected challenges into objects of fear and dread, they may well have decided never to venture outside the secure walls of their monastic home. Only keeping sight of their goal prepared them to face the challenges and begin the journey of discovery.

It was not long before they encountered the first difficulty. A raging river blocked their way. As they stood contemplating how best to ford it, something distracted their attention. Above the roar of the racing waters they could hear sad and desperate sobbing. After a little searching they found its source. A woman hid in the shelter of a rock, crying in violent sobs.

"I have been attacked and robbed," she uttered between her tears. "As I was coming home from the market with the only food my family could afford for the next week, a band of thieves set upon me. They stole my groceries and, at knife point, made me hand over most of my clothes, leaving me here cold, lonely, and nearly naked."

The first monk, compassionately and without hesitation, peeled off his outer robe. "Here, take this," he offered, gently wrapping it over her shoulders. He then inquired as to the whereabouts of her village.

"Across the river and several miles up the bank to the right," she said.

The monk asked if she would like to be carried across the river to ensure she arrived safe and dry on the other side. After she consented, he picked her up in his arms and walked across the river, gently placing her down on the opposite bank. He then escorted the young woman to her village several miles up the riverbank, concerned that no other misfortune should befall her on the way. Just before entering the village, he took the modest amount of food he was carrying for his own journey and handed it to her. He wished her safety and happiness, before turning to resume his travels.

The second monk could no longer hold back his emotions. "What have you done?" he asked incredulously. "We have taken vows of celibacy, we have sworn not to touch women, or have contact with them. Here you are picking up a semi-naked woman, embracing her in your arms, and carrying her across the river. You have engaged in an act of intimacy with a woman most unbefitting of a monk."

The first monk opened his mouth to respond but his fellow traveler gave him no opportunity. "You escorted her up the riverbank to her village. You made me go with you. You have added miles and miles to our journey. We may miss some of the master's teachings.

"On top of that you have given away your food and robe. We need them for our journey. Without food to eat and a robe to keep you warm at night we may never reach the monastery. Our whole journey could be ruined. Now we may not benefit from the master's teachings on spiritual development at all."

For hour after hour along the trail the monk continued berating his compassionate colleague. Eventually the monk who had carried the woman across the river stopped. He looked his companion caringly in the eyes and said, "At least when we got to the other side of the river, I let go of her."

STORY 28
A JOURNEY OF UNEXPECTED LEARNING

Therapeutic Characteristics

Problems Addressed

- Too much drive or purpose
- Failure to enjoy the moment
- Focus only on self
- Not receptive to new learning

Resources Developed

- Learning to appreciate the moment
- Discovering and enjoying simple pleasures
- Remembering to be playful and childlike
- Being receptive to new learning
- Accepting change and differences

Outcomes Offered

- We can learn from the young.
- Be mindful of the moment.
- Maintain an openness to change and discovery.
- Enjoy!

I recall a very idyllic day, made even better because my grandson was visiting. Thomas was about two years old and it was Spring. The sky was a vibrant swimming-pool blue, dotted with puffy white clouds. The air was washed with unseen waves of fragrant garden blossoms. That day I learned something from my grandson that I still remember.

I had our time together all planned. I would take him down the road to the neighborhood park. There the grass was mown, and the area was clean and tidy. The playground equipment was colorful, metallic, and relatively new. My mission was to get to the park as quickly as possible, spend our time together there, and then get home. To me it was all very clear. Little did I know that my grandson was about to teach me an important lesson.

You see, Thomas had a different mission. He was simply being in the moment, enjoying the experience of whatever happened to come along at the time. He had no need or purpose for getting to the park. He had no preconceived expectations or goals to be accomplished.

We had not gone a few yards from the front door before he stopped. He picked a wild daisy from beside the pavement. He looked at its color, studying the deep black center and bright yellow petals. He gently plucked a petal and looked with intrigue at the golden pollen dust that speckled his fingers. Only when he had lost interest was he willing to move on.

I was eager to get him to the park, so I took his tiny hand to guide him on. If we didn't hurry the afternoon would slip away before he had the chance to play on the swings and slides. However, within a few yards he stopped again. He had found a dandelion. He puffed at it and watched the fluffy seeds dance through the air. He followed their slow drifting arch as they flew lightly on the breeze and floated to the ground. He puffed again and watched in meditative silence. There was no hurry or urgency in his motion. Each puff brought a new experience, and he had all the time to discover it. He blew again until all the seeds had floated off to find fresh ground to germinate.

"Let's get to the park," I encouraged, but we had come to a vacant block of land between two houses. Two or three years back someone had dumped some rubble on the land. Wild grasses grew between old bricks and broken slabs of concrete. Flowers were springing up among the builder's debris.

Thomas made a direct line for it. He wanted to climb. Now we might never reach the park. I began to question the purpose of our afternoon, or at least the purpose as I had perceived it. Was it about his pleasure or what I thought he would enjoy?

He began to scramble up the rubble. I watched with the anxiety of a relatively new grandparent. He climbed the first mound with a look of delight in his eyes. He stopped at a stalk of wild oats that stood as tall as he. He picked the grain, peeled back the outer layers and rolled the seed in his fingers, feeling the texture, shape, and firmness. His attention was so focused that, for a while, the rest of the world evaporated.

Then he resumed his climb. He stood on a stick that snapped beneath his weight, dropping his leg into a gap between the rubble. I had to fight back my urge to race in and rescue him. I had to reassure myself that the unexpected can hold important lessons. This was part of his learning process.

High on the pile of rubble he discovered a trigger plant, and he gently reached out to investigate it with a tiny, chubby finger. The plant reacted. A hidden stamen snapped onto his fingernail, mistaking him for a visiting bee. He giggled in surprise and looked around to check whether I, too, had observed this trick of nature. He tested flower after flower, laughing with delight.

Neither time nor conquest was important. But eventually, without drive or mission, he stood on his summit—a mountain of rubble nearly twice his own height. From the look of triumph and delight on his cherub-like face, he may have just been the first to conquer Everest.

When we set out I was the one with a mission. I was on a journey of purpose. For me the walk had been seen as the means for reaching our goal: the playground in the park. Thomas, however, had been on a journey of discovery. For him the destination was not as meaningful as the process of simply enjoying the experiences along the way.

As a parent I thought I needed to teach my children many things. In fact, I thought it my duty and obligation to be their teacher. The responsibility weighed heavily. As a grandparent I've discovered there is much I have to learn from children. In many ways Thomas is *my* tutor.

We never made it to the park.

REFRAMING

STORY 29
WHEN YOU REACH THE END OF YOUR ROPE

Therapeutic Characteristics

Problems Addressed

- Feelings of stress and worry
- Symptoms of anxiety
- Parenting issues
- Self-doubts
- Lack of enjoyment

Resources Developed

- Learning to accept the unchangeable
- Finding way to change what you can
- Rediscovering your abilities to enjoy
- Choosing positive alternatives

Outcomes Offered

- It is possible to alter perceptions.
- It is possible to experience joy.
- There are means for self-nurturing.
- Stress can be modified.

When I first met Brenda, she said, "I am at the end of my rope."

Life is tough as a single mom, especially when your ex-husband moves overseas, has no contact with the children, and provides no financial support. Brenda devoted herself to work, in part because she enjoyed it and in part because she needed the money. She climbed from a basic secretarial job to a job as the personal assistant to the chief executive officer of a large corporation, but her career had not been without its stresses.

Her two children, in their late teens, were a handful. Her son was in jail for a string of driving offenses and unpaid fines. Her daughter had a drug addiction and had dropped out of the university. Brenda couldn't understand it, and neither could those who knew her, for there was no question that she was a good mother who cared deeply for her children and sought to instill in them strong social values. Where had she gone wrong? What more could she have done? Her questions only made her feel a greater sense of inadequacy.

The stress and worries began to take their toll, and Brenda developed a tremor in her right hand. Strangely, the tremor only occurred in her right hand and only when other people were watching her write. At such times, she just wanted to run and hide. Her doctors could find no physical reason for the tremor, which only increased her anxiety. Why could no one find the problem? The more she sought to learn what she didn't have, the more she worried and the greater her doubts and despondency.

Brenda took her work and motherhood—two roles that seemed to totally define her life—very seriously, which also added to her stress. When I asked what she did for fun, her answer was simple: nothing. When I asked about what she *used to do* for fun, she said she hadn't really enjoyed herself for a long time. When I invited her to recall a moment of childhood happiness or pleasure, however, something interesting happened.

She remembered swinging in a park. I asked her to close her eyes and imagine it as clearly as she could. She described the smell of the grass and the feel of the breeze on her face as she swung back and forth. She spoke of how nice it was to have someone there pushing the swing. She felt special, like someone was there solely to give her support, security, and enjoyment.

I showed her a Garfield comic in which the striped cat was sitting alone on a motionless swing saying to himself, "Sometimes in life I need a little push." Swings, like life, have their ups and downs, their back and forths. At times they swing off line, or twist out of balance, and the ride may not always be as smooth as we may have hoped. They can't always be controlled exactly as we wish for there are factors outside of our control, like the length of the ropes, the strength of the breeze, or the evenness of pressure applied by the pusher. Generally, the more we swing the better we become and the easier it is to manage, but swings also have the habit of settling down, losing any wayward motion, and centering themselves once again, even if we do nothing at all.

The fact of Brenda's life was that there were some things she could not change—and some that she could. As it *was possible* to alter her feelings and recapture those former experiences of being relaxed and carefree, I asked her to find a neighborhood park with a swing where she could spend some time swinging each day.

When she came back to her next appointment she said, "I know what you're asking me to do. I once heard someone say that when you have reached the end of your rope, it's time to tie a knot and have a swing."

STORY 30
WE ARE WHAT WE BELIEVE

Therapeutic Characteristics

Problems Addressed

- Feeling depressed and despondent
- Lack of drive or ambition
- Dissatisfaction with personal circumstances
- Discontentment with your lot

Resources Developed

- Being open to explore new options
- Learning to make choices
- Using knowledge and experience to make changes
- Finding and developing your inner strength

Outcomes Offered

- In choice is the power to change.
- New information can help you see yourself differently.
- It is possible to soar to new heights.
- Life can be different from what it has been.

A farmer inspected his property. As he knew, there are times when it is important to check your boundaries, see how the season is affecting your crop, and make sure things are in order. A little maintenance along the way can often prevent later catastrophes. Nurturing the things that need attention can help ensure that life flows smoothly. Naturally, he felt happier when it did, so he made sure he took the time whenever he could.

This particular day he deviated from his course to look at an eagle's nest high in a tree. He had been watching it with interest. He first became aware of it some months before as he observed the majestic bird bringing twigs to the site of its future home. Occasionally, he rode by to monitor its construction, while keeping his visits infrequent enough so as not to disturb the process. He was excited when the eagle nestled into the securely built bowl, and eagerly awaited his first sight of the hatchlings.

This day he was disappointed. The eagle was not on her nest. Nearby he found her body. She had been shot. Curiously, and apprehensively, he climbed the tree. The nest contained a single egg. He carried it carefully down the tree, took it back to his barn, and slipped it under a brooding hen.

The eaglet eventually hatched along with the other eggs that were lain under the hen. It was raised with the chickens and thought itself to be nothing but an unusual chicken. It spent its time scratching the ground for seeds, searching for worms, and clucking senselessly. That was the way it was, and that was the way the eagle spent its formative years. It had no concept of who or what it was. The opportunity to discover itself had never been there.

One day a dark, ominous shadow fell across the barnyard. In terror the eagle fled for shelter with its companions. Looking up, the eagle saw the outstretched wings of a huge bird effortlessly carrying itself in graceful circles as it glided on currents of warm air. Entranced by the majesty of such a huge and powerful bird, it turned to the chicken beside it and asked, "What's that?"

"That," said his companion, "is the king of birds. Its realm is the sky. It controls the air. It is called an eagle. We are chickens. We belong on the ground."

The eagle looked up at the bird and saw their similarities. It looked at the chickens and, for the first time, saw how different he was from them. The eagle's observation brought a new knowledge. Something changed in the way it experienced its reality. The new information opened up new options.

The eagle now had a choice. It could live and die as a chicken in the backyard coop or it could spread its wings and soar into the air with the majesty, skill, and power of the bird above.

STORY 31
MY DAD: FROM PROBLEMS TO SOLUTIONS

Therapeutic Characteristics

Problems Addressed

- Loss
- Unexpected tragedy
- Abuse
- Hard times

Resources Developed

- Drawing on inner resources
- Adapting to life's challenges
- Learning determination
- Developing lateral thinking

Outcomes Offered

- It is possible to overcome difficult times.
- Every problem has a solution.
- Problems can help develop skills and learning.

My Dad referred to himself as a "jack of all trades and master of none." He held neither trade qualifications nor professional degree. He claimed his schooling had been through the University of Hard Knocks.

Born at the beginning of the twentieth century, he was just one in a family of thirteen. It was a struggle to keep a family of this size fed, let alone finance their education. So my dad spent more of his childhood laboring in coal mines than sitting behind a school desk.

At the age of seventeen, he worked his passage on a steamship from England to Australia. Life was not easy, and, in his first job as a farmhand, he was treated like a slave. Abuse was not a common word then, so he had no language to describe the treatment he received, but his spirit was undaunted and he quickly learned to stand up for himself.

He saved his meager salary until he was able to buy a small but picturesque property on which the develop a market garden. He cleared the block, prepared the soil, planted his crops, and established his markets. All his efforts seemed to be paying off.

Then, just when he thought the end of the rainbow was in sight, a wildfire raced through the area. The fire destroyed his crops and razed his home. He lost everything that he had worked so long and hard to achieve. In debt and heartbroken, he walked off the land to obtain a job on a road gang carving a highway through precipitous coastal cliffs—a project on which several of his friends died. To add to his scant income, he caught snakes, grasping them by the tails, cracking them like a whip to break their backs, and selling their hides for fashionable snakeskin belts.

One of the many stories of this type of resourcefulness that he liked to share happened during his honeymoon. He and my mother had celebrated their marriage in a hills resort. Returning in their road-weary car to the home that he had built himself, they punctured a tire. Dad had spent every last cent on the honeymoon. Even if he walked back to the last town some miles away, he could afford neither the cost of a new tire nor a repair. Besides, he was a gentleman, and there was no way he would leave my mother by herself on an isolated roadway.

Instead, he removed the punctured tube, climbed over the roadside fence, and gathered an arm full of long wheat stalks that were growing in the farmer's paddock. He carried these back to the car, packed them solidly into the tire, and replaced the wheel on the car. As a result they were able to drive slowly, and safely, home. My father used to say, "A problem is just an excuse to help you find a solution."

EXERCISE

Use a notebook to jot down your own ideas for reframing metaphors. Look for the sources of such ideas. Where might you find them? Are they in the stories your clients tell you? Are they in the outcomes they achieve? Might they be in experiences of your own or the adaptations you have learned in life?

From these stories of life, start to structure your own reframing metaphors that include:

1. The problem or challenges faced by the main character.
2. The resources they have, or need to develop, to overcome the challenge.
3. The outcome that opens up new possibilities for perceiving and responding to the challenge.

CHAPTER 7

 Changing Patterns of Behavior

A common goal in therapy is for people to change particular patterns of troublesome behavior. These may be avoidance-type behaviors such as becoming panicky when faced with a feared object, withdrawing from other people, or being too anxious to speak up in a tutorial or business meeting. They may be approach-type behaviors like compulsively abusing an unwanted substance or object, such as tobacco, food, drugs, or a gaming table. They might be behavioral patterns in a relationship with a spouse, child, or employer.

Changing behavior has long been a core, and well-researched, goal of psychotherapeutic interventions with the result being that many behavioral and strategic approaches have been developed to help clients attain their desired behavioral changes. Consequently, there is much evidence-based data available for therapists to adapt readily into metaphors for change.

The outcome stories in this chapter seek to identify the behavior that a client wishes to modify, model the processes of change, provide the means for how to do it, and reach a realistic outcome.

STORY 32
WHEN ONLY THE BEST WILL DO

Therapeutic Characteristics

Problems Addressed

- Poor self-worth
- Low self-esteem

- Acceptance of second best
- Feelings of inadequacy

Resources Developed

- Acknowledging the patterns
- Seeing the available choices or options
- Choosing a balanced approach
- Learning how to care for yourself

Outcomes Offered

- It's OK to look after Number One.
- It is possible to achieve a balanced approach.
- It's OK to feel worthy of the good things.
- You deserve the best.

Some years back I read an interview with a well-known wine connoisseur. He said that there was a time when he believed you should occasionally drink inferior wine. Give yourself the second best, he had said. Taste the worst. That way, he suggested, you would really appreciate the contrasts when you tasted a truly great wine.

I have heard therapists talk about the "burned-chop syndrome" which refers to people who *always* give themselves the second best and *never* sample the elusive, truly great wine. The term typifies the scenario in which the chef burns one of the chops she is cooking and keeps the burned one for herself.

People who subscribe to the burned-chop syndrome never take the best chop for themselves and, most often, don't even share the burned one with others. They think, "If someone has to have it, it might as well be me."

The burned-chop syndrome is, in some aspects, a light-hearted way of defining people's actions when they invariably treat themselves as second best. Nonetheless, it does represent something important about the ways we care for ourselves.

I recall visiting a winery once and being fascinated by the different ways people were approaching the wine. At a table in one corner of the cellar sat a small group who looked like they had settled in for several hours of solid drinking. Bottles were lined up on their table, some already empty or partially empty. Merry, boisterous, and loud, the group drank like students sculling beer at a post-exam celebration.

As I watched, a minibus arrived with a group of people from a wine club. They carried a couple of stainless steel buckets and some bottles of chilled water. They had brought their own glasses rather than use the winery's disposable plastic ones. When the cellar assistant had provided each in the line with a sample and given the routine spiel about the wine's merits, the group moved out of the dimly lit cellar. They held their glasses to the light and engaged in an in-depth conversation about its color and viscosity. Only when they fully exhausted this sensory experience did they move on to smelling the bouquet and launching into a further lengthy discussion. Finally, the wine reached their palates, was held, swilled, and expelled into one of the stainless steel buckets. The group members then cleansed their glasses and palates with water before they approached the next wine.

A couple at the bar sat between these two groups. They, too, held their glasses up to explore the wine's color, but without stepping into the sunlight. They smelled its fruitiness with a few words of appreciation. They allowed it to linger on their palates, then swallowed.

What fascinated me was how the three groups approached this one object and situation so differently. The wine, like a chop, remained the same. The difference lay in how they treated it and themselves. The first group consumed without even tasting. The second tasted without consuming, while the third tasted and consumed moderately.

Perhaps there is no *right* way to choose how you drink a wine or select your chop, for our different choices are what make us interesting and unique as individuals. However, there may be some *better* ways to choose, ways that are more self-caring and self-nurturing while not harming or hurting others.

The interview I read with the wine connoisseur who believed you should occasionally drink an inferior wine to appreciate what a truly great one tasted like did not end there. Later, he reported that he realized his time on earth was finite, so he did some calculations. He could only expect to drink another 8,000 more bottles of wine, eat 2,500 more steaks, and make love on another 5,000 occasions during his life. That being the case, his attitude changed. "From now on," he said, "I deserve the best every time."

STORY 33
THE BEGINNING OF KNOWLEDGE

Therapeutic Characteristics

Problems Addressed

- Selfishness
- Lack of regard for others
- Feelings of anger
- Impulsiveness and impatience

Resources Developed

- Valuing the acquisition of knowledge
- Learning how to blend knowledge and experience
- Developing and employing patience
- Understanding others

Outcomes Offered

- Don't jump to conclusions.
- Look for alternative explanations.
- Consider other people's experiences.
- Be open to new discoveries.
- Be patient.

A group of four philosophy students were forced to spend the night in a small, backcountry village. They had been driving to a distant city when their car broke down, and the only mechanic in town could not finish the repairs for a couple of days as he was best man at a wedding the next day. The students seemed pretty dejected, so he invited them to the wedding. After all, everyone else in town would be there.

A local man was marrying his childhood sweetheart. The two had been born and raised in this isolated hamlet and had never ventured beyond its borders. During the wedding festivities the bridegroom overheard the four students talking. They spoke with authority and knowledge about things that he had never heard discussed in the village. "Where did you learn all this?" he inquired.

"We have spent many years in the city at the university," they replied. "We have studied for several degrees. We have engaged in independent research, and we tutor students. Now we are going to a conference where we will present papers on our work and ideas."

The groom was fascinated. He spent his wedding night thinking of the students and their knowledge. In the morning, he announced to his bride that he was leaving for the city. Assuming knowledge was something that he could gain as quickly as purchasing a loaf of bread, he said confidently that he would return shortly.

As the weeks went by he became engrossed in his studies. The weeks turned into months and months into years. Absorbed in his quest for knowledge, he forgot about his wife and backwoods village, until many years slipped by.

Then, thoughts of home began to haunt him until he could reject them no longer. It was time, he decided, to take his knowledge back to the village. Along the way he stopped to spend the night at a farmhouse. The old farmer, seeing many books in the man's luggage, asked, "Are you a man of knowledge?" With several degrees behind him, many published articles, and a university teaching appointment to his credit, the man replied in the affirmative.

"I am pleased," said the farmer. "I have long sought to meet someone who can tell me what is the beginning of knowledge."

The scholar had to confess after all his years of study he didn't know. The farmer looked up at him and said, "I think I can give you the answer."

"Please tell me," the inquisitive man asked.

"It is not that easy," the farmer replied. "To understand the answer to the question, you need both information and experience. To gain that you will need to work on my farm for the next year and then I will tell you the answer."

The scholar was trapped by his own curiosity. For the next twelve months he labored hard and long without pay, finally asking the farmer the question that had rested in his mind for all that time. "You promised that if I worked for you for twelve months, you would tell me about the beginnings of knowledge. I have fulfilled my part of the deal. Please tell me the answer."

"It is simple," said the old farmer. "The beginning of knowledge is patience."

The scholar got angry. "I have worked in your field a whole year for nothing," he exclaimed. "All you have told me is something I could have said myself."

The farmer waved him on his way saying, "Yes, but you also needed experience. Remember your lesson: The beginning of knowledge is patience."

Angry at having been so easily tricked into giving a year's free labor, the scholar stormed off down the road to his own village. He was furious at the farmer for conning him and angry at himself for being conned.

As he approached his house he saw a shocking scene through the open window. A handsome young man was embracing his wife! Impulsively, he turned on his heels and went to the backyard shed. He took down his old rifle from a high shelf and loaded the gun, preparing to shoot both his wife and the man he assumed to be her lover.

As he stormed back to the house, the words of the old farmer came to mind: "Remember the beginning of knowledge is patience." Patience, he thought. Yes, be patient. Think it through first. He returned the rifle to the shed and wandered dejectedly down to the local tavern. He needed time to think.

After more than 20 years the locals failed to recognize him. Using the opportunity, he made some subtle inquiries about his old friends and then eventually about his wife.

"She was deserted the day after her wedding," they told him, "by her own husband. Despite a hard life, she has remained loyal and has done an excellent job of raising their son who was conceived on her wedding night. He too, has done well and is now a much loved teacher in our village school."

"Speak of the devil," said one of the locals, "here he is now!"

A handsome young man entered the bar. The scholar was once again shocked. He was the very same man the scholar had seen embracing his wife. If he had acted on his impulse, he would have killed both his wife and his son. His anger toward them faded. His anger toward the old farmer also faded. Indeed, the farmer had taught him a valuable lesson. Patience *is* the beginning of knowledge.

STORY 34
RECOGNIZING AND USING ABSURDITY

Therapeutic Characteristics

Problems Addressed

- Relationship conflicts
- Arguments
- Narrow-mindedness
- Failure to appreciate differences
- Nonacceptance of others

Resources Developed

- Accepting differences
- Listening
- Appreciating absurdities
- Laughing at life

Outcomes Offered

- We are all individuals.
- Tolerate differences.

- Enjoy differences.
- Problems can be turned into fun or a resource.
- It is what you do with differences of opinion that counts.
- Share laughter, not conflict.

I have a friend who willingly shares an experience from his own marriage. He is a successful counselor of couples and perhaps this story illustrates why. I think it also illustrates that none of us are exempt from the challenges of our relationships. Because couples are made of two different people, and because the differences, as much as the similarities, may have been what attracted us to each other, there will be times we have different attitudes about the same thing.

Carl Rogers, when musing about relationships, once commented how interesting it was that as humans, we thrive on variety. We pause to watch a sunset because each night it is different. We love the variety that exists between cloudy or clear skies. We are awe-struck by the changing hues. Yet when it comes to relationships, we so often expect our partners to always be the same. We want, and, at times, demand consistency. Relationships thus seem to be one of the most challenging situations we face in life, and it was just such a situation that my colleague was facing.

He had gotten into an argument with his wife. There was no question about their love or devotion for each other. At this point they simply had different ideas and were either unable, or unwilling, to accept the position of the other. Even though the subject of disagreement was insignificant—perhaps even absurd—they managed to engage in a shouting match for more than an hour.

My friend and his wife were arguing about two old wire coat hangers. He wanted to keep them. One day they might be useful. She wanted to throw them out. For her, maintaining a neat and tidy home was a higher priority. After an hour of raging, they realized the absurdity of their argument. Then something important happened.

It is not so much a question of whether a couple has different ideas or not. That is probably inevitable. It is more a question of what you do or don't do with the differences when they occur.

What my colleague and his wife *didn't* do was use the argument to continue to berate each other. They *didn't* employ it as another weapon in the battle. They *didn't* keep bringing the argument up as a constant reminder of the other's lack of understanding. They *didn't* even try to forget it as though nothing had happened, when it really had. Instead, they *used it* as an invaluable aid to diffuse other times when they started to feel a conflict of interests or ideas.

"If we get into an argument now, all we need to do is say 'coat hangers,'" my friend said, "and we fall down laughing. It is impossible to fight when you are laughing."

STORY 35
A GESTURE THAT CHANGED A WHOLE VILLAGE

Therapeutic Characteristics

Problems Addressed

- Fixed patterns of behavior
- Need to change feelings

- Lack of influence
- Powerlessness

Resources Developed

- Discovering and sharing joy
- Feeling happy
- Communicating warmth and happiness

Outcomes Offered

- With a simple gesture, you can have a big influence.
- Happiness can be communicated effectively.
- One person can make important changes.

As I drove my son to school I encountered a man who, through one simple gesture, changed the behavior of the whole village.

This elderly gentleman was the new school crosswalk attendant. As I drove by, he waved as one would to a close friend. A broad smile accompanied the gesture. For the next couple of days I discreetly tried to study his features to see if I knew him. I didn't. Perhaps he had mistaken me for someone else. Perhaps he thought he recognized my car as that of a friend's. By the time I convinced myself that he and I were strangers, we were smiling and waving warmly to each other every morning.

Then one day the mystery was solved. As we approached the crosswalk, I stopped my car behind a line of others while a group of students crossed the road. Once the pupils had reached the safety of the sidewalk on the opposite side, the old man lowered his flags and motioned the cars through. I noticed that he waved and smiled at the first car with gestures I thought had been intended personally for me. The children in the first car were familiar with the warm morning greeting. They already had the window down and were happily leaning out to wave their reply. The second car received the same greeting. He did the same with each following vehicle.

Each day I continued to watch how this one man's gesture affected the morning commuters. I never saw anyone fail to respond. How did they feel, I wondered? What difference did the warm friendliness of a stranger make to their morning? For me, I looked forward each day to the pleasure of a greeting from a friend I had never met. His cheerfulness warmed the start of my day. With a simple gesture—a warm wave and smiling face—he had changed the behavior, and I suspect, the feelings, of the whole village.

STORY 36
IF YOU ALWAYS DO WHAT YOU HAVE ALWAYS DONE

Therapeutic Characteristics

Problems Addressed

- Stuck in a rut
- Repetition of the same old patterns

CHANGING BEHAVIOR

- Life changes
- Release of the past

Resources Developed

- Learning to question our old habits
- Discovering the available choices
- Saying goodbye to the past
- Creating change

Outcomes Offered

- Change is possible.
- Letting go of the past can create a new future.
- Prepare yourself for the changes.
- A whole new world of options lies in front of us.

If you always do what you have always done, you will always get what you always got. Dave reminded me of the truth in that statement. Every workday, Dave's alarm went off at precisely 6:30 A.M., He made a pot of tea, setting the breakfast table as the pot boiled and the tea brewed. He took the tea into his wife, then shaved and showered while she arose. After eating the same breakfast cereal he had preferred since his childhood, he caught the 7:53 bus into work to arrive before the rest of his staff and thus set a good example.

For more than a quarter of a century he had remained in the same department, and, although his job now had more responsibility and a higher salary, he said he was still doing the same thing—"pushing paper across a desk." Each lunchtime he left work at precisely 1 P.M., arriving (at 1:07) at his favorite café where he knew a table would be waiting for him along with his standing order of a chicken salad sandwich and a cup of coffee.

While discussing his weekend routine, Dave said he and his wife always set the alarm for 7:30 A.M. on Saturday so they could sleep in. After making a pot of tea, shaving, and showering, they went shopping, before puttering around the house for the rest of the day.

"And what do you do on Sundays?" I asked.

"Oh, we always go out," he replied.

Seizing on what I thought seemed like a light at the end of a tunnel, I inquired, "Where do you go?"

"Oh, to my favorite café," he answered, "where we lunch on a chicken salad sandwich and a cup of coffee."

I wasn't surprised that Dave was feeling depressed for he seemed to illustrate clearly the principle that *if you always do what you have always done, you will always get what you always got.* As we began to explore how he might alter this principle to change his experiences and the way he was feeling, Dave felt hesitant, uncertain, and even a little fearful—and naturally so, for what he had been doing not only felt familiar but also kept life balanced and stable. It worked in the sense that it limited the risk of the unexpected but, in doing so, it also limited his possibility of enjoyment.

In discussing what small steps he might take to commence this process of change, Dave came up with several suggestions—but he knew that change had to come at his pace. Although he was willing to alter his morning routine, catch an earlier bus, and possibly sit at a different table in his favorite café, he soundly rejected my ideas of wearing odd-colored socks to work, arriving late one morning, or trying a new café—at least at first.

As he started to examine whether he was *really* enjoying what he was doing and, if not, how he might do it differently, he started to experience more positive emotions. Soon he and his wife were trying new coffee shops, sampling different foods, and taking drives into the country for a Sunday lunch. One day as I was going through my mail I was delighted to find a postcard from Dave telling me how he and his wife were enjoying a weekend away at a little seaside town. He had even taken a day off work to make it a long weekend.

Sometimes change may seem difficult, foreboding, and maybe formidable, but Dave learned that making gradual changes at your own pace can you open up opportunities for new experiences and new possibilities.

He could understand the adage at the beginning of this story that a colleague of mine has elaborated and gives to his clients as a handout. It says,

If you always do what you have always done,
You will always get what you've always got.
So for a change do something different,
And do something different for a change.

STORY 37
BEING IN THE MOMENT

Therapeutic Characteristics

Problems Addressed

- A focus on the past
- Fixation on the negative
- A tendency to blame others
- Missed moments

Resources Developed

- Learning to appreciate nature
- Looking for beauty
- Taking time to appreciate

Outcomes Offered

- Appreciate the experience of the moment.
- Enjoy beauty.
- Take responsibility for your feelings.

Two travelers sat high on a crop of granite rocks overlooking the Serengeti Plains of East Africa. One was watching the fiery red ball of light that symbolized, for her, this parched, sunburned country. As she stared, it slipped slowly to the horizon, the shadows lengthened, and the heat fell from the day. The clear sky was a watercolor wash of pastel shades.

Her companion sat with her back to the sunset talking. She talked about how she had always wanted to come to Africa. How she had read so much about it as a child and been fascinated by the African documentaries on television. Something about the country had fired a yearning in her.

The first young woman listened and looked, not at her companion, but at the scene below. She raised her binoculars to study a pride of lions feasting on the corpse of a wildebeest. She was fascinated at how they followed a preordained pecking order, each patiently sitting to await their turn to eat. Hyenas fidgeted behind them, impatient for their turn at the table.

The second woman talked about how hard she'd worked and how long she'd saved to get to Africa. Sometimes she had worked at two jobs. She had taken whatever came her way. It didn't matter how tough or unpleasant it was. She had a goal and was going to achieve it.

The first woman watched, transfixed, as the lions wandered off and the hyenas moved in. Overhead, vultures had been whirling effortlessly on a hot thermal current rising from the parched plain. Some glided down from the sky, warily keeping their distance from the hyenas and hoping to be the first of their kind to hop in and pick at the bones.

The young woman with her back to all this continued to talk. Her journey to get here had been a nightmare. Her aircraft had experienced mechanical problems and she was forced to wait for several days in a North African airport for the aircraft's repair. While traveling through East Africa on a public bus, someone had slashed open her backpack and stolen her traveler's checks. She blamed the airline. She blamed the Africans. She blamed the government for the poverty and corruption.

The first woman heard, but did not really listen. She preferred to watch life on the plains. A herd of giraffe moved north against the backdrop of the sunset. Tall silhouettes stroked the painted sky. Giraffe necks waved like reeds being blown by the wind, and gangly, long legs caressed the dusty earth that rose in mini sun-touched clouds. The sinking sun touched the woman's heart with a warmth as tangible as the heat that had touched her body during the day.

Her friend still had not turned around, but continued to vent her frustrations. Finally, the first woman asked, "Don't you realize what you have just missed? Here you are talking to me *about* Africa, and missing the experience of being here. You are focused on the past and what has already happened, while missing the wonder of the present. You are telling me how much you wished to be here, but now that you've made it, you're not enjoying it!"

Hearing this, the traveler began to wonder how she might let go of what has been and enjoy what is.

STORY 38
WHAT YOU SOW

Therapeutic Characteristics

Problems Addressed

- Interpersonal problems
- Sibling rivalry

- Conflict and rivalry with others
- Anger and embitterment
- Greed and selfishness

Resources Developed

- Learning to be kind and compassionate
- Discovering ways to resolve conflicts
- Learning how to work cooperatively with others

Outcomes Offered

- What you give is what you get.
- Love and caring are what count.
- Be mindful of what is really important.
- Look for resolutions rather than problems.

A farmer had labored long and hard all his life to scratch a meager existence for his family from their humble plot of land. His labors and his carefulness were rewarded in time. On years of good crops, he put aside what monies he could and, by frugal saving, gradually expanded his lands.

Culture decreed that the eldest son should inherit his land, but the farmer was not one to be dictated to by tradition. Fairness and a sense of equality guided his principles more than tradition. Consequently, he bequeathed his property in equal plots to each of his three sons.

When the farmer died, the eldest son was furious about being deprived of his birthright. He was surely the rightful inheritor. Everyone knew the land should be his.

All three brothers received land that was equally as poor, arid, and hard to till as it had been for their father. Schisms split the family. The eldest would not talk to his siblings. The younger brothers found their relationship with the eldest so strained that they avoided him. Unfortunately, the father's desire to see each son happy had not worked, and when harvest time came, each tended his own plot, ignoring the brother on the other side of the fence.

As the youngest sowed grain across his plot, an elderly stranger rode by. "You look thirsty and hungry," said the young man, so he went to the well and drew water for the stranger to drink. He opened his lunch bag and offered the man his sandwich.

Before riding on the stranger thanked him and asked, "What are you planting?"

"Wheat, sir," said the young man courteously.

"Then," said the stranger, "wheat is what you shall reap."

It was only a short way down the track before the stranger encountered the middle brother, also spreading seeds across his land. "You look tired and weary," said the brother. "Come and stay at my place for the night. Let yourself rest a little."

The brother accommodated the stranger in the modest cottage he had erected on his plot of land. He fed him a warm meal and offered him his bed. In the morning the stranger thanked the middle brother and inquired, "What are you sowing?"

"Oats, sir," came the reply.

"Then," said the stranger, "oats are what you shall reap."

The stranger mounted his horse and rode on. Passing the land of the eldest brother, he received no greeting. The brother was too busy angrily striking the ground with his hoe to be bothered about a stranger. Nonetheless the traveler asked politely, "What are you planting, young man?"

"Can't you see, you silly old fool," shouted the irritable and bitter brother. "I'm sowing rocks!"

"Then," said the stranger quietly and undisturbed, "rocks are what you shall reap."

The seasons changed, the stranger was forgotten, and harvest time was soon upon them. The two younger brothers were delighted to reap abundant crops. Their efforts had paid off, and they made a tidy little profit. For this they offered thanks to their father.

The eldest was not so joyful. He had nothing to harvest. He stood looking across a barren field covered with rocks. At first his anger flared with an even more passionate flame. He cursed his father and his brothers. He cursed the stranger who predicted he would reap nothing but rocks.

But anger, like the seasons, can change. His brothers comforted him about his loss and offered to share their bounty. They promised him he would never go needy. After all his angry and evil thoughts toward them, he was touched by their generosity and caring.

"Forgive me," he asked them. They assured him that there was nothing to forgive. After all, were they not brothers? "Your kindness has taught me a lesson," he said. "My jealousy and anger were unfounded. They hurt me as well as you. The priority that I gave to property and assets was inappropriate. There is nothing more important than the love and kindness of those who care.

"Whenever I see a rock or stone," he continued, "I will be reminded of what I learned: What you sow is what you reap."

STORY 39
WHEN ACTIONS SPEAK LOUDER THAN WORDS

Therapeutic Characteristics

Problems Addressed

- Preconceived and fixed expectations
- Desire for a preplanned outcome
- A need to value words rather than actions

Resources Developed

- Appreciating and expressing human warmth
- Enjoying nature
- Valuing life in all its various forms
- Using behavior as a model

Outcomes Offered

- Enjoy life and nature.
- Show compassion in what you do.
- Remember that actions speak louder than words.

There is an old but beautiful story about the most appealing and endearing of all Italy's medieval saints. St. Francis of Assisi has won the hearts of generations of devoted followers for his gentle appreciation of life in all its many forms. People cherish him for his love of animals and his care of the ailing and less fortunate.

The story begins in the sheltered cloisters of his hillside monastery. There St. Francis invited a young novice to preach with him in a nearby village. The novice was delighted to be asked by such an esteemed elder. Surely he would learn by watching and observing his master preach.

They strolled together down the hillside, through country lanes bordered by farms. St. Francis smiled and greeted the householders along the way. He paused to pat an animal or two, stopped under a tree to listen to the morning song of the birds, and seemed to enjoy the leisurely beauty of life outside the dark hallways of the monastery. But the novice was eager to get to the village and hear the Father preach.

When they finally arrived at the town, they walked the length of the cobbled main street. Buildings blocked out the light. The streets were grimy and littered. Animals scavenged for food. People traded their wares. St. Francis wandered in and out the back streets, continuing to smile and greet people gently. The novice began to wonder when St. Francis would deliver his sermon.

After awhile the monk turned, retraced their steps through the village, emerged into the countryside, and began the climb back up to the monastery. The young novice tried to contain himself, but as they mounted the pathway to the monastery, he could hold his tongue no longer. "Father," he asked, "I thought we were going into the village to preach."

"We have been," came St. Francis's benevolent reply. "While we were walking, we were preaching. Sometimes there is no need for words. Our presence alone reminds people of what we represent. By our actions, we have been delivering our morning sermon."

Turning to engage the gaze of his novice, he concluded, "There is no point in walking anywhere to preach unless we preach as we walk."

STORY 40
LIFE IS NOT SO BAD

Therapeutic Characteristics

Problems Addressed

- Stress management
- Work pressures
- Family pressures
- A tendency to see the worst

Resources Developed

- Learning to perceive things differently
- Appreciating what you have

- Accepting difficult situations
- Tolerating tough times

Outcomes Offered

- Things could be worse.
- If you can't change what's happening, change the way you see it.
- Enjoy what you have.
- Find time for yourself and others.

Emma was a working mother. She taught children all day long and, at night, came home to three of her own who were constantly fighting. One would have the stereo up loud, blasting his favorite CD over and over and over again. Another would be watching television, continually increasing the volume to drown out the stereo and complaining about her sibling's noise. A third would play computer games and refuse to relinquish his control of the keyboard so the others could have their turn.

Emma was called in to settle the disputes, feeling she was supposed to be judge and jury—at least until she made an unfavorable decision. Then it would be challenged and the squabbles would resume all over again.

She would come home from teaching worn and frazzled, wanting a little peace. Exhausted, she sought out a therapist.

"I can't take it any more," she told her therapist. "I've reached my wit's end! What can I do?"

"What I am going to suggest," replied her therapist, "may sound a little crazy, and you may not want to do it, but if you want the situation to improve, this is what you need to do. Wait until the next school holiday. Invite every relative you can possibly think of to stay with you for the vacation. Ask them to bring all their kids and their pets. Let them sleep on the couch, on the floor, wherever you can squeeze them."

As you may guess, halfway through the first week of the vacation, Emma requested an urgent appointment with her therapist. "What have you done to me?" she demanded. "The place is a mad house. It is worse than ever. Now, instead of three kids fighting, there are nearly a dozen squabbling with each other. They can't agree on a thing. There is no room to put your feet. The house is a mess. The noise is horrendous. It's worse than living in a battlefield. And the pets! That is the final straw. I can't tolerate all those animals."

"I'm sorry," replied the therapist calmly. "You are right, the pets were too much. Find someone to look after them for the rest of the vacation."

Emma went home feeling a little relieved, but she was back in her therapist's office the next week. "Are you trying to make me crazy?" she asked. "I got rid of the pets, but the house is still hell. All those people, all that noise, all the shouting, all the fights. It's endless, dawn to dark. There's no relief. I can't take it. I'm tripping over kids everywhere I turn. There is no room to get into the kitchen with all my relatives. Everyone wants to watch something different on television. It's enough to make someone look for a short rope and a tall building."

"I am sorry," said the therapist again. "You are right. Send all your relatives back to their own homes."

The woman couldn't wait for her next scheduled appointment. She burst into her therapist's office. "This is wonderful!" she exclaimed. "You have saved my family and my marriage. Life is so peaceful and quiet now the relatives and their pets have gone. The house feels large and roomy. It is nice to hear the sounds of my own children going about their activities. I am making sure I take time out for myself, and my husband and I now appreciate the time we have to talk. Thank you."

STORY 41
ARE YOU BETTER THAN YOU USED TO BE?

Therapeutic Characteristics

Problems Addressed

- Challenge management
- Worry about past issues
- Guilt and self-recrimination
- Stuck in the past

Resources Developed

- Acknowledging that we are evolving beings
- Valuing and developing the blend of both skills and knowledge
- Learning to grow from our past mistakes

Outcomes Offered

- Learning is ongoing, not static.
- Keep striving to achieve your best.
- Understand how the past may be helpful for growing into the future.

Being a psychologist is an interesting profession. When I tell people what I do, I get different reactions. Some people back off, fearful that somehow I might discover their deepest secrets. Some try to get a free consultation and unload their burdens on me in the hope that I will wave a magic wand and make them disappear.

One night at a party a man approached me and said, "I hear you are a psychologist."

Eric Berne, in his book *Games People Play,* describes a game called "Now I've Got You, You Son Of a Bitch" in which a player will set out to trap another person in a way that puts him or her down and thus gives the player an upper hand. I didn't realize it at the outset, but I had just met such a player.

He asked, "Are you a better psychologist now than you were 10 years ago?"

Over the last 10 years, I had striven to develop my professional skills as fully and competently as I could. I had traveled around the world to attend conferences. I had sought out leading practitioners whose training would expand my skills. I had participated in workshops. I had read extensively in books and journals. I had received supervision from learned colleagues. There was no doubt in my mind that my experience, knowledge, and skills had expanded.

"Yes, I believe I am," I answered.

He was quick to retort, "Then don't you feel guilty about the people you saw 10 years ago?"

At first his question took me by surprise. Now as I look back on it, I thank him for challenging my thinking. Everyone knows that in hindsight it's easy to have 20/20 vision. There may have been things we could have done better. We may have made "mistakes," for, after all, we are human no matter what our profession. The question is not so much whether these things happened, but more what we do with the understanding or knowledge we gain from them.

We can feel bad about them, but will that change anything or help us to do things better next time around? If, in looking back, we can use those mistakes to improve what we do, they may serve as a valuable foundation on which to build our developing skills, whether in our profession, in a recreational pursuit, in a relationship, or in life generally.

As I contemplated his question, I realized that at the time of seeing each client, I had sought to give the best of myself, my knowledge, and my experience. Hopefully my work, as well as my life, has been one of progress. Certainly it would be more tragic for me to be still stuck at the same point I was 10 years ago than to be where I am in the present.

When I project my thoughts ahead, I hope that in 10 years time I will be able say again, "Yes, I have improved. I am better. I have progressed from where I was 10 years ago." If not, I am neither learning nor growing. If not, my career, as well as my life, is being wasted.

So, when I hear someone say, "I want to learn something new every day," I am filled with admiration. Life is not about being static. It is about growing and evolving in as many vast and varied ways as is possible. Life is about learning, and learning is living.

EXERCISE

Here is the chance to record ideas for your own stories of change, whether they are about modifying patterns of behavior, altering modes of thinking, or changing styles of feeling. Using your notebook, it may be helpful to

1. Think about, and write down, the desired therapeutic outcome of change as your first task.
2. Once this task is completed, work out the type of resources or abilities the client will need to achieve that change.
3. If the client has these abilities, how can they be used to reach the desired change?
4. If not, how might the metaphor help develop and employ appropriate resources?

CHAPTER 8

📖 Learning from Experience

We often hear that experience is the best teacher but, like any teacher (no matter how good), there are some pupils who learn much and some who learn only a little. Just having an experience doesn't guarantee the quantity or quality of learning that may be derived from that experience.

Aldous Huxley once said, "Experience is not what happens to a man; it is what a man does with what happens to him." Metaphors are a means for creating learning experiences a client may not have had, or of replicating a past experience to help modify the learning gained from it. Therapy's goal in this area is not just about creating or using events that happen, but it is also about helping clients maximize the learning that may be gained from that event to better equip them to deal with subsequent life events.

It follows that if experience is the best teacher, then the more we experience, the more we are capable of learning. Throughout history, stories have been a way of sharing and communicating essential life experiences and how to use these experiences for our future health and well-being.

The following metaphors focus on how to learn from the experiences we encounter. They illustrate how we may grow and develop from difficulties, or unexpected and seemingly tragic events. A loss, for example, may be tragic, but it is even more tragic if we lose the potential learning that may be gained from that experience. These are stories about new learning, new possibilities, and new perceptions.

STORY 42
USE WHAT YOU HAVE

Therapeutic Characteristics

Problems Addressed

- Deprivation
- Feeling powerless
- Perceived lack of resources
- Tough circumstances

Resources Developed

- Developing an acceptance of what life brings
- Finding and using your resources wisely
- Being creative and innovative
- Making the most of what you have

Outcomes Offered

- Use your skills and abilities to the greatest advantage.
- When life is tough, look for the positives.

In the small Tibetan town of Tingri, Tom and I hired yaks and yak handlers for our journey to Mt. Everest. Chomolongma, or Mother Goddess, (as the world's highest mountain is known to the Tibetans) lies several days trek across the stony and arid Tibetan plateau. To the south of us lay the snowy white peaks of the Himalaya, stretching high into clear and rich blue skies. Like a tall fence, these mountains that border the plateau shelter it from the moisture-laden clouds of the Indian monsoons and thus form the world's highest desert. Not a tree or bush can be seen. The only vegetation is low, coarse tufts of occasional grass that fight for survival on the rocky terrain. The only animal that seems to survive is the yak, and only the yaks' capacity to manage these desolate, high-altitude areas enables humans to survive alongside them.

For the Tibetans, yaks are transport, clothing, food, fuel, and, indeed, life itself. Their wool is knitted into apparel and tents to stave off the bitter cold. Their hides make jackets, boots, and bed-clothes. Their meat, combined with ground, roasted barley, called *tsampa,* provides the Tibetans' staple diet. Yak milk churns into a rancid-tasting butter which, when blended with tea and salt, makes a nutritious, cold-climate beverage. No product of the yak is wasted. Even its dung is used. On the treeless plateau there is no wood to burn for heating or cooking—and both are essential at these chilly altitudes. The Tibetans found an innovative solution. They gather the yak dung, mix it into watery pats, throw it onto the walls of their stone homes, and leave it to dry. These dung discs are subsequently stacked on the flat roofs of the houses, awaiting their use as fuel to warm the home and cook the food.

As Tom and I shared the hospitality of a yak herder on the plateau one evening, we sat in his yak wool tent, sipped yak butter tea and choked on the smoke of a somewhat green yak dung fire. Despite the smoke we huddled close to it for the warmth. It was better than no fire, and as I sat there, I was filled with admiration. "What a resourceful people," I thought to myself. "When life gives them nothing but shit, they can turn even that into something useful!"

STORY 43
CONFRONTING AND BEFRIENDING YOUR MONSTERS

Therapeutic Characteristics

Problems Addressed

- Pain
- Suffering
- Discomfort
- Discontent
- Unhappiness

Resources Developed

- Learning to think through issues rather than act impulsively
- Discovering and adapting to different perspectives
- Being open to discover the positives
- Developing a willingness to change

Outcomes Offered

- Turn monsters into friends.
- Try managing problems by befriending rather than fighting.
- Look at suffering and discomfort differently.

Often in life we confront monsters of various sorts. They may be people, circumstances, or events that we wish weren't there. They may be elements of our past that have come back to haunt us. They may be circumstances or powers we perceive to be outside of our control. It is not a question of whether we encounter the monsters, so much as how we manage them when we do encounter them.

Long ago, a monster slayer learned how to handle such forces. His father had been a deity who wanted to free the world of monsters, and knowing the need for a brave young warrior to fulfill this task, he came to earth, married a young woman, and left when she became pregnant. The child was born and grew into a self-sufficient young man. His mother never revealed the identity of his father, despite the child's requests, and so the time came when the young man decided to find his father.

The search took him on a dangerous journey. He encountered many challenges and hazards along the way, each testing his mettle, each strengthening his resolve, each enhancing his capabilities and strengths. With time, determination, and good luck, he eventually came to his father's palace.

His father was so pleased to discover his son had adopted the mission to free the world of monsters that he presented him with a magical bow and arrow. Thus equipped, the young warrior set off to find and eradicate the monsters that terrified his people.

He hadn't gone far before he encountered the Monster of Hunger. He raised his bow and arrow, pointed it toward the monster's heart and shouted bravely, "Prepare yourself to die. You have been causing my people to be hungry. They suffer and feel discomfort. I shall eliminate you and free them from hunger."

The monster looked him in the eye and asked, "Is that what you really want? I acknowledge I do cause your people discomfort, but think what benefits I bring them as well. Without hunger, they would have no desire to go hunting for their own food. Without hunger, they would sit and die. I give them the drive to find food and survive. Instead of trying to destroy me, look at the ways I might be useful. Stop seeing me as a monster and examine how I might keep people healthy, contented, and happy."

The young warrior saw the truth in what the monster said. Perhaps he was not so monstrous after all, and the discomfort he created had its essential benefits. So the young warrior spared the monster's life, thinking perhaps it was better to befriend, rather than destroy this powerful force.

Later, he came upon the Monster of Winter. Here was a monster that surely needed to be eliminated, so he raised his bow and arrow. "You bring cold and darkness into the life of my people," he challenged her. "You make us shiver and, at times, you are so cold that people die. I must destroy you."

"Yes," replied the Monster of Winter. "What you say is right. I do bring cold and darkness into your lives, but think how much you need me. I bring rain that fills your rivers, waters your crops, and feeds the animals that you hunt. I pave the way for the warmth and beauty of spring. Without me, there would be no spring and, without spring, the animals you need for food and clothing would not mate and reproduce."

The young warrior realized that what the Monster of Winter said was true. She was not all bleak and evil, as he had originally perceived her but offered much that his people needed. If people could enjoy these benefits rather than think only of the cold and misery, their lives would be richer. So he spared her life and befriended her.

As he continued on, he encountered the Monster of Suffering. "Ah hah!" shouted the young warrior. "At last I have found a monster that humanity can do without. Nobody wants to suffer. Prepare to be slain."

"I know what you are thinking," said the Monster of Suffering. "You think that I cause people needless pain, discomfort, and unhappiness. You think they would be better off without me. But have you thought about what benefits I bring to people? It is because of me that people learn, grow, and develop. Remember as a child when you put your hand too close to the fire and experienced the pain of the heat? Your suffering was brief, but you learned from the experience. That learning has protected you, maybe even saved your life. People grow from pain. They learn through their suffering. Like me or not, you need me."

The young warrior lowered his bow, for he had discovered another truth. Nobody likes to suffer or experience pain, yet somehow there was something paradoxical about it. Through pain we learn to avoid pain and grow from the experience. Through suffering we learn to avoid suffering and discover something about attaining happiness. Even suffering has its place if we learn how to benefit from it.

The young warrior changed the purpose of the mission that initially engaged him. His goal now was to befriend what he thought were monsters, for he had much to learn from them.

STORY 44
LEARNING TO LOVE YOUR DISCOMFORT

Therapeutic Characteristics

Problems Addressed

- Pain
- Fear
- Discomfort
- Unpleasant past memories
- Powerlessness

Resources Developed

- Acquiring new knowledge, which can change an old attitude
- Learning to acknowledge and alter past experiences
- Discovering how to do something different
- Being willing to accept wise advice

Outcomes Offered

- Feel good about being empowered.
- It is possible to modify past experiences.
- Make the feared useful.
- Use present experiences to change the past.

Claire lived and worked on a commune. She was delighted to have been allocated the task of tending the vegetable garden because she loved gardening, save for one aspect: the stinging nettles. No matter how much she covered up with protective clothing, the nettles, like moths drawn to a light, always seemed to find that one little spot of flesh that happened to be unwittingly exposed. In an allergic reaction, her skin would welt and become itchy. As a result, she approached the garden with fear and dread, rather than with anticipation and enjoyment.

Apart from the immediate discomfort, the nettles triggered memories of past unpleasant experiences, for our minds can be quick to remind us of past pain. As uncomfortable as it may be, such memories are self-protecting. They are there to alert us, to signal danger, and thus to help us avoid creating new unpleasant memories.

As a childhood hobby, Claire's brother had raised fowls, including one particularly aggressive rooster which, on one occasion, attacked young Claire. She fled, and, sensing victory, it flew after her. Her shortest route to safety—a direct line to the back door of home—was through a patch of nettles. They stung her from head to toe, and she cried miserably from fear of the rooster and pain of the nettle stings.

It took days for her welts to subside, but the family stories of the incident never ended, so she continued to be reminded, again and again. Years later it would come up in conversation, "Do you remember when you ran through the nettles to escape the pet rooster?" Claire and nettles were linked. The mere mention of the plant brought recollections of pain, fear, and embarrassment.

In the communal garden, all these memories and fears came flooding back, and Claire felt powerless against the nettles. The commune would not permit sprays or chemical controls to be used, and for Claire to rip out the nettles by hand meant the risk of being stung. This seemed fruitless, for the nettles grew back almost as quickly as they were pulled.

Claire took her problem to the commune meeting. She wanted to work in the garden, but something had to be done about the nettles. One of the other commune residents gave her a book about nettles and made a comment that stuck in her mind. Claire wasn't sure whether it was the book or the comment that made the difference.

To her surprise, the book praised nettles and their usefulness. It prescribed them as a treatment for several ailments. The book said that sipping nettle tea was good for arthritis. Claire carefully gathered the nettles and made them into tea for the communal breakfast. When she called it "nettle tea," people refused even to try it. The next day she made the drink again but called it "fresh, garden herb tea." Her fellow residents drank it with the eagerness and enjoyment of a camel arriving at an oasis after a long desert journey.

Back in the garden, this incident led her to think, *It is not so much what an object is, but rather how we see or label it that makes the difference.* The tea remained the same. Only the name Claire gave it determined whether others in the commune rejected the tea with repugnance or accepted it with enjoyment.

The second thing she discovered was that *doing something different makes a difference.* No matter how much she advocated nettle tea, or tried to sell people on its health benefits, the other residents may still have avoided drinking it. By changing the name, she changed the outcome. To bring about a change she needed to do something different.

Perhaps, she began to think, the experience of the past is not immutable. Today people will drink a beverage that yesterday they thought unpalatable. Maybe now I can enjoy the benefits of something that terrified me as a child. Perhaps *the experiences of the past can be altered by what we do in the present.*

Her friend who had given her the book said something that also stuck in her mind. "We can't rid the garden or the rest of the property of nettles for it is their home as well as ours. You can't change the physical reaction that you have to them. If it is outside your ability to alter those realities, then I suggest that you learn to love them."

STORY 45
PROBLEMS MAY OPEN NEW OPTIONS

Therapeutic Characteristics

Problems Addressed

- Loss
- Disappointment
- Frustration

Resources Developed

- Discovering how to reframe attitudes
- Learning to focus on the positive aspects of experience
- Being open to the new or novel

Outcomes Offered

- Experiences are mutable and our responses to them are mutable.
- A "negative" event may create the opportunity for a "positive."
- Enjoy what experience brings.

I had traveled halfway around the globe from Perth in Western Australia to Phoenix, Arizona for two reasons. The first was to attend a conference in which I was presenting a workshop and the second was to visit the National Parks of the Southwest United States.

On a previous visit 18 years earlier, the Grand Canyon was under snow and the paths were too icy to hike the trails down to the Colorado River. Now, I had a mission to get to the bottom of the Canyon and photograph this world-renowned natural spectacle.

As I stepped over the Canyon rim and pressed the shutter button for the first time, the winding mechanism on the camera jammed. Damn! I felt so frustrated. No matter how much I jiggled, twisted, or pulled at things, it obstinately refused to work.

I spent the next two days walking to the bottom of the Canyon, with my eyes framing dozens of spectacular photographs I couldn't capture on film. On top of that disappointment, I had to carry several pounds of useless camera gear up and down the vertical walls of the Canyon. The frustration grew as I was unable to find a camera repair shop until arriving at the tiny town of Kanab several days later. In the hour that Terry took to repair my camera, I had the delight of exploring the streets of this quaint, movie-set town that John Wayne, Clint Eastwood, and many other big screen stars had also walked. Nature, like a caring mother, embraced the settlement protectively in the encircling arms of the vividly warm, and true-to-their-name, Vermilion Cliffs. It had a sense of self-sufficiency like it always had, and always would, survive on it own resources.

Terry not only fixed my camera but also gave me tips about photographing in the harsh desert light and through the dark, dappled, recesses of slot canyons. He talked about petroglyphs, where to find them, and how best to photograph them. He described several brilliant, off-the-beaten-track walks that led me into beautiful areas I would not otherwise have discovered. Had the camera not jammed I would not have met Terry, wandered the uniquely memorable streets of Kanab, or found spectacular, little-known slot canyons.

A second unwanted event occurred when I locked my keys in the rental car. They lay, frustratingly, in full view on the front seat while I stood on the outside looking at them helplessly.

I approached the receptionist at the hotel to inquire whether their maintenance staff may be able to assist me. "We are not allowed to touch anyone's car," said the receptionist. "You could sue us. It is hotel policy."

I phoned the park rangers. "Sorry," they said, "we assisted someone recently, damaged the car slightly in the process, and got sued. It is policy. We are not allowed to touch anyone's car."

I had noticed a gas station on the way in, so I phoned it for assistance. "No," replied the mechanic. "How do I know it is your automobile? I could be aiding and abetting you in stealing someone's vehicle. Then I could get sued. It's management policy."

I was struggling to break in with a wire coat hanger I got from the hotel receptionist when two Navajo men saw my difficulty and came to my assistance. As we worked together I heard the men talking in Navajo.

The frustrating experience of locking the keys in the car gave me the opportunity to hear this soft and gentle language for the first time. I learned it was so difficult for nonnatives to speak that the U.S. military selected it as the basis for a World War II radio transmission code that was never cracked.

They spoke to me about their culture, their pow-wows, and the maintenance of long-held traditions. They described the Navajo as a "nation within a nation," and discussed their system of government. They talked about their canyons and pointed out a pair of thermaling Golden Eagles. By the time the coat hanger finally gripped the door lock sufficiently to reward us with a welcome click, the two Navajo and I had shared an experience that I will not forget.

Who can tell how one unexpected frustrating event may lead to an unexpectedly beautiful new experience? Losses, disappointments, and frustrations do happen. What matters is how we see them. I've heard it said, "If you experience a loss, you don't have to lose the experience."

STORY 46
FINDING TREASURES IN TRAGEDY

Therapeutic Characteristics

Problems Addressed

- Unexpected disaster
- Loss of objects or possessions
- Loss of life's labor
- Disappointment
- Uncertainty

Resources Developed

- Acknowledging that losses occur
- Accepting grief as a natural, healthy process
- Being open to new discoveries
- Looking for the "silver lining" even on darkest clouds

Outcomes Offered

- Even in tragedy it's possible to find a treasure
- Adjust appropriately to loss
- When one door closes, another opens

Mesa Verde is a uniquely spectacular and mysterious wonder. Visiting this archaeological site made me realize how many questions in life are still unanswered, for, despite all the research that has been done on this civilization, there is still much we do not know.

One of those mysteries is why the Anasazi Indians who lived in this area for about 700 to 1200 A.D. left their accessible homes on flat mesa tops and moved into the less accessible overhangs of cliff faces. When they were constructing their homes, they could not have predicted what unknown factors would force them to leave, any more than the park rangers could have predicted an event that occurred in 1996.

That year the national park celebrated its 90th birthday, a period in which archeologists surveyed every site they could find. But during the summer, lightning triggered a wildfire in Soda Canyon. Within four days its tongue of destruction had devoured nearly 5,000 acres. Charcoal and soot covered the walls of historic dwellings, original woodwork was burned to a cinder, and building stones either flaked or fractured in the intense heat.

If the loss of so many millennia-old buildings was not enough to render decades of scientific studies meaningless, one event alone was sufficient to move lovers of this site to tears. At a place called Battleship Rock, a large petroglyph panel with irreplaceable carvings up to four feet tall, cracked, splintered, and fell from the rock face. For the archeologists, their loss was real and significant. Any grief they felt was surely appropriate.

Imagine, if you will, being one of those archeologists. You are feeling the loss, and, although you know that, like all feelings, it will pass in time, your head keeps telling you the object of your loss is gone forever. Then you find a new field house here, there a multi-roomed pueblo, and beyond that, an underground kiva. The fire has burned away the woods and undergrowth that had successfully hidden exciting, previously undiscovered sites.

It is true that they could never replace what was lost, but the new sites were unique and provided new knowledge about a mysterious society. The fire that had seemed so devastating exposed 400 previously undocumented sites, revealing along with them that, in the face of apparent tragedy, it is possible to discover new treasures.

STORY 47
FINDING PEACE

Therapeutic Characteristics

Problems Addressed

- Conflict and struggle
- A fight against the odds
- A need to cling to the unnecessary

Resources Developed

- Learning to choose what is important
- Learning to let go of what is not important
- Learning strategies to avoid conflict
- Affirming your own skills and resources
- Finding and enjoying what brings peace and happiness

Outcomes Offered

- Feel good about freeing yourself of conflict and struggle.
- Let go of what's not needed.
- Use your skills wisely.
- Enjoy life's pleasures.

One evening, a couple strolled along a beach, found a peaceful spot to spread their rug, and nestled down to watch the sunset. They brought a chicken picnic and a bottle of fruity, dry wine with them. He poured the wine and toasted their happiness. She spread out the picnic. The scene was peaceful and romantic, but they were not alone.

The woman looked at the flock of begging sea gulls and threw her last piece of meat into its midst. One gull could not believe its luck. It opened its beak and launched itself at the piece of meat. Wings beat about it in a desperate flutter. Discordant shrieking pierced the air. Dozens of birds swooped at the small morsel—and the first gull won.

It wheeled urgently into the air, turning toward open sea and sky, but the other gulls did not give up. In hot pursuit, 20 or so birds began their greedy attacks. Each wanted what the one gull had. There was no mercy in their relentless struggle to get it. Some tried to snatch the piece of meat from the bird's mouth. Others, seeming to have forgotten the object of their desire, attacked the gull itself. They screeched at it, flew at it, and pecked at it, but the gull flew on. It had acquired the piece of chicken in fair play, fortune had bestowed it with this gift, and it wasn't about to give up what it had won.

But the battle was not over. The other gulls were also reluctant to give up. Temptation was in their sight, and they wanted the prize. It grew harder and harder for the winning gull to hang on to the piece of chicken. Finally, feeling the exhaustion and fatigue of trying to fight against the odds, the gull began to question whether it was worth hanging on. What price did it have to pay to keep this piece of meat? Was it really worth the effort?

At some stage the gull realized there would come a time when it had to let go of what it had been hanging on to. There would come a point where the consequences of the struggle outweighed the benefits of the reward. It opened its beak, let the piece of chicken fall, and watched as another bird darted below to snatch up the morsel. Its attackers swiftly found their new target, the battle moved to a different field, and the gull felt relieved.

It remembered a saying that sea birds liked to repeat: There are plenty more fish in the ocean. It knew that it would not go hungry or be deprived. It knew its own skills at hunting and was aware of the opportunities that awaited it. With the battle behind, it was free to take its own time to look leisurely for another meal. Now it had a choice of where and when it sought out the things that would nurture, satisfy, and make it happy. The battle was not necessary for its survival.

Once more it wheeled in the air. This time it was not to avoid attack, just purely for fun. It soared up on the refreshing sea breeze, a contrasting dot of liberated whiteness in the rich blue of the sky. Above the struggles and battles that continued among others, the gull enjoyed its freedom and peace.

The couple, sitting on the beach for their sunset picnic, watched as a lone seagull separated itself from the crowd of squabbling birds. They followed its silhouette as it drifted leisurely across the soporific golden rays of the setting sun. They embraced, feeling the serenity and intimacy that accompanies a day as it draws to a close.

The seagull, too, felt at one with the tranquility of its world. It thought to itself, "I may have lost a piece of meat, but I have gained the peace of the sky."

STORY 48
DRAWING BOUNDARIES

Therapeutic Characteristics

Problems Addressed

- Relationship difficulties
- Interpersonal conflict
- Self-imposed restrictive boundaries
- Desire for what the other has
- Envy, or seeing the grass as greener on the other side
- Lack of communication

Resources Developed

- Building better communication skills
- Developing a willingness to negotiate
- Learning to seek resolutions instead of dwelling on problems
- Discovering the benefits of a give-and-receive attitude

Outcomes Offered

- Conflicts can be resolved.
- Restrictive boundaries can be relaxed—with mutual benefit.
- It is possible to find ways to work together.
- Be willing to communicate.
- Relationships are based on sharing.

Some years ago I visited a marriage counseling agency to give a talk to colleagues. As I entered the building my eye was immediately drawn toward a large poster behind the reception desk. I don't know whether it had been hung deliberately to illustrate some metaphoric statement or whether it was purely an unconscious act. Whichever, I found it amusing.

The poster was a farmyard scene. There was a barn on the horizon. The foreground was a large, green field divided into four fenced paddocks, with a cow in each paddock. Each cow leaned over the fence chewing the grass on the other side! Would an agency specializing in relationship counseling deliberately hang a poster communicating the message that "the grass was greener on the other side of the fence?"

But is that not the way it is? As soon as we construct fences or draw boundaries, do we not start to become a little curious about what might lie on the other side? Do we not create myths and fantasies about what or who exists on the other side of the border?

Once there were two countries that faced this very dilemma. Over the years, and as a result of many struggles, they had drawn a boundary that defined the extent of their lands. As one country was very stony, and the other did not have stones, they simply followed the geological line of where the stones began and ended.

At first all was well, then the people on the stony side began to envy those on the stoneless side, thinking if their own land was clear, they could till the soil, grow crops, and feed their people without having to move rock after damn rock. The people on the stoneless side envied those with the stones, thinking how stones would be useful to build houses and construct fences.

Each wanted what the other had, and did not appreciate what they already possessed. The people on the stony land went to their queen and complained about all the stones. Eventually she relented to their demands and said, "OK, if you don't want the stones, throw them across the border."

The people of the stoneless country went to their king and complained, "The people in the queen's country are throwing stones at us." The king said, "How dare they invade our territory. This is an act of war."

The war continued for some time with stones being hurled back and forth across the border until the king had a bright idea. He said to his military chiefs, "Don't we want stones? Let's keep waging war with the queen's people, for they are poor and have no other weapons apart from their stones. That way we will have all the material we need to construct our buildings." So the war continued until the stoneless land was full of stones and the stony land had no stones.

Again, for a while, both the king's and queen's subjects were happy. The queen's people tilled the lands and produced crops. The king's people built homes and stone fences. Then discontentment arose again. The queen's subjects had no materials to build new homes and the king's subjects had so little clear land that they couldn't grow crops.

The countries declared war once more and hurled the stones back across the border at each other. And so the cycle of conflict continued, broken only by brief periods of peace when the two countries were busy growing crops or erecting new buildings. But neither king nor queen was happy, and each began to think how much nicer it would be if their countries could live in harmony instead of conflict. Musing with the idea of what it would be like to talk instead of fight, they arranged to meet in a neutral country where, for a while, they could distance themselves from their history of conflict.

The talks weren't easy at first, for there had been many years of bitterness. "It is all your fault," said the king. "You started this by throwing stones at us."

The queen replied, "Maybe there are accusations I can make about you, too. There have been many bad feelings between our countries, but it will not help us to find a resolution if we fall into the trap of blaming each other."

The king acknowledged that to reach a resolution they would have to put aside the feelings of anger, hostility, and bitterness that had built up in the past. "What has been is something we can't alter," said the king. "Maybe, by looking forward together, we can begin to shape a harmonious future for the both of us."

The queen asked the king, "How can we have a harmonious future together?"

For a moment the king thought. "The stones are yours," he said. "The pastures are ours. Yet we both want what the other has. Maybe we could share. Maybe we could trade. Perhaps we could exchange the produce of our country for the stones of your country. Maybe our people could share their knowledge of farming and your people their knowledge of building. That way we could work together."

The queen agreed. "Perhaps," she suggested, "we may even relax the restrictions on the border. Maybe you and your subjects could cross into my country and we into yours. We could trade freely. Share what we have to offer each other and exchange our knowledge."

The countries became the envy of other nations for the way they lived in peace and harmony. True, there were occasions when one desired more stones or the other wanted more produce. That happened from time to time, but now they had a means for resolving differences by understanding, negotiation, and trade.

In time, not even an expert geographer would have been able to define where the original boundary had been. There no longer seemed to be any clear distinction between what had been the stoneless country and the stony country. While maintaining their own unique characters, they had learned to share and exchange what they had with each other.

STORY 49
GETTING INTO, AND OUT OF, WRONG PLACES

Therapeutic Characteristics

Problems Addressed

- Loss of direction
- A tendency to be in the wrong place
- A need to follow inappropriately others' footsteps
- Tough times
- Self-recrimination
- Fear and anxiety

Resources Developed

- Discovering how to manage in the face of adversity
- Learning to explore the available options
- Enjoying beauty—even in tough times.
- Seeking and finding solutions

Outcomes Offered

- It is important to challenge our own beliefs—they may be wrong.
- Learn from the experiences you have.
- Choices are available to you.
- Enjoy your unexpected discoveries.

I remember once being stuck in a wrong place. In fact, it was a *very* wrong and *very* dangerous place. Only later was I to discover how wrong and how dangerous. To make matters worse, I was thoroughly convinced I was in the right place. Where I was—and hadn't planned to be—was up a glacial valley in the Stubbai Alps of Austria.

I had left the warmth and security of a cozy mountain hut to follow a trail for the day. The route looked simple and achievable—at least on the map. It would take me into a valley, across a glacier, over a ridge, and down into the next valley where another warm hut should await me.

But problems arose from the beginning as snow had fallen overnight and covered any clear signs of the trail. I studied my map, convinced the valley to my left followed the contours of the one I needed to enter. I studied the shape of the mountain peaks and the curve of the valley and checked my compass. To top it off, there was the faint trace of footsteps leading where I thought I needed to go. But still I had questions. Should I follow in others' footsteps, or should I step out and carve my own direction ahead? I hesitated for a while, then chose to follow where others had been, trusting they knew where they were going.

Soon the prints were obliterated by fresh snow, and I had to forge my own path anyway. Toward the ridge at the head of the valley, the going got tougher and the snow became deeper. At times I sank to my knees, and even my waist. It was obvious I was no longer on the trail and I was quickly growing fatigued.

The only way to confirm my location was to climb the ridge to see the valley beyond and, hopefully, the hut that was my destination. Ascending the wet, near vertical rock face was a risky venture. Yet turning back seemed pointless because if I was in the right valley I would have lost a whole day's effort. Slowly, anxiously I edged my way up. What greeted me was a stunningly beautiful expanse of white, unblemished snowfields with sharp black peaks cutting like shark's teeth into a crisp blue sky. Save for the soft hush of the wind, all was still, as if I had stumbled on nature's moment of meditation.

It was beautiful, but wrong. There was no sign of what should have been a visible hut. This was not the valley that my map said I should be looking at. I was definitely in the wrong place. Shaky, fatigued, and frustrated, I found a rock on which to have my lunch and contemplate my choices, but my head filled with self-rebuke. Words from the past flooded back as I chastised myself for such a foolish mistake. It took some time before I assured myself that such thoughts would not provide a solution. I needed to find my way out, and the first step was to accept where I was. Wishing myself somewhere else was not going to fix the dilemma. My mistake had been a temporary error of choice. It had led me into a place that I didn't want to be, but, just as I had made a choice that got me here, so I could make a choice to get out.

The question now was, "which direction to go?" Would I be better to go back the way I had come? I knew the way and could anticipate a warm hut and hot meal at the end. Should I stay where I was and hope that someone would eventually rescue me? Should I choose to move on? To do so would take me into unfamiliar territory. It would mean crossing several ridges to find the hut I needed for the night. I might not make it before dark. That would mean being trapped out in the elements on a snowy, cold night.

I decided to retrace my steps, and the descent was fun, first tobogganing on my waterproof jacket, then glissading across the glacier on my boots. Only when I got back to the hut and was talking about my day's embarrassing adventure did I learn where I had been. The season before, two backpacks emerged from under the tongue of the very glacier I had traversed. They were thought to have belonged to a couple of trekkers who disappeared down a crevasse twenty-five years ago—and were never seen again.

Ending up in the wrong place can happen to any of us. Just as the choices and decisions we make can lead us into such places that we may not want to be, so we have the power to make those choices and decisions that get us back on track. But, if you find yourself somewhere you hadn't expected to be, look out for the opportunity to discover something new.

STORY 50
TRUSTING YOUR ABILITIES

Therapeutic Characteristics

Problems Addressed

- Feelings of fear
- Lack of confidence
- A feeling of burden
- Self-restricted freedom
- Pain

Resources Developed

- Learning to recognize and use our abilities
- Choosing to follow appropriate role models
- Coordinating mind-body processes

Outcomes Offered

- Trust in yourself.
- Use your inner resources.
- Have confidence in your personal capabilities.

At the end of a long, hard day, trekking solo in Nepal, I found myself weaving down a narrow, stony track into a steep river valley. The path clung hesitantly to the steep face of the ravine, zigzagging down at varying widths and shifting gradients. The burden of my backpack heightened the sense of challenge. Like many of the things we carry around with us in life, it weighed heavily on my shoulders. I cursed its encumbrance as I labored up hills and plodded down, thinking how much more freely I would move without it. Frequently during the hike, my hips and shoulders cried for freedom, and at the end of the day, invariably, I was relieved to cast it aside.

Yet, like there are two sides to every coin, there were aspects of the burden that I needed. It carried my clothes, my medical supplies, and my camera. There was a unique pleasure in washing with a soap that had the smell of home, or snuggling into a down sleeping bag that had been my only nocturnal companion in many isolated parts of the world. No, I would not choose to be without them.

As I plodded down the side of the ravine, the path hurled itself frighteningly and rapidly towards the roaring river below. In addition to the effects of a tough day in my body and limbs, I felt fear that tensed my muscles, restricted my joints, and cautioned my gait. Beneath the weight of my backpack, my feet wobbled uncertainly on the uneven, stone-littered trail. While my knees and ankles suffered from the concussive impact of each deliberately planted footstep, my mind turned inward, focusing on burdens, fear, and pain. Briefly, I might have been distracted by the sight of a distant, snow-capped peak, or seen the color of a rhododendron tree in blossom, but it was not long before I was back in thoughts of my own misery.

Then something did capture my attention. A noise came from behind, the sound of laughter and merriment from a group of local Nepalese. Though we shared the same path, there seemed a vast difference in our mood and manner.

They carried loads much heavier than my own, with greater ease, and, apparently, little ruminative thought. Thin leather bands across their foreheads supported woven wicker baskets that were heavily laden with compost. From their homes in the mountains above, they bore fertilizer to fields in the river valley below. Their task was joyful as they traversed the trail like mountain goats, leaping from stone to stone. Despite the weight of their loads, they moved lightly and quickly. As they overtook me, they sang and laughed their way down the mountainside as if they participated, not in a group for labor, but in a party for merriment.

I watched their light, fast movements. If these were the people who lived here, if they were familiar with carrying their loads up and down the ravine each day, surely theirs was an example to follow. I adopted them as my model and started to replicate their gait. "Spring rather than plod. Move lightly," I told myself. And the results were rapid. The pains in my knees and ankles began to ease.

Then I let fear resume its grip. What if I stepped on a loose rock and twisted off the path? What if I slipped on the uneven surface and plummeted down the side of the ravine? What if I stumbled under the weight of my pack and somersaulted over the cliff face?

In fear, I again slowed my pace, deliberately watching each footfall. As I did so, I felt the full weight of my burden, and the concussion of each firmly planted step brought the pain back into my joints.

The laughter of the Nepalese compost bearers came wafting up from below, their merriment a timely reminder. "Surely," I thought, "my eyes are capable of seeing the path ahead. My legs have supported me well through my life and know how to move. I just need to feel confident in the abilities I already have."

Somehow, reminding myself at a conscious level what I already knew at a deeper level freed my body to move comfortably and lightly. Permitting myself to be in touch with long-held capabilities allowed my feet to travel easier. As I traversed the stumbling blocks of my mind, I moved over the ground with a greater freedom, and the load of my baggage felt less burdensome.

Every now and then I stopped, a little fearful again. If I looked down the side of the ravine and started to think about the prospects of falling, I found myself becoming tense, and my freedom of movement curtailed. Reminding myself that what I wanted was within my capabilities, I felt the fear fall away and my gait become freer. All I needed was to trust my inner mind to do what it was already capable of doing.

STORY 51
TURNING PAIN INTO PLEASURE

Therapeutic Characteristics

Problems Addressed

- Pain
- Powerlessness
- Focus on the negative
- Loss of self-esteem

Resources Developed

- Discovering how to shift awareness
- Developing skills for managing pain
- Learning to acknowledge your competencies

Outcomes Offered

- Turn pain into pleasure.
- Learn to attain empowerment over the seemingly uncontrollable.
- Feel confident in using self-management strategies.

Joanne had cancer growing through the bones of her right leg, but the recommended treatment terrified her even more than the diagnosis. Her surgeon said her leg would have to be amputated. It was a choice: her leg or her life.

She lost her leg from the hip down and, with it, her life-long passion for running triathlons, along with the associated feelings of self-worth and self-esteem. But what she didn't lose was the pain. Six months after the amputation, she was still in agony. "How could she have pain in a leg that isn't there any more?" asked her surgeon. The cause of the pain had been removed. There was no physical explanation. "It must be in your head," her physician told her.

"I'm not imagining it," she protested. "It is as real as it was before surgery. Who would want to imagine such agony?" Nonetheless, she accepted a referral for psychotherapy.

Joanne struggled into the consulting room, still unfamiliar with the skills for managing her crutches. The task was not only difficult but also extremely frustrating and humiliating for someone who prided herself so much on her elite level of athletic achievement. She sat in the chair angling her hips so as to take the pressure off the missing leg and grimaced with the facial expressions of someone suffering very genuine pain. It was as incredulous for her that her pain had not remitted as it was for her surgeon.

Pointing to her remaining leg I said, "You must have taken some bumps and knocks while you have been learning to use the crutches. If you hurt your left leg, if you have pain in your left leg, what do you do?"

"I usually rub it or scratch it," she replied.

"And when you rub it or scratch it, how does it feel?"

"It helps ease it for a little," she answered.

I gestured to the absent space on her right and asked, "Where do you feel the hurt on this side?" There was no point in telling her, like everyone else had done, that she should be pain-free now the leg had been surgically removed, for obviously she was still in intense pain. Sometimes it is easy to become so blinded by the immensity of a problem that we lose sight of the abilities to resolve it. Joanne had already let me observe some of the abilities she possessed. First, she was able to feel pain in a leg that wasn't there any more. Second, she could feel it intensely. Third, pain in her other leg was responsive to actions she took to help ease it.

"My knee," she responded.

I asked, "Would you like to give it a rub or a scratch?"

She looked perplexed but, following my request, bent over and rubbed an absent knee.

"How does it feel?" I inquired.

"A little better," she answered, looking surprised and even more perplexed.

This was no magical response, and it had not been hard to predict. It was a simple fact that had become shrouded in her focus on the overwhelming, and seemingly inexplicable, intensity of her pain. What Joanne was experiencing was a normal pain. It followed the laws of normal pain, and thus was likely to respond in the same manner as the feelings in her left leg.

Pointing back to the left leg, I asked, "What things help you to feel pleasure in this leg?"

"It feels good when my husband is caressing it." And, as she spoke, I watched the first faint smile I had seen lift the corners of her mouth. "I like the sensations," she continued, "of the warm baths I have been having recently to help me relax. It is also nice feeling the warmth of the sun on it when sitting out on the back lawn. I used to enjoy the pleasures of having a massage, but I haven't done that since the surgery."

By changing her thoughts she changed her feelings. She shifted her focus from the problem to what means she had available to manage and alter it. Instead of thinking about what she could not do, she started to become aware of what she *could* do. Through these simple actions she was able (at least to some degree) to bring a previously overpowering pain into her control and to enable herself to alter her experiences.

I cannot explain exactly how Joanne began to create feelings of pleasure in the leg that wasn't there any more. Maybe it had something to do with the feeling of empowerment about her abilities, or the fact that she could, and had, faced tough battles before, or an innate desire to be healthy and well, or a determination not to be beaten, or the discovery of hope.

I can only say that change is possible, and Joanne discovered it can happen. For, if it is possible to feel pain, then maybe it is possible to feel pleasure—and to do so with equal intensity.

EXERCISE

Record in your notebook metaphor ideas about learning from experience, whether they are from your own experiences, client cases, or stories you may have heard.

Let your story follow the same format as provided for the Therapeutic Characteristics at the beginning of each story.

1. Begin your story by addressing the problem or problems that parallel those of your client.
2. Move on to the resources that the client can use or needs to develop to reach a resolution.
3. Conclude with the outcome which, for this set of stories, reflects what has been learned from a certain experience.

CHAPTER 9

Attaining Goals

Kierkegaard, the nineteenth-century Danish philosopher, commented that we live life by looking forward and understand it by looking back. Though these two perspectives need not be mutually exclusive, our objective will determine in which direction we need to focus attention. If it is that we want an understanding of what has happened, we may need to explore the past. It is indeed possible to learn from the experiences of the past and such learning is essential to our survival in the present. For example, the child who burns its fingers in fire learns to avoid touching fires in the future, but continuing to dwell on the fire and the suffering that resulted from it is likely to lead to feelings of unhappiness.

If life is about what lies ahead then that is where our gaze needs to be directed. As a species we are equipped to look and move ahead. We have eyes in the front of our head, and our anatomy is built to move forward easily and quickly. Conversely, our reverse gear is clumsy and inefficient. Our physiology and psychology are closely interactive in this perspective. If we bow our head and look down, we become introspective and our mood can easily swing into one of depression. When we stand tall, look forward, and have our goals in front of us, we feel better and more energized, both physically and emotionally. Life is about experiencing the moments of the present while looking at our directions for the future.

Most therapy clients want to improve their circumstances now and in the future. They want things to be better than they were. The stories in this chapter provide ideas for helping clients to set goals, to develop the means for achieving them, and to appreciate the success of asttainment. They cover many examples, from facing a challenge, to finding an appropriate path, to developing strategies for reaching a desired outcome.

STORY 52
REACHING THE ULTIMATE GOAL

Therapeutic Characteristics

Problems Addressed

- Failure to achieve
- Knowledge but not action
- Reliance on others to provide
- Lack of self-reliance or commitment

Resources Developed

- Finding your goal
- Learning about the way or means to reach it
- Doing what is necessary to get there
- Taking action

Outcomes Offered

- Choose your destination.
- You must walk the path yourself.
- Reaching a goal involves *doing* as well as knowing.
- To gain you must act.

Legend has it that a young man once approached the Buddha to ask about reaching the ultimate goal. He had been attending the Buddha's teachings every day for many years. He had listened to talks on enlightenment. He had spent time meditating on principles that he never put into practice. Some people may have interpreted this as resistance, rebellion, or anger, but it seemed more likely that he just never got around to acting on what he was offered.

One particular evening he mustered up the courage to ask the Buddha. "Oh, Learned One," he began, "for years I have been coming to your teachings. I have tried to learn about the path to enlightenment but found that it has not altered my life in any way."

"Then," inquired the Buddha, "what is your question?"

"Over the years," said the young man, "I have seen many people come to your teachings. Some stay. Some leave. Among them are monks and nuns, rich and poor, men, women, and children. Some of these seem to have reached their goal. They show a sense of inner peace. They care for others. They are alive in their joy and happiness. But this is not true for everyone, or perhaps even the majority. I would say that most are no different from when they first came to hear you. For some, life's circumstances have even deteriorated. You are obviously a great teacher. You are caring and concerned for these people. Why don't you use your power to help them? Why don't you assist them to reach the ultimate goal?"

The Buddhist's expression was compassionate but his reply seemed irrelevant. The man thought he had missed the point of his question.

"Where is your home?" asked the Buddha.

The man told him the name of his home town and state. He spoke of where he had been born and raised. He also explained how, a few years ago, he had moved in search of employment.

"Do you still return to your home?" asked the Buddha.

"Yes, as often as I can," said the young man. "My family still lives there. I have friends there with whom I grew up. I even have a girlfriend there and one day we hope to marry."

"Then," observed the Buddha, "if you travel it so frequently, you must know the path very well."

"I know it like the back of my hand," replied the young man. "So well, I think I could walk it blindfolded," he joked.

"If you know it so well then, could you to describe it to someone who was planning to do the journey himself? Would you be truthful and clear in your description?"

"Why, yes. I have described it often to people who have asked me the way, and I have sought to do so as clearly as I can. There is no point in sending them off on the wrong track."

"Of those who ask you for directions," inquired the Buddha, "does everyone set out on the journey?"

"No," said the young man. "Many inquire but not all of them attempt it. Some never find the time or purpose. Some would like to but somehow just don't seem to get around to doing it."

The Buddha inquired further. "Of those who do set out, how many make it to the final destination?"

"Well," said the young man, "usually only those who have set my hometown as their goal. The path is not easy and some give up on the way. Some choose only to go part way and don't have the full journey as their objective."

"Then," said the Buddha, "we both have a very similar experience. People come to me, seeing me as someone who has made a particular journey and knows the path well. They ask me to explain it to them. They may enjoy the description of the path, and like the way I talk about it, but not everyone steps onto it. Of those who do, not everyone chooses to walk its full distance, and, consequently, not everyone reaches the ultimate goal.

"Like you," continued the Buddha, "I seek to describe the path as clearly and truthfully as I can, but I cannot push, pull, or carry someone along the trail. All I can say is, 'I have walked the path. There are things I have learned from the journey. This is my experience of it. I am happy to share my experience of it with you. I can do no more. If you want to reach your goal, you must walk the path yourself.'"

STORY 53
FLYING FREE

Therapeutic Characteristics

Problems Addressed

- Conflict of desires
- Facing a dilemma
- Being fearful or phobic
- Feelings of responsibility

- Guilt
- Neglect of your own needs.

Resources Developed

- Acknowledging dilemmas
- Facing fears
- Finding alternatives
- Seeking pleasure and enjoyment

Outcomes Offered

- Discover new options.
- Develop strategies for managing fear effectively.
- Learn how to discover enjoyment and happiness.
- Attain goals through patience and persistence.

Anna had a dilemma. Would she try something new or be held back by old fears? Would she do something crazy or keep her feet solidly on the ground? It had been a lifelong dilemma. As long as she could recall, there had been part of her that wanted to break free and part of her that was grounded in security and stability.

In her childhood she was torn between wanting to run off to play with her friends and staying inside to do her homework. She wanted to play but knew she should meet her commitments. When she left school, she wanted to travel, but there was a degree to obtain and a career to establish. She needed to think about the future.

Then there was a marriage, a home, and a mortgage. With children came the ultimate responsibility. But the yearning for freedom never ceased. As she said several times, "Oh, how I would love to feel free enough to have time to myself without feeling guilty."

Then she told me a dream. She envisaged that she and her husband were driving along a coastal road on a summer's day—together, alone. This was not a usual activity for her, but in the dream it felt part of a common summer routine. They were planning to visit their favorite beach for a swim, unaware that something unusual was about to happen.

On the way to the beach they pulled off the road to take in a cliff-top view across the ocean. Below, they heard the joyful sounds of laughter and, looking down, saw a group of people. It looked like a party was happening. The sounds of merriment were so pleasant and inviting that they decided to wander down the steep pathway and investigate.

On the golden sands below they discovered the source of joy. People were learning to fly. They were not using aircraft, hang gliders, or parachutes. Like Peter Pan and Wendy, they were soaring into the air, bobbing on the sea breeze, and chuckling with delight about their achievements.

Anna, not surprisingly, had a dilemma. It looked like fun. She wanted to join in, but knew it couldn't really be happening. She saw people flying but told herself it was impossible. She struggled with the conflict between her knowledge and her immediate experience.

As she watched she felt a compelling urge to try. She wondered how it would feel to be free of gravity, to know life without restrictions. At the same time, a part of her was scared to try. What if she failed? How would she handle the unfamiliar experience of doing something so different? What if she fell? Would she hurt herself? What if she screwed up in front of all these other people who were doing it so well? What if she embarrassed herself among people who were so joyfully soaring and lifting, rising to new heights?

Excitement won out. In her first attempt she could not get off the ground. Fear held her down as effectively as if her feet had been cast in concrete. With such a burden, there was no way she would be able to fly free. Nonetheless, she so desperately wanted to share in what the others were experiencing. She let her excitement and anticipation rise. As they started to soar, so did she. Her feet began to bob gently above the warm sands. "This is not possible," she said to herself. "I can't do this." Instantly, she fell into the soft sand.

She recalled a childhood story about a spider struggling to climb a strand of web. Each time it slipped back, it tried again, and each time it tried it rose a little higher. She remembered the punch line: If at first you don't succeed, then try, try, and try again.

Anna tried again. She bobbed on the breeze and lifted into the air. Wow! This was great. The sea sparkled jewel-like in the sunlight below. A warm current of breeze that caressed and gentled her floating body lifted from the sands.

When fear crept in, she began to sink back to the sands below. But she learned there were several ways she could avert an unwanted descent. If she distracted her attention, by looking into the joyful faces and excited eyes of others, she would start bobbling upward again. She could focus her appreciation on the beauty of the natural seascape surrounding her, or she could remind herself, "I am capable," and again she would find herself lifted by the nurturing hands of the breeze.

Anna only needed to do it one time to know she could. While, in some ways, it felt like a new achievement, in others it felt as familiar as learning to walk or ride a bike or drive a car. It wasn't necessary to do it perfectly the first time, for wasn't that just a normal part of the learning process? Maybe she had her falls or setbacks, but each time, like the spider, she tried again. Each time she felt that much stronger and more capable.

"Now that I know I can," she said, "I am free to enjoy my freedom."

STORY 54
MAKING A DIFFERENCE

Therapeutic Characteristics

Problems Addressed

- Difficult circumstances
- Overwhelming odds
- Uncertainty about where to begin
- Feelings of powerlessness

Resources Developed

- Developing kindness and compassion
- Finding a place to begin
- Looking for the attainable

Outcomes Offered

- See what *can* be done rather than what cannot.
- Reaching a goal may be a step-by-step process.
- Find a place to start.
- Take one step at a time.
- Even little steps may be important.

A young couple was walking along a beach after several days of wild storms. The sea had been whipped up to a frenzy. Turbulent waves and high tides had littered the shores with hapless sea creatures. The debris of sea life was so dense that the couple found little space to place their feet. Jellyfish, sea slugs, starfish, and other marine animals coated the beach like a dying blanket.

As they walked along they saw an old, weather-beaten man on the shoreline, wading in and out of the water. They paused to observe his curious behavior. He bent down and picked up one of the sea creatures. He cradled it gently in his hands, waded out into the water, and released it back into its home. He returned to the shore, picked up yet another creature, and gently carried it back into the water.

The couple began to laugh. As they approached, they asked, "What are you doing, old man? Can't you see the futility of your efforts? The shore is covered with thousands of dead and dying creatures. Your efforts won't make any difference."

The man picked up a young octopus that seemed almost lifeless. He nursed it carefully in his hands and walked back into the ocean as if ignoring the couple. He lowered the octopus into the water, tenderly washing away the sand and seaweed that had collected over it and entangled its tentacles. Slowly lowering his hands, he let the little creature again feel the caress of the sea. It spread its arms, sensing the reviving pleasures of its familiar home. Supportively, his hands cupped the young animal until it mustered the strength to propel itself forward. He stood watching, a faint smile on his face at the pleasure of seeing another creature safely on its way.

Only then did he turn and retrace his steps to the shore. He lifted up his gaze, looked the couple in the eyes and said, "It sure made a difference for that one!"

STORY 55
MAKING A COMMITMENT

Therapeutic Characteristics

Problems Addressed

- Life in unhappy circumstances
- Work and life stresses
- Abuse
- Indecision and uncertainty
- Unrealized dreams
- A desire to break free

Resources Developed

- Learning to create dreams or goals
- Being responsible for goal attainment
- Doing what is necessary to reach an objective
- Being committed to your goal

Outcomes Offered

- Dreams can become reality.
- It takes effort to achieve your goals.
- Seize the opportunity when it presents itself.
- Commit yourself to change.

I once saw a nun as a client. She was a delightful person with whom to work, and we shared a lot of fun on her journey of recovery. I think one of the reasons I remember her so well and enjoyed our time together so much was because she communicated in proverbs, parables, and metaphors. Stories stick in our mind and form a bond between teller and listener. Together both participants share a special experience. And that is how it was with the nun.

On our last session I recall her saying, "It is like you gave me a manual and a wrench. I knew if I wanted the job done, it was up to me to fix it." In another metaphor she told me the tale of a chicken and a pig who lived together on the same farm. Although I wasn't sure whether she offered her story with the intent of giving me information or telling herself something important, the tale made it clear that life was not happy for either the chicken or the pig. They felt confined and restricted, they had no sense of job satisfaction, and their diet was monotonously boring. Not surprisingly, they felt they were being used, or even abused. They were giving but not getting. So, frequently, their conversation drifting to topics of breaking free.

They dreamed of a new life, living in liberty and freedom, but their conversations were no more than wasted words, for they did nothing to make their dreams a reality—until one night when the chicken noticed the farmyard gate had been left ajar. Perhaps now was the time to seize the opportunity. The chicken awakened the pig with the news that they could gain their freedom, but the pig hesitated. It seemed ambivalent and indecisive.

Suddenly, faced with the prospect of gaining what it had for so long dreamed was scary. The pig grew fearful, not knowing what lay ahead. Was life on the farm really so bad? It had shelter, food, and security. Were those things worth putting at risk?

"Come on," urged the chicken as it strutted towards the gate. "I am going even if you are not."

With a groan the pig arose and began to follow. Together they walked through the long night, seeking to put as many miles as possible between them and the farm. As the first golden rays of morning began to light the sky, the chicken and pig felt both tired and hungry. They came upon a roadhouse not much further along the road. Outside was a large sign that read "Breakfast Special—Bacon and Eggs."

"Great," exclaimed the chicken. "Let's go and get ourselves a feed."

Again the pig was hesitant and uncertain, unable to make up its mind. As it procrastinated, the chicken voiced its feelings of excitement. "Can't you see this is the beginning of our new life, just the way we have always dreamed about?"

The pig remained hesitant. It was frozen with doubt and uncertainty, immobilized by indecisive thoughts that petrified both mind and body, leaving it powerless and helpless.

"Come on," encouraged the chicken. "What is the matter?"

"Well," said the pig finally, "it is all right for you if we have a breakfast of bacon and eggs. For you it is only a partial commitment. For me it is a total commitment."

STORY 56
WRITING A BOOK

Therapeutic Characteristics

Problems Addressed

- An overwhelming task or challenge
- Uncertainty about where to begin
- Uncertainty about ability to achieve
- A tendency to give up

Resources Developed

- Learning to acknowledge your abilities
- Doing what you can do
- Taking it one step at a time
- Accepting things can go wrong
- Managing when things do go wrong
- Looking at the big picture
- Discovering how to make achievement fun

Outcomes Offered

- Establish the means to achieve your goal.
- Break goals into achievable parts.
- Have strategies for when things go wrong.
- Keep focused on the goal, not the problem.
- Enjoy your success.

I am currently writing a book with the assistance of three valued assets: a handwritten note, a cartoon, and a trophy I won playing polo. Why do I need them, you may well ask. Why don't I just sit down and write? Well, making a decision to do something is an important step in the process of achieving a goal, but it is also important to have the means for achieving it, for without them you may never reach the goal.

The first of my means is the hand written note. It reads,

I am *not* writing a book.
I am *not* even writing a chapter of a book.

I know that I can tell a story,
and, if I can tell a story, I can write a story.
I can tell enough stories to make a chapter,
and enough chapters to make a book.

So I am just writing one story at a time.

It reminds me to break the task down, look at it one step at a time, and consider it in bite-sized bits. If I see the book one story at a time, the task becomes easier and, indeed, more enjoyable.

My second aid is a cartoon. In the first frame a character is seated in front of his computer with a look of contented accomplishment on his face. "After years of writing," he says, "finally, I have completed my autobiography." At that very moment a lightning bolt rips across the face of his computer screen, the computer crashes, and his whole book is lost. In the final frame his fingers are back on the keyboard. With a resigned look on his face he says, "Oh well, now to the Reader's Digest version."

The cartoon reminds me that, though my goal or object might be clear, and my step-by-step plan for reaching it might be defined, things do not always go according to plan. Energy may fade, memory can be lost, and a direction might change. There *will* be hiccups along the way, and some of them may even be major. The journey to a destination is not always smooth. Unexpected interventions, though unplanned and unwanted, may add to the challenge and increase the learning that we gain.

My third aid is the polo trophy. It reminds me about shoveling manure out of my horse's paddock, something I detested and could rarely find the energy or time to do. Fifteen minutes every second day was all it took, but that was enough to have me complaining to a friend.

He laughed out loud. "You lack the energy," he confronted me, "to spend fifteen minutes shoveling manure, but you have plenty to gallop a horse around a field for a two-day polo tournament!"

He was right. I could always find energy to do what I wanted to do but had very little time to do what I did not want to do. I needed to see the things that I did not enjoy or want to do as part of the big picture. If I didn't clean out the stall, the manure would attract flies that would attack my horse, causing it to be ill—and that would mean I couldn't play a game I loved. It was a simple law of cause and effect. Seeing each task as part of the whole enabled me to see a different—though still not entirely pleasant—perspective. I needed to keep my focus on the goal.

The second reminder in the polo trophy is that success is possible. Our team was never particularly competitive. We were playing for a giggle rather than a gain. We set out to have fun rather than be champions, so the trophy came somewhat as a surprise. The surprise was that in having fun one can be successful, and that in success, there is still the opportunity for pleasure.

STORY 57
CLIMB EVERY MOUNTAIN

Therapeutic Characteristics

Problems Addressed

- Previously unattained dreams
- Facing challenges

- Goal attainment
- Being fearful
- Dealing with conflicts of interests

Resources Developed

- Learning to strive for your goal
- Developing self-initiated plans
- Learning to cope with setbacks
- Anticipating success
- Building resilience

Outcomes Offered

- Realistic goals are achievable.
- Seek to find the path to your goal.
- Enjoy the attainment of success.
- Take a risk if you wish to win.
- Learn to look ahead.

Most of us have a dream we seek to follow, for without it life may seem somewhat meaningless. In various ways we all have our mountains to climb, valleys to traverse, or rivers to ford. And when one thinks of following a dream, climbing a mountain, or reaching the pinnacle of achievement, it is hard to think beyond Edmund Hillary and Tenzing Norgay who were the first to summit Mount Everest around half a century ago.

If the world has a collective image of these men it is of heavily clad, black-goggled, near faceless figures suddenly arriving on the planet's highest peak—two men from two different worlds on two different, yet similar, journeys. But the image of arriving suddenly is far from the reality, for both had long-held dreams and a lifetime of preparation.

Hillary was a country-raised New Zealander, university drop-out, bee-keeper, and would-be student of philosophy who fell in love with his country's Southern Alps and began a mission of climbing to the top of the world. For Tenzing, the lesser known of the duo (at least in the West), it began with the dream of a boy who looked up from his herd of yaks to a mountain over which legend said no bird could fly. Unlike Hillary, his mountain career did not start off with the lower peaks and build up to the big ones, as his first expedition with a large British team took him straight to the grandfather of all mountains.

After this initial encounter with Everest, he avidly sought out every expedition he could, enthusiastically wanting to develop his experience, hone his skills, and establish his reputation among the climbing elite, but his efforts were not without their drawbacks. He compared the life of a Sherpa mountain man to that of a sailor whose work frequently took him away from family and home. Tenzing constantly tried to balance the scales between love of family and love of the work that provided their income. When weighted in one direction, the other always seemed to be light. "So it has gone with us through the years," he said, speaking as a family man. "Funny things and sad things: ups and downs—in our lives no less than on the mountains."

At times, striving for a dream can be tough, and many times he seemed to assess whether the struggle was worth it. A young family, an ill and dependent mother-in-law, a post-war slump in expeditions, and a battle with malaria were just some of the obstacles that thwarted his ambitions. Then, when the expeditions resumed, he was on three consecutive climbs in which mountaineers died. This was not a good omen and even this "man of Everest," as Tenzing was to be called, admitted to being "a little afraid." Hillary shared the emotion, saying, "In a sense, fear became a friend—I hated it at the time, but it added spice to the challenge and satisfaction to the conquest."

While still in a hospital bed recovering from a bout of malaria, Tenzing received an invitation to join a British team for his seventh attempt at Everest. The choice was not easy for he was in poor health, his wife argued strongly against it, he was not particularly happy about climbing with the British, the porters were bound to squabble, and how would his family survive if he died? But he never lost sight of his goal, and, while trekking into base camp, he commented, "As I looked (up at Everest) all the rest was gone. The trouble and arguments and bickering meant nothing. Nothing in the world meant anything, except Everest. Except the challenge—and the dream."

In the expedition's grand plan, Tenzing and Hillary were not meant to be the first to the summit, but their chance came when the front-liners fell back exhausted and unsuccessful. After a sleepless night at the highest camp anyone had yet pitched on the mountain, they inched their way toward the summit, cutting steps in the ice, treading carefully to avoid avalanches and, even with supplementary oxygen, struggling for breath.

Their breathless and labored arrival was anything but sudden. For Tenzing, it had been seven attempts and 18 years of physical, emotional, and financial seesawing since he first set foot on this mountain, and many more since, in yak fields far below, he wistfully dreamed of the summit over which no bird could fly. Now, for 15 minutes at the top of the world, he could reap the rewards and experience what no other human had yet done.

In the stories of his life and mountains Tenzing says, "It has been a long road. Yes. From the bottom of Everest to the top. From the yak pastures . . . to a reception in Buckingham Palace. . . . Sometimes, like all roads, it has been hard and bitter; but mostly it has been good. For it has been a high road. A mountain road."

Describing himself as a lucky man, he concluded, "I have had a dream, and it has come true. . . . Everest is climbed. My life goes on. In (my) book I have looked back at the past, but in living one must look ahead."

STORY 58
MANY ROADS

Therapeutic Characteristics

Problems Addressed

- Inability to find a means to an end
- Uncertainty of how to attain a goal
- A tendency to look at the outcome without the processes
- Ambivalence

Resources Developed

- Being willing to explore the options
- Developing choices
- Opening up possibilities
- Creating experiences
- Seeking enjoyment

Outcomes Offered

- There are many means to an end.
- Look at the process as well as the outcome.
- Develop and explore the choices.
- Create new possibilities.
- Enjoy the journey.

An old proverb says, "Many roads lead to Rome,"—but Rome wasn't where Tracey wanted to go. San Francisco was her choice. She had been born and raised in New York. She had never traveled beyond the range of her local zip codes, but somehow she had always had a yearning to visit San Francisco.

Having decided where she wanted to go, the next question she faced was how to get there. Her first thought was to fly. To do so she would have to take a cab through the New York traffic, wait at the airport, and sit uncomfortably in a plane for five hours while it whisked her to her destination—surely the quickest possible route

On the other hand, she could get onto Interstate 80 and drive straight across the country to San Francisco. With steady hours of driving and nights spent in roadside motels, she would be there in four or five days. That would be the quickest and shortest route by road. Of course, she could opt for a more leisurely trip. She could visit Niagara Falls or the Great Lakes, then follow the footsteps of the early pioneers across the continent's mighty interior. She might extend her journey southward to Colorado, weaving through high mountain passes and towering Ponderosa Pines. As she thought about it, there were so many things she could see: the Continental Divide, Salt Lake City, Reno, and Lake Tahoe. From there, she would not be far from the Bay area—and her destination. The journey would be a week or two longer but the experience would be much greater.

As she thought about this, she considered her other options. To get to San Francisco, she could fly from New York to London. She hadn't thought, at first, that going in an apparently opposite direction could get her to her destination. In London, she could visit all those famed sites that she'd only read about in history books: Parliament Houses, Big Ben, The Tower, Buckingham Palace.

She could ferry across the English Channel, sample the wines of Bordeaux, and explore the cosmopolitan capital of Paris. She could walk the banks of the Seine and stand at the top of the Eiffel Tower. It all felt romantic.

In Italy, she could tour the Coliseum, see Michelangelo's handiwork on the ceiling of the Sistine Chapel, and visit the ruins of Pompei. From Brindisi she could ferry across the Adriatic Sea to Greece, stand in the stadium where the first Olympic Games were held, take in a symphony concert in the ancient ruins of the Herod of Atticus Theatre, or bathe in crystal clear island waters under a warm Grecian sun. The thought of tasting different cultures was truly delicious.

And that would just be the beginning. There would be Turkey, Israel, India, and the whole of Asia just waiting to be explored. Beyond, she could travel through Australia and the tropical Pacific islands before a final stop in Hawaii where she could learn to surf or watch volcanoes pour their fiery lava straight into the sea. Another flight is all it would take to be in San Francisco. She would still reach her destination and have had a very different experience along the way.

Yes, thought Tracey, just as there are many roads that lead to Rome, there are also many roads that lead to San Francisco. Then another proverb came to mind. In fact, many people in many different cultures have repeated it in various forms. Robert Louis Stevenson quoted it, the Japanese use it, and ancient travelers knew it from their personal journeys. Now it began to have some meaning for her. *The experience is in the journey, more than the arriving.*

STORY 59
BUILDING A NEW LIFE

Therapeutic Characteristics

Problems Addressed

- Feelings of anger
- Hostility
- Revenge
- Dejection
- Deceit
- Failure

Resources Developed

- Learning to develop and practice tolerance, patience, and compassion
- Developing a willingness to learn
- Finding your own resources.

Outcomes Offered

- The answer lies within.
- Negative feelings can and will pass.
- Learning comes through doing.
- Experience is the best teacher.

Milarapa was an angry young man who sought to achieve mystical powers to gain revenge against those who had done him wrong.

On his quest for power he engaged a teacher named Marpa, who quickly recognized the anger and hostility in Milarepa's motivation. "I am willing to help you," he said, "but I cannot give you everything that you ask. You ask for food, shelter, and instruction. It is important that you learn to care for yourself. What I offer will, at best, enrich what you are already capable of doing.

"I can give you food and shelter *or* instruction. Whichever you chose from me, the other will be your responsibility. What is your choice?"

Milarepa responded without hesitation. "I can care for my own physical needs," said Milarepa. "What I seek from you is instruction."

Marpa laid down the rules. "If you want my instruction, you will have to do everything I say. You will do it without question, because the *doing* will contain the experience that will help you reach your goal. Do I have your vow?"

Milarepa consented and was given his first clear instruction. He could not understand how it would help him reach his goal, but he had agreed to do as instructed, and he stuck by his agreement. The instruction was to build Marpa a two-story house of a particular design and in a particular place. "When you have finished," said Marpa, "I will teach you the things you want to know."

Milarepa labored long and hard. He worked diligently from dawn to dusk because he wanted to learn quickly. When he finished he proudly called Marpa to inspect the home. Marpa did so thoroughly. "It is a very good house," he said. "There is no question that you have completed your task as instructed, but we do have a problem. My brother claims that the land on which you built it is his. You must now demolish it and rebuild it on that next hill which is definitely my land."

Not surprisingly, Milarepa protested. He had done what he was told. He should now receive his instruction. Marpa replied, "If a material object such as a house matters to you more than your education, then you must make that choice."

More than anything Milarepa wanted to learn. He wanted the powers of revenge, so he tore down the house that he had built, carried the building supplies, brick by brick and log by log, to the next hill where he rebuilt Marpa's house. He cursed every brick he carried. He cursed Marpa. He seethed with hostility. He berated himself for being manipulated, but he completed the building. The house was built, not through desire, but through the energy of hatred.

When Marpa came to inspect, he gave clear and quick instructions. "Tear it down," he said. Milarepa looked at him with disbelief. "It is tainted," said Marpa, "with all your negative thoughts and actions. How can I live in a house with such negative energy?"

Milarepa began to think of how he could escape the responsibility. He did not want to have to demolish a whole house and rebuild it for a third time. Cunningly, he thought about how to cut corners. How could he pretend to do the job without all the effort? He had a solution. He would simply rebuild the front. If Marpa came by, he would see the activity and assume the whole house was being rebuilt. Milarepa even sat back and rested for long periods to pretend the reconstruction had taken an appropriate time. Only then did he advise Marpa the task was complete.

"You have tried to deceive me," said Marpa. "You have been dishonest with me. How can you expect me to instruct somebody who does not respect the truth? If you want my instruction, you must build it again."

Milarepa was no longer angry. That had passed. He had worked out the energy of his hostility. Now he felt dejected, and for sometime sat in utter despair. He wanted the instruction of this most learned master, but how could he attain it? So far, whatever he did had failed. The first time he built the house begrudgingly, and though it was perfectly constructed, it was not in the right place. The second time he had gone about it with anger and hostility. Again, the structure was perfect, but the energy that went into it would not make it a comfortable home. On the third occasion, he had tried to cut corners and be deceitful. Now he saw that by using deceit and dishonesty, he was only cheating himself.

To complete the task, he needed to do it wisely. He needed to put his heart into the project. If he truly esteemed this teacher, it must be a befitting gift of love. With this in mind, Milarepa set out to build a home that was truly appropriate for his master. He tended to every aspect, not just with detail, but with love. He built a house that stood nine stories tall, and even then he wondered whether he might have done more. When Marpa came to inspect the final achievement, the master said, "Now I can instruct you."

"Thank you," said Milarepa, "but I have learned what I need to know for now. I have received your instruction in a way more powerfully than I could have imagined." As he departed he felt the weight of anger and revenge had been left behind. He was free to continue his own journey of discovery.

STORY 60
THE SECRETS OF SUCCESS

Therapeutic Characteristics

Problems Addressed

- A rivalry
- Confrontation of a challenge
- Goal-setting
- Ways to find the means to succeed

Resources Developed

- Learning to acknowledge your strengths and weaknesses
- Developing your abilities
- Making choices about weaknesses
- Discovering the value of training and preparation

Outcomes Offered

- Focus on your strengths.
- Apply yourself toward your goal.
- Aim to develop your personal best.

"Grandpa," asked Thomas on the phone, "can we hike the Bibbulmum Track and camp out at Hewitt's Hill Hut?" Grandpa knew Thomas was in training for the school swimming competition but there was something else he did not know.

"Can I bring some friends? Daniel, Corey, Luke, and Willo?"

Daniel was the school's best swimmer and top favorite to be this year's champion. He and Thomas were cousins of the same age, and they were in constant rivalry like two young bucks clashing antlers in seriously playful challenges.

When it came to schoolwork, Thomas was usually the victor. But Daniel tended to excel in challenges of physical prowess, and those were the things more valued among little boys. It was not that Thomas wasn't good, it was just that Daniel always seemed to run faster, climb higher up a tree, and throw a stone further.

Some days they would take the long walk home from school through the woods. There they would climb to the top of a granite outcrop and engage in the ultimate little boy challenge: to see who could pee the furthest. Again Daniel always seemed to win, but what hurt most was when Daniel taunted and laughed at him in front of his friends. That struck Thomas to the core of his juvenile masculinity.

Some weeks before the planned overnight hike, Thomas arrived at his Grandpa's looking forlorn. Daniel had beaten him again. Twice. Once when they stopped at the granite outcrop and once in the swimming trials.

"No matter what I do he's always better than me," complained Thomas. "The competition is coming up soon and I'd love to beat him, just once."

"In my experience the best athletes have a few secrets that you never hear them talk about," his grandpa, who was once a champion swimmer, confided as though he were a master magician finally consenting to tell his apprentice those safely guarded tricks of the trade.

"First, it is important to know what you are good at. You see, there are some things you do very well and some things Daniel does very well. We all have our different strengths and abilities. The secret is to concentrate on your strengths. Know what they are and how to use them. Be aware of what you are not so good at, too, and choose whether you want to focus on them less, or try to develop them. Thinking too much about what you can't do may stop you from doing what you can.

"The second secret of top athletes," continued his grandpa, "is that they train. Have you ever seen Daniel training? No, he never puts in the effort. It is no good having the ability if you don't develop it. Set your goal, work hard toward it, and you can make it.

"Finally," said Grandpa, "aim to improve your own abilities. Strive to attain *your own* personal best rather than concentrate on beating your opponent. That is more important than winning."

Thomas took Grandpa's words to heart. He wanted to do his best, so he began to train, getting up early every morning to practice. In particular he worked hard at improving both his distance and speed. He watched swimming champions on television, followed their example, and realized, after Grandpa's talk, how much effort they put into becoming the best. He noticed that they often carried water bottles with them. That, he thought, was a good idea and always kept one in his school bag. He drank plenty.

A couple of weeks after he spoke to his grandpa, they went hiking. They cooked on a campfire, toasted marshmallows on sticks they had whittled, and played spotlight in the dark. They watched the moon rise, and then snuggled into their sleeping bags full of anticipation, for the competition was getting close.

Thomas had prepared himself: He drank constantly from his water bottle all that day and even sipped on it when he awoke during the night. He certainly had been training.

First thing in the morning, before Grandpa awoke, Thomas led his friends out into the woods because here, near Hewitt's Hill Hut, was the tallest granite outcrop that he knew. This was the day of the competition. Thomas practiced holding back as long as possible. Now he was ready. He let fly, peeing the furthest he had ever done. Not only was it a personal best, but Thomas was declared the Grand Champion.

That night when they had walked out of the woods and returned to Grandpa's house, Thomas gave his grandpa a big hug. "Thanks for teaching me the secrets of success," he said with a smile his grandpa could only begin to wonder about.

STORY 61
ONE STEP AT A TIME

Therapeutic Characteristics

Problems Addressed

- Uncontrollable thoughts and behaviors
- A need to tackle a big goal
- Feeling powerless
- Relationship conflict and tension
- Desire for a "magic wand" solution

Resources Developed

- Being willing to seek expert assistance
- Learning to see the exceptions
- Developing patience
- Being committed to change
- Taking it one step at a time

Outcomes Offered

- What seems uncontrollable may be controllable.
- Find the exceptions to the rule.
- Look for positives in a relationship.
- Seek what gives you control and power.
- Don't expect a magical solution.
- Take it one step at a time.

I had a friend, a horse trainer, who taught me something very wise and very helpful. He thought he was teaching me something about horses. I think that he taught me a lot more.

What do you do when you are fighting to achieve something and all of your efforts seem to be in vain? Sometimes thoughts race ahead of us in directions that we don't want them to go. No matter how much we try to reign them in, they don't respond. Sometimes we slip back into unhealthy patterns of behavior that we feel powerless to control. How do we regain control? Maybe there is a goal that we want to attain but the leap from where we are to where we want to be seems impossibly huge and unattainable.

I once had a horse that I couldn't reign in. Her name was Jasmine. When my kids were young and learning to ride their own ponies, I wanted to take them for quiet rides in the woods, but once out of the paddock and free of her confining boundaries, Jasmine wanted to gallop like the wind. I just wanted a peaceful ride with my children.

Jasmine saw tracks along which to race, fallen logs to jump or wildlife to chase. I would battle to hold her back. Looking behind, I saw my kids trotting along on their little ponies, desperate to keep up with me, but fading in the distance. I would fight with the reins but, inevitably, she would win. I felt powerless. I was not in control. I was losing the battle.

It became such a problem that my relationship with her grew unpleasant. I saw our interactions becoming ones of increasing conflict and tension. Not being able to resolve the issue I consulted my friend, the horse trainer. Initially, he asked a very astute question, "When you go for a ride with the children, do you always have this conflict?"

"Always," I said, without hesitation.

"And what about on other occasions?" he asked. "Like times when you are riding by yourself and not with the children?"

For a while I thought. Jasmine was my polo horse. On the polo field, we were definitely a team. I often thought she played the game far better than I did. She loved the fun and excitement of the match. During a game she was responsive to my most subtle suggestions of control. I knew, too, that I could trust her initiative.

So, as I pondered my friend's question, I realized the battle we had in attempting to go for a quiet bush ride with the children was not such a huge problem. There were times when we worked well together, times when she was responsive, times when we enjoyed our interactions. I had to acknowledge that there were exceptions to the rule, as I had perceived it. I had allowed the problem to gain such weight that I had lost sight of the times when things were different.

My friend's advice was sound. He said, "Next time you go out, stop fighting. That hasn't been working and there is no point in continuing to do something that isn't working.

"Use your reins to check her back, instead," he advised. "If she starts to race off, bring her back on the bit. When she responds, loosen your grip. You will find she will race off again. When she does, check her back. Stick with it and you will find it pays off.

"On the next ride, you might have to do it 100 times. On the ride after that, you may still have to check her back 100 times, but perhaps on the next ride you might only need to do it 99 or 98 times. Within a few rides, you might have brought it down to 80 or even 70. The more you do it, the more she is going to get the message.

"It may seem tedious at first," he continued, as if reading my disappointment that he was giving me a laborious task rather then offering a magic wand. "You may not want to put the effort in, for it is a matter of constantly thinking about what you are doing at first, constantly checking back that force that is running away with you. But, if you are willing to work at it, it won't be long before you will be down to 50 or even 40 times. If you continue to do what I say, quietly and persistently, it will drop to 30 or 20, then 10 or 5, and it really won't be long before you don't have to do it at all."

I had hoped there would be some instant remedy, a quick fix that would keep Jasmine a fast-acting horse on the polo field, but a docile and gentle nag on the trail. But my friend's advice proved to be right. With time and the patience, change occurred. By taking it one step at a time, we moved forward, slowly but steadily. In retrospect, it seemed hardly any time at all before I was enjoying pleasant country rides with my children and still had a willing games horse. To this day, I thank my friend for his wise advice. I think he taught me about a lot more than just how to bring a horse under control.

EXERCISE

Use your notebook to record your own stories about reaching a goal. In doing so, you might like to consider the following steps:

1. Think of an appropriate, relevant, and attainable goal.
2. Describe the circumstances that lead to its attainment.
3. Build in the feelings, sensations, and mood of the story.
4. Write in the setbacks and achievements, the challenges and progress that make up the journey.
5. Incorporate the rewards or feelings of achievement when the goal is attained.
6. Examine how they can be used when confronting similar challenges in the future.

CHAPTER 10

Cultivating Compassion

We are social, interactive creatures, and, therefore, creating and maintaining warm, caring, and compassionate relationships are essential parts of our well-being. Such qualities in early parent-child relationships determine, to a large degree, not only our future interpersonal skills but also our overall psychological health. One of life's quests is to find another person with whom we can share love and intimacy. In fact, whatever we do in life brings us into contact with others. If those interactions are warm and positive, we blossom. If they are aggressive and hostile, we suffer.

There is a solid body of research that confirms the benefits of caring relationships on our well-being. People who lack close social ties tend to suffer from poorer health, higher levels of unhappiness, and greater vulnerability to stress. Having social support and intimate relationships appears to improve immune system functioning and lower rates of cancer, cholesterol, and premature death.

By seeing things from the other person's perspective, by thinking about how that person feels, and by acting out of loving kindness, we prevent and diffuse emotions of anger, hostility, and aggression. Compassion may be an act of altruism, but it is also an act of pragmatism, because caring for others is a way of caring for ourselves and our needs as social beings.

Acknowledging and developing compassionate, caring interactions is the basis for the stories in this chapter. They speak about establishing and maintaining healthy relationships with our fellow beings. They talk about caring, kindness, giving, and empathy toward others.

STORY 62
THE FUTILITY OF BICKERING

Therapeutic Characteristics

Problems Addressed

- Relationship conflicts
- Communication difficulties
- Arguments
- Self-centeredness
- Lack of regard for others

Resources Developed

- Learning to become more insightful
- Developing awareness of the consequences of our actions

Outcomes Offered

- Gain insight into the futility of bickering, selfishness, and lack of compassion.
- Recognize paradoxical suggestions of change.

There once was a husband and wife who argued constantly. In all their long years of marriage, they could not recall anything they had ever found to agree on. After decades of practice they could find even the slightest, most inconsequential thing about which to bicker.

Like two young children watching to see whether one got more sweets than the other, or whether one's glass of drink contained more fluid, each lived with a sense of unfairness and injustice. "You got more than me." "Yours is better than mine." "You had the big one last time." "I want the one you have."

One day the man was walking home from work when he passed a neighbor's orchard. Seeing three ripe peaches on a tree full of otherwise green fruit, he climbed through the fence and stole the peaches.

When he arrived home, the husband handed his wife one of the stolen peaches and kept two for him. Seeing this, the wife started yelling at him. "Why do I get one and you get two? I have been home all day slaving around the house. I deserve the extra peach. Besides, how do I know you haven't already eaten some on your way home?"

The husband's fury rose. "I, too, have been out working all day," he shouted, "and harder than you. I am accountable to a boss. I can't just quietly sit back and pretend I have been working like you do. I can't spend my day watching TV or chatting with the neighbors. Anyway, I gathered the fruit. I deserve to have all three. You're lucky I've given you one."

And so the argument went on. Tempers and voices were raised. Neither wanted to compromise their self-righteous stance. For an outsider, a few pieces of fruit might not have seemed to be worth the tension and unhappiness of such a conflict, but, for the husband and wife, the matter was to become one of life and death.

Either could have offered the extra peach to the other, but neither was willing to make the sacrifice. They could have considered cutting the third peach in half, thus having equal portions, but, in their greed, neither was prepared to be so considerate. Both husband and wife believed they deserved the extra peach more than the other one—and they were not prepared to give in. A mere equal share was not enough.

Sick of the wife's nagging, the husband wagered a bet. "I bet you my extra peach," he shouted at her, "that you can't shut up and remain silent. The one who stays quietest the longest gets the two peaches."

The wife went to bed. The husband stretched out on the couch. Each of them was so determined to win against the other that they maintained their silence. They persisted throughout the first day and on into the second. Day followed day. They declined to move. Neither ate nor drank.

After a week of silence from the house, the neighbors began to grow curious. When they went inside to investigate, they found the husband and wife stretched out, pale and silent. Thinking the couple dead, the neighbors began to arrange a funeral service.

Husband and wife were laid out in separate coffins. As the undertaker began to nail the lid on the husband's coffin, he screamed out in fear of being interred or cremated alive. "You fools, can't you see I am still alive?" he shouted. The wife leaped from her open coffin. "Ah, hah!" she screeched with delight. "I win. I get the extra peach."

Both husband and wife raced back to the house, trying to beat the other to the prized fruit. When they arrived they found the three peaches still sitting in the kitchen—rotten!

STORY 63
FEEDING A FELLOW

Therapeutic Characteristics

Problems Addressed

- Separateness
- Selfishness
- Greed
- Lack of concern for others
- Lack of cooperation with others
- A seemingly insoluble problem

Resources Developed

- Developing an awareness of others and their needs
- Seeing different solutions
- Finding ways to be cooperative
- Developing care and compassion

Outcomes Offered

- Working cooperatively with others can have mutual benefits.
- Think laterally about seemingly insoluble problems.
- In giving, you receive.
- Discover what makes effective relationships.

A woman died, and on her journey on to the next life, she found herself standing in an amazingly elaborate banquet hall. The walls were lined with the most expensive timbers, crystal chandeliers hung from the high ceilings, and original paintings of all the great masters decked the walls. A huge banquet table ran through the center of the hall and was loaded with every possible delicacy and the most awarded of the world's wines. "This must be heaven," she thought, a little surprised. She didn't believe she had led a life so good or holy as to deserve such a reward. Undeterred, she eagerly raced to her place at the table, dropped into her chair and then noticed something dreadful.

Both her arms were in splints. She could not bend her elbows. Her hands felt like they were at the end of a distant pole. She had no trouble taking hold of the luxurious delicacies that lavished the table but was unable to maneuver them to her mouth. As she paused to look beyond what she had initially, and greedily, desired for herself, she saw other people sitting around the table. Their arms were also in splints; they cursed, grew angry, became frustrated, and cried, but it seemed that nothing could save them from their fate.

"I was wrong," thought the woman. "This is not heaven but hell. I wonder what heaven is like."

Her wish transported her into another, identical banquet hall. Similar expensive chandeliers hung from the ceilings. Original artworks by all the great masters were on the exotic wooden walls. A similar carved wooden table stretched down the center of the hall. It was equally laden with every imaginable exotic dish and award-winning wine. Again, she eagerly rushed to her seat hoping to share in the delicacies. Then again she perceived the same unnoticed fact: Her arms were still in their rigid splints.

About to despair, she looked around the table. There was something very different about this group of diners who all appeared happy and well-fed. She looked at their arms which, like hers, were bound in splints, but her fellow guests were jovial and communicative in spite of their confinement.

At last, she finally saw what made the difference. They were not struggling to bend immovable arms, nor greedily trying to force food into their own mouths. Instead, each person would pick up a delicacy politely requested by the person opposite him or her. Rather than seeing the restriction as a disability, they used it to benefit their fellow diners. Having secured an item of food, they reached across the table to feed the other person. She found that in giving to another, she gained. Others fed her, just as she fed them.

"This is not just about food," she thought, for as the people shared food, they also shared conversation. They exchanged stories, spread feelings of optimism, and joined in an experience of joyfulness. "Yes," she decided, "this is truly heaven."

STORY 64
LOVE AND LET GO

Therapeutic Characteristics

Problems Addressed

- Parent-child relationship issues
- Dealing with a "problem" child

- Uncertainty about what to do
- Nothing seems to be working

Resources Developed

- Learning to focus on outcome rather than problems
- Letting others have their experiences
- Knowing that learning can be tough at times
- Doing what you believe is right
- Learning to let go

Outcomes Offered

- Care without interfering.
- Be available without being controlling.
- Permit others their experiences.
- Love—and let go.

Joanna told me a story not unfamiliar to many parents. She was a mother of a teenage daughter around whom the whole family seemed to pivot. She said if it were not for this child, life would be peaceful. She felt that her daughter was the source of all the family's problems and conflicts. She was smoking marijuana. She mixed with friends her parents did not like. They suspected she was involved in a sexual relationship—at an age too premature and with a guy too old. She had lost all interest in her studies, stayed out past curfew, and had been drinking. As if all this wasn't enough, she lied to her parents about her behavior. They found this hard to handle. They had raised her to be honest. They prided themselves on being an open family. Naturally, they were worried and concerned. They wanted the best for their daughter.

No matter what they did, it seemed to be wrong. If they tried to be loving, caring, and empathic, she turned a cold shoulder and walked away. If they ignored her, she did what she wanted to do anyway. If they got angry, she responded in kind. Everyone was left feeling hurt, bitter, and tearful. What could they do when nothing was working?

In the middle of this dilemma, Joanna had a dream. She dreamed that her family was on vacation by the ocean. As she was walking along the beach one morning, she noticed a young dolphin washed up on the shore. It was out of its element. She knew it wasn't happy there, but what should she do?

She looked at the dolphin's cute face, its prominent beak, and the faint glimmer of a smile. Its eyes were lonely and pleading. She reached out to touch it, but it flinched slightly as if wishing to draw away. Even the hint of withdrawal left Joanna feeling hurt that the dolphin rejected her gesture. Should she try and help the dolphin back into the water or should she let nature take its course? For a while she sat on the beach and looked into its baleful eyes. As she did, a wildlife officer strolled along the beach. She asked what she should do. Later she couldn't remember whether the officer answered her or whether the thoughts were already there in her own head. "Hard as it might be," was the message, "there are times when we must sit back and let nature take it course. Though we may care, and care deeply, we need to let others learn from their own mistakes. Although we can offer understanding and comfort, this experience may be an important lesson. To continue to survive in the big world, everyone must learn to look after themselves—even if the lesson is tough."

The woman walked back to the cottage where she was staying, gathered some towels, wet them, and placed them over the dolphin to keep it cool. She would give it comfort. She would prevent it from suffering the heat of the sun and ask nothing in return.

All day she kept an eye on the dolphin. She kept the towels moistened. She dug holes in the sand to take the weight off its pectoral fins and allow it greater feelings of comfort. She let it take time to recuperate. All she could do was watch, with care, and give what support she could.

She often met the wildlife officer who was also keeping an active vigil on the stranded creature. New understandings came to mind as she sat beside the dolphin. Again, she wasn't sure whether it was from words spoken to her or her own thoughts. "Experience is the best teacher," she heard. "Those experiences may not always be pleasant. They may not necessarily be what we want for someone or something we care about. They may, at times, be hard and difficult to cope with, but it is from our experiences that we gain our deepest and most profound learning. Would you really want to deny this creature its learning experiences?"

She desperately wanted to ease the dolphin's pain and suffering. She didn't want to rob it of what might be important, so she kept watch over it. At times she left it alone so she could go and do whatever she needed to do. She thought about her relationship with the little dolphin, and, again, she wasn't sure whether the thoughts were something that came from outside or inside.

"As a caregiver, no matter what you do, it may be wrong. There is a risk that you may make a mistake. There is a risk that the choice you make at any time might not, in the long run, prove to be the best. No matter what you do, it may be perceived by the other person as being wrong." She finally said to herself, "If there is a risk that what you do may be wrong, then you might as well be wrong while doing what you believe is reasonably and ethically right."

Late in the evening the tide washed high up the beach. The cool, refreshing waters lapped around the little dolphin. The woman watched the life come back into its eyes and saw the excited quiver of its muscles. On a wave that was a little larger than average, the dolphin flipped itself back into the water. The towels washed off its spine, and it flapped its fins joyfully in the shore break. Swimming out deeper, it leaped enthusiastically from the sea, and, Joanna was sure, sent an unspoken message of gratitude. Then it disappeared beneath the waters, finding its own way home.

"You need to give," were the words she heard, "without expecting to receive. You need to be available without being controlling. You need to trust without wanting to manipulate. You need to love—and let go."

STORY 65
LOVE, VERSION 4.0

Therapeutic Characteristics

Problems Addressed

- Hate
- Bitterness
- Selfishness

- Denigration
- Resentment
- Past hurt
- Low self-esteem

Resources Developed

- Learning to accept compliments
- Encouraging yourself and others
- Accepting kind words
- Communicating effectively
- Sharing
- Accepting yourself

Outcomes Offered

- Love can be the basis of how we feel and relate.
- Let go of the things that block love.
- Develop what facilitates love.
- Share good feelings.

A customer phoned the HEART System Software Company to inquire about their latest program, LOVE, Version 4.0. "Can you help me?" he asked. "You see, LOVE is new to me and I don't really understand it."

"Certainly," replied the service representative. "The first thing to understand is that LOVE is unique and there is nothing else like it in the world. It operates quietly in the background, helping everything else run smoothly.

"You won't see LOVE on your monitor, but you will notice its effect on every application you have because, with it, your good programs will run better. It helps smooth out the bugs in bad programs and may even delete ones that are a nuisance."

"That sounds wonderful," said the new customer. "How do I make it work for me?"

"Well, the good news is that it is all relatively easy," answered the service representative, "but LOVE won't show its full potential unless you use files like COMPLIMENT.WAV, ENCOURAGEMENT.WAV, KINDWORD.WAV, and FORGIVENESS.EXE which can help prevent and resolve those annoying 'unable to connect' messages."

"This sounds like it is exactly what I need," responded the customer. "I feel I have grown stale sitting alone in front of my computer, replaying the old programs over and over again."

The service representative acknowledged, "That can be a danger, but LOVE searches your memory for old, unwanted programs, even those you have tried to delete unsuccessfully. Although files like HATE.TIF, BITTERNESS.EXE, SELFISHNESS.DOC, and SPITE.EXE cannot be entirely deleted, LOVE overpowers them and stops their commands from being executed.

"With LOVE, you will no longer need INSULT.WAV. Certain fonts will also become redundant. BADWORDS12, DENIGRATION10, or HARSHNESS, even if only 7, will not be necessary for communication. In fact, LOVE will make communication more meaningful and enjoyable."

COMPASSION

"Is LOVE a program I need to upgrade?" asked the customer.

"LOVE is not static," answered the service representative. "It is a dynamic program, always growing and upgrading itself. Once you have LOVE installed and running, it copies a module, or piece of itself, to every Hard drive, E-mail, And Remote Terminal (HEART) that it comes in contact with. These external devices run whatever version of LOVE they have. They return a module of their version of LOVE to your HEART.

"This is why we have LOVE as shareware. Each time you share a little of your version, you receive a little of someone else's. Your upgrades thus come automatically and the program keeps growing. Your HEART can learn and develop from what other HEARTs have learned."

"What is the first step," asked the customer, "in making sure it is installed and running properly?"

"First," said the representative, "you need to ensure your HEART is open. Then you need to be willing to open COMMUNICATION.DOC, for LOVE cannot operate without COMMUNICATION.

"Second, there are some programs with which LOVE is incompatible, like PASTHURT.EXE, GRUDGE.EXE, RESENTMENT.DOC, and LOWESTEEM.EXE, so invoking FORGIVENESS.EXE will help. Although they may remain in your memory, they will no longer be disruptive."

"Thank you," said the happy customer, now confident that he could install and run LOVE in his HEART.

"Remember," said the service representative, as if reading his thoughts, "you need to connect to other HEARTs in order to get your upgrades and keep LOVE operating effectively. In addition, the HEART you work from needs to be cared for properly. You have to LOVE your HEART before it can LOVE others."

"How can I do that?" asked the customer.

"First, find the directory called SELFACCEPTING," the rep replied. "Click on the files named FORGIVESELF.DOC, SELFESTEEM.TXT, REALIZEWORTH.TXT, and GOODNESS.DOC. Then copy them to the MYHEART directory. Finally, you need to find and delete SELFCRITIC.EXE from all directories. This is one you never want to see again."

"Hey!" cried the customer, "Look at this! MYHEART is filling up with some wonderful files. SMILE.HPG is already running. As I watch, I can experience WARMTH.JPG, PEACE.EXE, and CONTENTMENT.TIF being copied into MYHEART. This feels great."

"Well done," said the service representative. "You now have LOVE installed and running. But there is one final thing to remember. LOVE is freeware and only operates effectively when it is shared. Be sure to give it and its various modules to everyone who contacts your HEART, for, in turn, they will return some really beautiful modules to you. Just imagine every HEART in the world running on LOVE."

"Thank you," replied the customer, eager to sign on and discover more about LOVE.

STORY 66
APPRECIATING EACH OTHER

Therapeutic Characteristics

Problems Addressed

- Failure to appreciate fellow beings
- Failure to see others' skills and resources
- Arrogance
- Egocentricity
- Self-righteousness

Resources Developed

- Learning to observe what others have and are
- Developing an appreciation of others' skills
- Seeing the need for change

Outcomes Offered

- Listen to others.
- Appreciate the other person for who he or she is.
- Be less self-righteous.
- Be open to learn from others.

A university professor and his wife decided to cruise the Caribbean—their fantasy vacation—after his retirement. On his last day at work, the professor packed his briefcase and walked away from the university. Although they were excited about their trip, it was not easy to leave behind a lifetime of work. He was used to standing in front of students, impressing them with both the depth and expanse of his knowledge. After decades of teaching, he could not stop, even on vacation.

Maybe he didn't see the need to stop. Maybe he lacked the insight to appreciate how others reacted to his pedantry. Either way, he never missed an opportunity to pontificate.

"Tell me," he asked his cabin boy as they were shown into their shipboard accommodation, "have you ever studied psychology?"

When the cabin boy replied no, the professor asked, "How could that be? You are working in a people industry. Surely you need an understanding of how people think and behave, not only to do your work, but also to understand more about life. I hate to say this, but if you haven't studied psychology, you have wasted half your life."

On deck he approached a sailor who was merrily whistling away as he polished the brass-work. "Have you studied philosophy?" inquired the professor.

"No sir," said the sailor, courteously. "I am happy with what I do. I get paid to see the world. Why would I need to study . . . what was it . . . philosophy?"

"By studying philosophy," replied the professor, "you would know more about the meaning of life. You would understand in greater depth the experiences that you have. You would be able to converse with other people at an intellectual level. If you are not doing this you are wasting half your life."

A day or two later, the professor encountered another sailor. This one was leaning over the stern fishing in a bay where the ship had anchored. "Have you studied anthropology?" he asked the humble fellow.

When the man said no, the professor told him how knowledge of other people and cultures would greatly enrich his travels and journeys to exotic islands. "If you learn about the tribes in the lands you visit, your experiences will be richer," he said. "Anthropology will teach you about rituals, rites of passage, legends, and folklores of the natives you encounter. You will be able to communicate with them better. Without doing this, you are wasting half your life."

Not surprisingly, the professor's reputation quickly spread around the small ship. Sailors and cabin crew alike avoided him in dread of facing his questions and lectures.

Then, one inky, black night in the middle of a boundless sea, a hurricane struck. Buffeted with high winds and pounding waves, the small ship's hull creaked and cracked under the strain of nature's fury. The professor and his wife donned their life jackets and hurried to the lifeboats where sailors were organizing passengers in preparation for abandoning ship. One sailor, seeing the professor stagger through the gloom and spray, asked the learned gentleman, "Have you studied swimming?"

"No," said the terrified professor, gripping tightly to the handrail with one hand and holding his wife with the other.

"What a shame," said the sailor. "If the ship sinks you may have wasted your *whole* life."

STORY 67
LEARNING TO CARE

Therapeutic Characteristics

Problems Addressed

- Parent-child relationship difficulties
- Lack of love and caring
- Lack of joy and happiness
- Grief
- Anger

Resources Developed

- Learning to care for yourself
- Finding happiness
- Managing grief and anger
- Developing relationship skills

Outcomes Offered

- It is possible to overcome grief.
- Happiness is attainable.

- Relationships can be restored.
- Loving care is the basis for good relationships.

Once there was a very unhappy little girl. Her unhappiness was the sort that seeps into every cell and stops your mouth from wanting to smile or your legs from wanting to move. Even the brightest of days seemed miserable or pointless. The little girl didn't like how she felt, but she didn't know how to change it. This made her even more unhappy.

The little girl didn't really understand why she was so sad. All she knew was that her father, with whom she now lived, didn't seem to care for her. He never had time for her and never showed her the love and caring she craved. They never laughed and joked like other families. He didn't have time or interest to teach her all the things that a child needs to learn to prepare herself for adulthood. They never played together.

It had been hard enough when her mother died. Although she had been told it would happen, she never wanted to believe it. When her mother did die, the little girl suddenly felt very alone and unsupported. At first she felt she'd lost a mom, but now it felt like she'd lost her dad as well. She could *understand* that he must miss mom, too, but his grief *felt* like a personal rejection of her.

In the years following her mother's death, her body changed from that of a child's into that of an adolescent's. But she felt she hadn't grown emotionally or spiritually, for she had not learned how to grow from a mother and a father.

One day, in her loneliness and unhappiness, she wandered from home, not knowing where she was going. She just walked. Anywhere but where she was had to feel better. Her footsteps led her down lanes, across fields, and into the woods where, after a while, she came to a clearing. She sat down on a log at the edge of the tree line, pensively ruminating on her melancholy thoughts.

As she sat quietly pondering, a pair of young bear cubs that ambled into the clearing distracted her. They started to play tag. Then they started tumbling. Then they just played at playing. While she watched she felt a sense of childish delight lift her heart, and she asked the bears if she could join them. Soon all three were tumbling amidst grunts of laughter, and the sound of her merriment surprised her, for she could hardly recall the last time she heard it. In fact, she could not remember ever feeling so joyful.

But her joy came to an abrupt halt as a dark, ominous shadow fell across the clearing. Looking up, she saw the towering, fear-inducing figure of a mother bear.

Meanwhile, back home, her father became worried after he did not see his daughter all day. When she didn't come home that night and wasn't there the next day, he became more concerned but, still debilitated by grief, failed to put his concerns into action. Eventually, his worry won out, and he commenced searching for his daughter.

He traced her footsteps into the woods, coming to the clearing where she'd sat on the log. Finding her tracks intermingled with those of an adult bear and two young cubs, he became really worried. What could have happened to her? Had the bears killed her? Could he handle another loss?

He followed the foursome's trail to a cave, but the mother bear, ever watchful for her cubs, detected his approaching scent. Quietly shepherding the cubs and the girl back into the cave, she attacked and chased the girl's father from her territory.

Back in his village he sought the wisdom of the local sage who was known for his knowledge and healing abilities. The sage said to the father, "I can offer you advice, but there is nobody else who can get your daughter back. This is your responsibility as her father. Your daughter is in need of caring. She needs the experience of growing and playing. The mother bear and her cubs have been providing her with what you haven't. That's why she stays. If you want to get her back, you must follow their model. You must give her the love they have shown her."

At first he went to the cave and pleaded with his daughter to return, but, being happy where she was, she chose to stay. The mother bear, as if aware, towered up on her hind legs and growled. The father hurried away.

By the time he got home, he was angry. This was a surprise for him because he had felt grief for so long he thought it was the only emotion he could feel. The intensity of this new feeling helped him realize how deeply he cared for his daughter. What would he do without her?

He gathered his bow and arrow and set off back to the cave, ready to kill the mother bear and reclaim his daughter. As he approached quietly through the trees, he saw his daughter playing happily with the bears. How could he kill the bears? How could he destroy what was bringing her such happiness? Were they not giving her what he had failed to provide?

He lowered his bow and arrow and retreated. He walked home deep in thought, wondering how to keep his daughter happy *and* have her return, willingly, when an annoying bee started to buzz around him. That was the answer! He followed the bee back to its hive, lit a smoky, green-leaf fire directly beneath it, and, when the bees were calmed, extracted some of their honey.

The father carried the honey to the bear's cave, placed it on a rock, and stepped back. He addressed the mother bear saying, "I have brought you an offering of thanks. I have seen the way that you have cared for my daughter, and I have learned what I need to do to show her how much I love her. Please accept this honey as an offer of my gratitude."

The mother bear emerged from the cave first and cautiously tasted the honey. It was good, and, as the gift was acceptable, she called forth her cubs and the daughter. While the bears ate, father and daughter were reunited.

Then the father saw something he had not noticed before. His little girl had grown into a young woman. She stood tall, with confidence, pride, and joy. He saw how love and care were so necessary for her growth and maturation. He could feel bad about what he had not given her, as some of the villagers thought he should do. He could seek her forgiveness. He could try to make amends, or he could decide to enjoy their relationship from here on. Perhaps there was a little of each in his thoughts and feelings, but he knew that what mattered was that they were together again.

"The bears have taught me many things," the young woman explained to her father. "They have shown me how we must care for one another. If we care for each other, we are truly father and daughter. If we care for each other, we are a family. If we care, we can be friends with each other, and with the bears."

The father felt proud of his daughter. He could not have expressed it any better himself.

STORY 68
LEARNING TO GIVE MORE

Therapeutic Characteristics

Problems Addressed

- Fear
- Anger
- Loss
- Self-centeredness

Resources Developed

- Using the power of reason
- Developing the ability to change emotions
- Developing the ability to change thoughts
- Using your personal resources
- Practicing the art of compassion

Outcomes Offered

- Inner peace is attainable.
- Empower yourself.
- It is possible to adjust to loss.
- Learn an other-centered focus.

One night a meditation teacher returned home to find the door of her apartment ajar. Thinking back to her departure earlier that day, she thought to herself, "Surely I closed and locked the door before I left." She was a private person and there were things she liked to keep to herself, hidden from others.

She entered cautiously only to find herself confronted by a burglar. At first she was swept with a wave of fear. Would he attack her? She gasped for breath, her heart pounded, and tremors shook her body.

"Face your fear," she found herself saying. She had read it and heard it said before. Indeed, it was something she often taught her trainees. Now she had the chance to put these words into practice for herself.

Her training also emphasized compassion, and now she taught this to her students. "Put yourself in his place," she reminded herself. It wasn't easy to let go of her self-focused fear and begin to empathize with this intruder of her privacy but, nonetheless, she tried.

"You must be in great need," she said to the thief, "to want to take somebody else's possessions. Come, sit down, and have a cup of coffee. Maybe there are ways that I could help."

As they sat and talked, she learned about the robber and his life. She discovered that he was unemployed, had a young family to support, and was desperate to provide them with food and clothing. The robber, she thought, is becoming my teacher. He was teaching her important things about fear. First, by coming to know and understand the feared object she became less afraid. The robber was a person like her, driven by his own fears and worries. He, too, was scared and vulnerable. It is easy to fear what we don't understand, she thought. Generally, the more we know about someone or something the less we need to be afraid. Second, she discovered that by focusing her attention on someone else, she wasn't as aware of the feelings in her own body. But when thoughts returned to her situation, the fears welled up once more.

In spite of this new awareness, she still had problems letting go of her feelings. Knowing what to do doesn't mean we have the ability to do it. Emotions sometimes dictate our actions. She started to feel angry that the robber was trying to take advantage of her. She had tried to be a good person. She had very few possessions. Why should someone take what little she had? Why should he be allowed to get away with it? How dare he!

With such thoughts, her jaws clamped, her body became tight, and she found her fingers rolling into fists. She wanted to teach the thief a lesson. He should pay for what he had done. She should call the police and see justice done.

Then she began to think that, perhaps, she could learn from these thoughts and feelings. Perhaps the robber had created an experience that could facilitate her growth. She was a teacher, not only of meditation, but also of the philosophy of meditation. She taught her trainees about the need to be detached from material possessions. She taught them about the nature of impermanence. "Nothing lasts forever," she had often said. Sooner or later it will cease to exist, and what did it matter in the big picture if it was a little sooner?

After finishing her coffee, she put together clothes, blankets, and food, then handed them to the burglar. "Here," she said, "please take these home for your family." As he left she sat cross-legged on the floor of her now bare home and began to meditate.

Meanwhile, the burglar had not got far before he began to feel guilty. It was easy to take things from someone you didn't know. Now that he had met the woman, he felt like he was stealing from a friend. "This is not the way I want to live," he thought to himself. He retraced his steps and left the teacher's possessions quietly on her doorstep. On the way home he thought about other ways that he could provide for his family.

Back at her apartment, the meditation teacher gazed out her window. The sun set in a golden dazzle that seemed to illuminate not only the sky, but also her soul. Night fell silently and sleepily toward the horizon. Stars twinkled like reassuring dots of warmth in a sea of darkness. Despite her loss, she felt a sense of inner tranquility and happiness. Absorbed in the view before her, she thought, "I wish I had given that poor man more. I wish I could have given him this."

STORY 69
TAKE HER HAND

Therapeutic Characteristics

Problems Addressed

- Fear
- Depression
- Confrontation of the unknown
- A tendency to be "clinical" in relationships

Resources Developed

- Developing the art of caring
- Showing kindness
- Being warm and human

Outcomes Offered

- Empathy can be healing.
- Care helps ease fear.
- Kindness can diminish depression.
- Wisdom comes from combining knowledge and compassion.

In a hospital ward a patient lay very ill, so ill that she had begun to give up hope. Her condition remained undiagnosed. That in itself was enough reason for fear. Nobody seemed to know what was wrong with her. If they didn't know, how could they treat her? And if they couldn't treat her, would she go on deteriorating, and possibly die? She certainly had shown no signs of recovery. None of the assistance offered to her so far had worked. It was not surprising that she began to despair.

In another part of the hospital, the professor of medicine and his registrars had just finished their rounds and were discussing each patient's case. The professor led the meeting, offering advice from his years of accumulated knowledge and experience.

"How is Ms. Smith?" he asked of the woman who lay undiagnosed.

"She is no better," said the registrar responsible for her care. "I have done everything I can. No matter what I do, we can't find what is wrong. She is not responding to treatment, and her condition has deteriorated. On top of everything she is becoming depressed."

"What have you done?" the professor inquired gently.

"To start with, I took her temperature, which was normal," said the registrar.

"What else?" asked the professor.

"I have taken her blood pressure, which is also in the normal range," said the registrar.

"Have you done anything more?" inquired the professor.

"Yes," replied the registrar. "I have taken a blood sample and developed a full blood picture. The pathologist was unable to find any abnormalities."

"Go on," encouraged the professor. "Have you done any more?"

"I took X rays. The radiologist studied them thoroughly. All of the X rays seemed to be clear. Her skeletal structure seems to be sound."

"I see," the professor said with a look of quiet wisdom reflected in his eyes. "Go on."

"I have taken an MRI and a CT scan. Once again everything came back negative. We are totally puzzled as to what is wrong and even more puzzled as to why she isn't getting better."

The professor rested his elbows on his desk and nestled his head into his hands thoughtfully. He reflected quietly for a few moments, then spoke softly. "You have taken her temperature, her blood pressure, and her blood sample. You have also taken X rays, an MRI and a CT scan. You have not found any abnormalities on all these investigations, but still you find she is deteriorating and even becoming depressed."

Slowly he raised his eyes, looked at the registrar and asked, "But, have you taken her hand?"

STORY 70
THE STORY OF COMPASSION

Therapeutic Characteristics

Problems Addressed

- Interpersonal difficulties
- Panic
- Life's disasters
- Egocentricity

Resources Developed

- Learning to care for others
- Learning to care for yourself
- Developing compassion

Outcomes Offered

- Avoid egocentricity.
- Appreciate compassion.
- Give time and caring.

Once upon a time, long ago, there was an island where all the Human Attributes lived. This was long before they resided in humans, and long before we pigeonholed them as being good or bad. They just existed, each with its own characteristics. Indeed, each was as uniquely individual as humans are. Maybe that is why they eventually got together.

On the island lived Optimism, Pessimism, Knowledge, Prosperity, Vanity, and Compassion. Of course others lived there too. One day it was announced that the island was sinking. Panic erupted when the Attributes heard the news. They ran everywhere, like ants whose nest has been disturbed. In time the Attributes began to settle down and plan some positive action. Living on an island, most of them possessed boats, so they all repaired their vessels and organized their departure.

Compassion was not prepared. She had no boat of her own. She had probably lent it or given it to someone in years gone by. She delayed her departure until the last possible moment so that she could help the others to get ready. Finally, Compassion decided she needed to ask for help.

Prosperity was just casting off from the pier in front of his mansion. His boat was grand, equipped with all the latest technology and navigational aids. Traveling with him would certainly be a comfortable passage.

"Prosperity," called out Compassion, "can I come with you?"

"No way," answered Prosperity. "My boat is full. I have spent days packing it with all my gold and silver. There was barely room for the antique furniture or art collection. There is no space for you here."

Compassion decided to ask Vanity, who was passing by in an intricate and beautiful vessel. "Vanity, will you please help me?"

"Sorry," said Vanity, "I can't help you. Have you seen yourself? You are wet and dirty. Just imagine the mess you'll make on my clean decks."

Compassion saw Pessimism struggling to push his boat into the water. She put her hands on the stern to help push as he pulled. He complained endlessly. The boat was too heavy, the sand too soft, and the water too cold. It was a miserable day to be putting to sea. They hadn't been given enough warning, and the island shouldn't be sinking. Why did everything always happen to him?

He may not have been the most desirable companion, but Compassion's situation was getting desperate. "Pessimism, will you let me go with you?"

"Oh, Compassion, you are too good to sail with me. Your selfless caring makes me feel even more guilty and miserable. Imagine if a wave should swamp us and you drowned. How do you think I would feel? No, I can not take you."

Optimism was one of the last boats to cast off. She hadn't believed all that doom and gloom stuff about the island sinking. Someone would surely fix it before it sunk. Compassion called out to her, but Optimism was too busy looking ahead and thinking of the next destination to hear. Compassion called out again, but for Optimism there was no looking back. She had left the past behind—and sailed on into the future.

Just when Compassion was beginning to despair, she heard a voice, "Come, I will take you." Compassion felt so tired and weary that she curled up in the boat and fell asleep almost immediately. She slept all the way until her skipper announced they had reached dry land and she could disembark. She was so grateful and overjoyed at having been given a safe passage that she thanked him warmly, and leaped ashore. She waved farewell as he sailed on his way. Only then did she realize she had forgotten to ask his name.

Meeting Knowledge on the shore, she asked, "Who was that who helped me?"

"It was Time," answered Knowledge.

"Time?" asked Compassion. "Why would Time help me when no one else did?"

Knowledge smiled and answered, "Because only Time is capable of understanding how great Compassion is."

STORY 71
GIVING WHAT IS NEEDED

Therapeutic Characteristics

Problems Addressed

- Ability to handle a helping relationship
- When caring is not enough
- When knowledge and skills are not enough
- Inability to listen appropriately

Resources Developed

- Developing effective listening skills
- Learning to observe astutely

- Learning from others
- Giving what is needed

Outcomes Offered

- Listen with your heart *and* mind.
- Give of your knowledge, skills, and compassion.
- Give what is needed.

A young woman once approached a wise and famous physician to see if she could become his apprentice. She wanted to learn, especially about the science of medicine. She wanted to help others and ease their suffering. The doctor noted her compassionate motivation as well as her understanding that caring was not enough. She also needed skills.

"No," he said at first, "I will not take you on." He continued to explain, "You are too young. You do not have the experience of life. The time is not quite right."

The young woman, however, was not ready to be rejected. She persisted, pleading with the doctor to give her a trial. Even a temporary period would do. Let him then assess if she was ready.

The doctor conceded and she became his temporary apprentice. For the first few weeks she sat at his side, closely observing everything he did. The weeks turned into months and the months into years. She studied in detail the different sorts of medicines he used, both natural and manufactured. She learned about illnesses and what treatments were applicable for what conditions. Not only did she observe the physician diligently during his consulting hours, but, at night she studied from the extensive collection of books in his library. Gradually she acquired the necessary knowledge.

The physician had no doubt that she *knew* what she needed to know about her subject. He also knew that compassion and healing are about more than knowledge. They are about more than giving from the storehouse of information in our memory banks and from the various professional skills we have learned. Compassion and healing also have to do with giving from the heart.

Confident in her knowledge, the apprentice asked her medical mentor several times if he would allow her to treat a patient. Every such request met with rejection until the doctor commented, "Here is a man that needs treatment."

They had just walked through the waiting room into the doctor's office. As was his habit, he closely observed the waiting patients on his way. When he entered the consulting room with his apprentice he said, "Did you notice the first man in the line?"

"Yes," replied the apprentice.

"Good," said the doctor, "tell me about his condition and your recommended treatment."

The student was stuck. She might be able to describe him and what he was wearing, but she could not offer a diagnosis or formulate a treatment.

"Pity," said the physician kindly. "You might have noticed that he is a patient who requires pomegranates."

The apprentice eagerly seized on the opportunity. "Doctor," she said, "you have observed the patient astutely, you have made the diagnosis, and you even know the prescription. Let me administer it."

To her surprise the doctor agreed. She called the patient into the consulting room. As he sat in the chair, she said, "I know your problem. You need pomegranates." The man leaped from the chair. "Pomegranates!" he shouted and stormed from the room.

As he slammed the door behind him the apprentice asked, "What went wrong? Why didn't he accept the prescription?"

The doctor said calmly, "Wait. The opportunity will arise again. You will have the chance to learn from this experience."

Some months later as they walked into the consulting room, and shut the door, the doctor said to his apprentice, "Did you notice the elderly woman in the waiting room?"

"No," replied the apprentice, hesitant to say she had, and be told how little she had observed.

"Pity," said the doctor. "If you had, you would have observed that she is a patient who needs pomegranates."

He called the patient in, gently directed her to the chair, and sat beside her. "Now tell me," he began, "how can I help you?"

She described her problems to the doctor. He listened carefully. He did so with empathy, nodding in the way of one who genuinely cares. He did not interrupt. He just quietly heard her story.

Only then did he begin to speak. "I have heard what you have told me. I think that your treatment needs to include something that is natural, healthy, and recuperative. Let me see. It needs to be round with little sacks inside. Perhaps lemons are what you need."

Observing a subtle twitch in the corner of her mouth as if responding to the taste of a sour lemon, he continued, "No, lemons are too acidic. That is not what you need. Maybe it is oranges. But oranges may be too sweet. I think perhaps they are the wrong color and texture."

He paused for a moment as if contemplating the matter with great seriousness. "Let me see. Ah hah. I know what is going to be most helpful. If you incorporate pomegranates regularly into your diet, you will soon begin to notice an improvement."

The woman rose with a smile on her face. She shook the physician's hand, thanked him profusely, and left happily.

The apprentice could not wait until she was gone. "What is the difference?" she asked. "When I prescribed pomegranates, the man rejected my prescription and stormed out of the office. But the woman thanked you profusely for the same prescription."

The doctor looked at his apprentice patiently and said, "As well as pomegranates, she needed time and understanding."

EXERCISE

Use your notebook to record your own stories about cultivating compassion. The emphasis here is on tales of empathy; kindness; consideration of others; and genuine, human caring. As these qualities are central to all interpersonal interactions, whether they are professional, social, recreational, familial, or marital, the stories may include several characteristics:

1. The discovery and acquisition of compassion and caring.
2. The cultivation or development of those qualities.
3. Their application for effective, happy relationships.

Note not only the story line, but also the emotions, for these stories are about the heart.

CHAPTER 11

Developing Wisdom

Increasingly, both psychology and psychotherapy emphasize the development of a "worldview" as an important ingredient for a healthy psychological existence. Worldview refers to a philosophy in which people see themselves as part of a larger picture, in contrast to an individual, inward, and reductionist perspective. Maintaining an outward-looking perspective and seeing oneself as part of an interactive whole (whatever that particular philosophy is) allows a person to develop more meaning and sense of purpose in life.

I define wisdom in the context of a therapeutic goal as being comprised of several components. First, wisdom is about acquiring knowledge and information, but knowledge alone does not necessarily make one wise or provide the essentials for a healthy philosophy on life. Second, wisdom includes experience: knowledge that goes deeper than the intellect and incorporates an understanding of both the head and the heart. Finally, wisdom should be practical and applied for our own benefit and the benefit of our fellow beings. The stories in this chapter address how to acquire and develop both knowledge and experience of ourselves and our relationships with the world in a way that enables us to live considered and considerate lifestyles.

STORY 72
THE RIVER OF LIFE

Therapeutic Characteristics

Problems Addressed

- The journey of life
- Obstacles and challenges
- The stages of development
- Desire to reach a goal or destiny

Resources Developed

- Accepting the ebb and flow of life
- Developing a philosophy or worldview
- Appreciating the various stages of development
- Receiving and giving

Outcomes Offered

- Take time out to appreciate.
- Take time out to think and learn.
- Accept the flow of life.
- Develop a helpful worldview.
- Enjoy the beauty of life.
- Observe the lessons of nature.

At the bottom of the Grand Canyon, I stood on the suspension bridge, gazing down into the powerful waters of the Colorado River and remembered something Winnie The Pooh said when he stood in a similar position.

I have long thought that a flowing river speaks to us about the journey of life. At its origins, it often seems small and insignificant compared to its potential growth. Who would believe looking at the mouths of the Mississippi or the Rhine that they began as a trickle tiny enough for a child to leap over? Yet that seemingly insignificant trickle or spring has challenged people to find its origins. Explorers have gone in search of the source of many of the world's mighty rivers—the Nile, the Euphrates, and the Amazon—as though seeking the meaning of life itself.

From its humble origins, the river begins a journey of challenge and excitement. Each drop of water that bubbles forth at its source knows not what lies ahead. But from the moment it emerges, it becomes part of an inevitable, uncontrollable flow that leads it forward. Its life lies before it, and it begins a journey that will take it through various stages of life.

An individual drop of water cannot flow by itself. It needs other drops of water to join it on its journey. It needs to be fed by rains that fall from the sky. It is nourished and expanded by encounters with other streams. Each meeting contributes to its growth and maturity as a river.

Just as it cannot reach its destiny without *receiving* from others, so, on its journey, it *gives*. Its waters give life to fish, birds, animals, and humans. It picks up nutrients from the soil it embraces along its banks. It carries these downstream to enrich the land and feed others along the way.

Despite its kindness and generosity, its flow is not without obstacles or difficulties. No river flows straight to the sea. It encounters unevenness in its journey. It meets obstacles that temporarily hold it back or force it to spread out into tranquil pools. At other times the world closes in around it. It may be compelled to travel a narrow channel that has it rushing and roaring ahead. Its mood alters with its circumstances. There are times for racing, times for dancing, times for bubbling happily, and times for sitting peacefully.

With each obstacle the river needs to find a new solution. If a tree falls across its path, does the river wash the trunk away? Does it seek to find an alternative course around the obstacle? Does it give in and lie still, eventually becoming stagnant? Does it dam up until it has raised to a height where it can flow over the tree and again move on in its own direction?

In its infancy, the river seems joyful as it dances over rocks and pebbles. In its adolescence, it is energetic and purposeful. In its maturity, it broadens, as if wanting to spread and share its experience, wisdom, and tranquility.

Its pace slows as it journeys quietly toward the sea. In meeting, the river and ocean become one, not just with each other but with all the waters of the planet. The warmth of the sun evaporates the water. It gathers in the clouds, is deposited back in the hills, and the journey of another river begins.

As I looked at the Colorado River from the suspension bridge, the waters twisted in green eddies, washing back on themselves in what canoeists call "stopper waves." The river flowed with a rushing urgency, fighting with itself and against itself.

When I gazed straight down and focused on the swirling, clashing energies of the immediate, I felt caught up in its destructive dash. As the water ripped through the canyon, its painful roar tore at my ears. I felt as if I were being drawn into the waters, about to be swept away to my death. I felt both respect and fear for its power.

Yet, it also lay peacefully in little riverbank bays. The river was both tortured and tranquil. If I looked up and followed its path ahead, through the canyon, the view—and experience—was different. Beneath my feet, it roared with energy. Ahead, it flowed smooth and steady. It *was* powerful, but it was also peaceful. The perception varied depending on which part I was focused.

The river held more than one paradox. There was something about this mighty waterway that was and always would be. Long before it ever had a name, either from its original settlers or European explorers, the Colorado was the same river from source to sea. As I looked down on it, there was a sense of permanence, a feeling of eternity, an experience of something that had and would long outlive my own fleeting existence.

But in its permanence was something temporary. The river was constantly changing, forever adapting, always altering. Each molecule of water that washed under my feet was different from the one that had washed by a millisecond before and would wash by a millisecond later. Though the Colorado was one river, it was never the same.

From the suspension bridge at the bottom of the Grand Canyon, the river looked huge. As I shifted my gaze up the mile of vertical ascent to the rim above, I realized how small the river was in comparison—a matter of yards across. Yet it was what had carved this great impression that brings people from around the world to stand in awe. It took time, patience, and energy, but with these, it carved out its destiny. Its journey has left its mark and will continue to do so throughout the ages.

Gazing at the eddying, swirling waters of the river, I was reminded of something Winnie the Pooh had said when he stood on a bridge looking down into the waters of a river just as I was doing. He said, "If you stood on the bottom rail of a bridge, and leaned over, and watched the river slipping slowly away beneath you, you would suddenly know everything there is to be known."

STORY 73
CREATING CHOICES

Therapeutic Characteristics

Problems Addressed

- Confrontation with choices
- Impractical or unrealistic expectations
- Uncertainty
- Inability to accept what life brings
- Discontent with what you have

Resources Developed

- Seeing the options
- Making choices
- Choosing the practical and obtainable

Outcomes Offered

- Choose what works.
- Learn to be pragmatic.
- Hold to views that match reality.
- Be content with what you have.

A wife awoke one Sunday morning to the smell of brewing coffee and baking croissants. A few minutes later her husband emerged through the bedroom door carrying a breakfast tray. Before her husband even had a chance to wish her good morning, she began to speak.

"There is nothing as sweet as honey on your croissants in the morning. Have you ever noticed how many different honeys there are? Each honey, like each wine, has its own unique characteristics. Honey has been valued for generations across many cultures. Collectors risk their lives climbing cliff faces and high trees to gather wild honey. It is known for its curative value. We call places with rich and plentiful soil a land of milk and honey. Honey is definitely my favorite breakfast spread!"

Her surprised husband asked, "What's all this? Why are you waxing so lyrical about honey?"

The wife ignored him and continued, "On the other hand, honey is unhealthy. Have you ever thought of all those dirty little insects gathering it, carrying it on their bodies, manufacturing it in unhygienic conditions, and storing it out in the woods somewhere? Bees have never heard of Louis Pasteur.

"Anyway, too much honey is bad for your blood sugar. Regardless of its impurities, honey itself can cause health problems. And how can you tell if you've had too much? How do you know your own level of tolerance? No, on second thought I loathe honey."

The husband was taken aback by this monologue. He thought it would have been a romantic surprise to bring his wife breakfast in bed. He was surprised by his wife's emphatic, yet conflicting, comments. "Hang on a minute," he said. "How can you simultaneously hold two such strong contradictory opinions about the same object at the same time?"

"I don't," said the wife. "I have a choice about which opinion I want to hold—and that depends upon whether we have any honey in the pantry."

STORY 74
EXPECTATIONS OF OTHERS

Therapeutic Characteristics

Problems Addressed

- Desire for perfection
- Discontent
- High expectation of others
- A reliance on others to fulfill our needs
- A tendency to place demands on others to give us happiness

Resources Developed

- Accepting reality
- Using reason
- Taking responsibility for your own satisfaction
- Valuing what others have to offer

Outcomes Offered

- No one is perfect.
- Be responsible for your own happiness.
- Enjoy what others have to give.
- Don't demand what others cannot give.

When people find out that I am a psychologist, they often ask, "Don't you get depressed listening to other peoples' problems all day long?" If that is what I did, I probably would become depressed, but I find a lot of satisfaction from seeing people achieve their goals and feeling that I might have contributed a little to their enjoyment and happiness.

Much of this satisfaction comes from the many interesting and enjoyable people I have met. Many clients hope to learn something from me, but, like any human relationship, the process is a two-way street. My clients have exposed me to many experiences that I may not have otherwise understood. They have taught me about the strength of human resources in the face of adversity, and they have shared with me the richness of their wisdom. Libby was one such tutor.

In telling me about the men in her life, she spoke first of a gay friend. He was a businessman who traveled the world attending meetings in New York, Paris, London, and other major cities. Together they would visit museums, explore the local sights, or take in a symphony concert. She cherished his cultured nature, his gentleness, and his sophistication, in part, because it complemented and nurtured those aspects of herself.

She described another man as her best friend. Together they would go to the movies or live theatre, then visit a coffee shop where they would sit talking until all hours of the night. They would discuss the show that they had just seen, politics, philosophy, and other intimacies of their lives, for there was nothing they could not discuss. She felt relaxed and open with him in a way she could not be with anyone else.

She mentioned a third guy with whom she'd had an exciting and passionate sexual relationship. So charged was their emotional arousal that they quickly moved in together, but living together proved to be a disaster. Ultimately, they went their separate ways, but he would occasionally phone her, and they would re-ignite their passion. She enjoyed these encounters, for she had never known such passion, and it fulfilled a need that she acknowledged was a part of her total being.

Then she told me about a fourth man. He was someone she said she loved. He was divorced and not ready for a fulltime commitment, at least, not just yet. Besides, his only daughter lived with him during the week, and she topped his list of priorities. Together Libby and her beloved spent most weekends quietly at his home. She felt special to love and be loved, for this gave her a sense of wholeness and completeness.

Libby must have seen my jaw dropping lower and lower with astonishment as she talked about each consecutive relationship in her life. Whether I agree with her morality, the choices she was making were hers. She paused, caught my eye, held my gaze, and spoke words that I remember to this day. She said, "I cannot expect any one person to satisfy all the needs I have as an individual."

STORY 75
DEVELOPING CHOICES FOR SURVIVAL

Therapeutic Characteristics

Problems Addressed

- Issues of survival
- When life is tough
- A life-dilemma
- Lack of support
- Adjustment to illness and injury

Resources Developed

- Developing appropriate adaptations to our circumstances
- Finding skills for survival
- Discovering your own abilities

- ■ Making choices
- ■ Learning what to sacrifice and what to save

Outcomes Offered

- ■ Observe the lessons of nature.
- ■ Survival is a normal and natural process.
- ■ Find the skills that work best for you.
- ■ Discover your own strengths.
- ■ Adapt to circumstances.

If ever you visit Arches National Park, Utah, look up at the cliffs on your left-hand side on your way to the spectacularly elongated Landscape Arch. High up the stark, rocky face, on the narrowest of ledges, grows a Utah juniper. It is hard to imagine where it finds sufficient soil or water to nourish itself. Limbs stretch out from the cliff, reaching toward the light like open fingers in an act of supplication. Somehow the tree tenaciously hangs on to that thin ledge of security.

Such trees fascinate me. The way they grow and survive is reflected in their shape and appearance, in much the same way as a person's face may show something of his or her life and character. Trunks and branches twist and turn to adjust to the various forces that effect their life span. Like us, their present is determined by their past. Like us, they live on in anticipation of the future.

An old eucalyptus tree grows near where I live. As I walk by, I often pause to circle its bulbous base, or meditate on its ancient sagacity. I touch it affectionately, longing to hear its untold tale of life. Fires have blackened its trunk. Disease has caused branches to die back. Children have hammered bolts into it as steps up to the remnants of a tree-house that once nestled in its arms. It has embraced each illness or injury and has continued to grow around a dead branch or over a rusty bolt, accepting them as unchangeable and incorporating them into its continuing development. The tree is an inspiring example to me of life and survival.

The Utah juniper tells a similar tale. All trees in the southwest United States must adapt to the harsh extremes of the local climate: scorching summers and snowy winters. In one day a visitor can be burning in the sun and shivering in the shade. There are times when life feels tough for all living things.

Yet, each finds its own way to adapt to what the circumstances might deliver. The deciduous trees lose their leaves to protect themselves from the accumulated weight of snow. They let go of what is useless or detrimental for their survival in those conditions. When summer returns they regrow their leaves for shade and shelter. They create what is necessary for them to survive the cycle of altering circumstances.

Other plants adjust rather than alter. In summer, they turn the edges of their vertical leaves toward the sun, thus reducing exposure to heat and loss of precious fluids through evaporation. They move away from what is harmful and toward what is most beneficial for them. In winter, they turn to the light, seeking to aid their photosynthesis and processes of self-nourishment. Adapting, adjusting, and altering, they continually find the best ways to ensure their survival.

The Utah juniper is unique. It faces a complex dilemma of survival. It needs its leaves to feed and nourish it, for without them it can die. On the other hand, it loses essential moisture from its leaves through evaporation. With them it can die. It resolves its conflict in a selective and intelligent manner, seeming to make choices. By sacrificing the leaves on some branches, those branches die. But sacrifice also means survival. Letting go of what it does not need means that it gets to keep what it does. It lets some limbs die so that the whole tree survives.

Somehow, against the odds, it has learned to adapt to its circumstances. It has adjusted to the harshness life seems to have dealt it. It has used what little it has available and has made choices about what it needs to sacrifice and what it needs to save. So look out for the Utah juniper. Or maybe there is another tree, like the old eucalypt near my home, that has a story to tell for you.

STORY 76
KNOWING VERSUS DOING

Therapeutic Characteristics

Problems Addressed

- A tendency to feel stuck and without direction
- Being fixated on asking "Why?"
- Bogged down in the "analysis paralysis"
- A search for explanations rather than directions
- Theory versus action

Resources Developed

- Learning to ask helpful questions
- Seeking action
- Avoiding explanations
- Doing what is practical

Outcomes Offered

- If you don't get the answer you want, ask a different question.
- Some questions are more helpful than others.
- Be pragmatic.
- Seek solutions rather than understanding.
- Smile at your own foibles.

People seeking therapy often ask, "Why am I depressed?", "Why is this happening to me?", or just "Why me?" When they do, I have to confess that often I don't know the answers, because at times there are some questions to which we don't have answers.

One of my favorite cartoon characters, Hagar the Horrible, offers the best answer to the question "Why me?" that I know. Hagar is shipwrecked alone on a desolate, rocky island. Waves crash relentlessly on the shore. The sky is full of foreboding, black clouds, and bolts of lightning stab threateningly from above. Hagar looks up to the heavens and asks, "Why me?"

WISDOM

The next frame is exactly the same. Hagar stands alone on the same rocky island. His boat remains wrecked on the same shore. Waves pound on the same rocks. Bolts of lightning flash from the same black clouds. The only difference is that a little balloon descends below the clouds, and in it is written, "Why not?"

While knowing may help us understand things, knowledge alone doesn't necessarily create change. To do that we need to ask another question than "Why?" Fortunately, just as there are some questions for which we don't have answers, there are also questions for which we do.

Some years ago I took flying lessons. I had just started flying solo when I moved to another part of the country. Much to my disappointment, the cost of flying lessons in my new town was almost double what I had been paying. With a young family and a high mortgage, my flying career, at least at a practical level, ground to a quick halt. I completed the theory exams but just because I knew why an aircraft stays in the air did not mean that I was capable of flying one.

If I want to get back flying, there is no point in my asking *why* I'm not doing it, as that won't create the action I need. If I want to make it happen, I need to ask questions to which I can find clear and practical answers—questions like, *how* I can go about it? *What* do I need to do to resume my lessons? *Where* can I get the lessons? *When* will I begin? Such questions will give me direction and put me on the path to achieving my desired outcome.

At this point, you would be wise *not* to fly with me, for in that choice, you would show your appreciation of the fact that making something happen has less to do with the question "Why," and more to do with the question "How." If we want to change a pattern of behavior, we have to learn *how* to do it. Knowledge may be useful, but action makes the difference.

STORY 77
TAKING A DIFFERENT VIEW

Therapeutic Characteristics

Problems Addressed

- Relationship conflicts
- Sibling rivalry
- Seemingly insoluble problems
- Selfishness and greed
- Lack of compromise and negotiation
- Fixed-mindedness

Resources Developed

- Learning to broaden your perspectives
- Listening to others
- Learning from challenges
- Seeking other possibilities
- Valuing relationships

Outcomes Offered

- Learn from wisdom.
- Problems have solutions if we broaden our thinking.
- Work cooperatively in relationships.
- Value relationships.

A traveler was riding along on his camel when he encountered three brothers deep in argument. He stopped, dismounted, and inquired why they were fighting.

The eldest brother explained that, some months earlier, their father had died and bequeathed all his camels to his three sons. His will was clear and explicit. The eldest son was to receive one half of the camels. The second was to receive one third. The third was to inherit one ninth. They had no dispute about that. The problem, and reason for their conflict, arose from the fact that the father had left them seventeen camels.

Almost anyone could appreciate the brothers' dilemma. Seventeen is not divisible by those proportions. "We have tried every mathematical approach we can think of," they explained to the traveler. "We have even considered killing and dismembering one or more of the camels to ensure that each received his bequeathed proportion. However, our father's will was clear on that, too: The camels were to be passed on as livestock and not killed." Each brother agreed that there was no value in receiving the odd limb or two of a dead beast.

In their failure to find a solution, they became frustrated and fell into argument. Half of seventeen was eight and a half. They couldn't kill a beast to divide it, so the eldest suggested he take nine. The younger two objected. His greed would deprive them of their rightful inheritance. He should take eight, according to them, but he was not willing to receive less than his father had willed him. The argument raged, tempers became frayed, and the brothers fought bitterly. Each wanted what he rightfully considered his. None was willing to compromise.

"I see your dilemma," said the stranger. "Your father has given you a difficult challenge. I also think I see a solution." He led his own camel across to the corral that contained the seventeen left by the young men's father. He pushed the slip-rail aside, let his own enter, then closed off the corral again. Eighteen camels stood in the enclosure.

"Now," he said to the elder, "you take your portion of one half." The brother counted out the nine camels that he delightedly claimed for himself. He thanked the stranger for getting him his rightful share.

Turning to the second brother, the traveler said, "Now you take your portion of one third." This brother happily took his six camels and led them aside. To the third brother the stranger said, "Now it is your turn. Take your one ninth." With relief, the last brother took his two camels and tethered them to the railing. This, of course, left behind the saddled beast on which the stranger had arrived.

"Your father has bequeathed you more than his camels," said the traveler. "He has also left you something of his wisdom. In setting you this challenge what else do you think that he has given you?"

"I think," said the first brother, "that he was trying to teach us that every problem has a solution. No matter how impossible something might seem, we may solve it by seeking a different perspective."

The second brother added, "I think it is more than that. As brothers we are always fighting. Father was always our arbitrator. He wanted us to realize that to survive as a family without him we needed a constructive and cooperative relationship. He set us a challenge that meant we needed to work together to find the solution. When greed and selfishness separated us, no one was happy."

"I believe," said the third, "he was possibly teaching us even more. He was saying that no matter how much each of us thinks we are right, we may not have the answer. Sometimes we need to look outside of ourselves. Sometimes, somebody else can offer us a different perspective and thus enable us to find a solution."

The stranger smiled as he mounted his camel and prepared to move on. "Perhaps one of you is right," he said. "Perhaps all three are correct. Then again, maybe he was teaching you something even more."

STORY 78
USING WISDOM WISELY

Therapeutic Characteristics

Problems Addressed

- Perceived disability
- Conflict
- Interpersonal difficulties
- Lack of negotiation skills
- Overemphasizing certain issues

Resources Developed

- Seeking prevention rather than cure
- Using what you have
- Turning perceived disabilities to advantages
- Deemphasizing conflict
- Learning to negotiate effectively

Outcomes Offered

- Use what you have.
- Minimize conflict and issues.
- Emphasize solution and outcome.
- Negotiate resolutions.

Vietnamese history celebrates a famous statesman named Ly who was known for his honesty. He could negotiate solutions to the trickiest of problems.

He was also well-known for his short stature. Ly was very short, even by Vietnamese standards. The top of his head rose no higher than the average man's waist. Many might have perceived this as a disability. To be so different from others might have caused another person to have feelings of self-doubt, inferiority, or lack of confidence, but not Ly.

At the time of this story, relations between Vietnam and its border country, China, were bristly.

Politics, more than people, marked this hostility. Although the two were not in all-out conflict, there was the imminent potential for hostilities to escalate. The Vietnamese emperor, seeking to defuse the tense situation and thinking prevention was better than cure, decided to send statesman Ly to China as his ambassador.

When Ly arrived in China, he was granted an audience with the emperor. The ruler was seated in a high, intricately carved throne on a raised platform. Ly prostrated himself respectfully before the emperor, then rose to his feet. The emperor looked down at tiny Ly and asked, "Are all the people in Vietnam so small?"

Statesman Ly replied humbly, "Your majesty, in Vietnam there are both short and tall people. Our emperor, in his wisdom, uses ambassadors who represent the importance of the problem. As the matter that I wish to discuss with you is such a small issue, they have sent me to negotiate. When a big problem arises between our two countries, they will send a larger man for such discussions."

STORY 79
IF I ONLY HAD THE TIME

Therapeutic Characteristics

Problems Addressed

- A need to take without giving
- Lack of regard for others
- A rushed or stressed life
- Lack of time
- Lack of self-nurturing

Resources Developed

- Learning to question what we do and how we live
- Learning to be aware of stressors and stresses
- Discovering the value of giving *and* receiving
- Discovering what we have
- Using time wisely
- Developing self-caring

Outcomes Offered

- Give and take are both necessary in life.
- Stop and reassess life.
- Take time to self-nurture.
- Take time to relax.
- Knowledge *plus* action equals wisdom.

One afternoon a traveler journeyed through a forest, looking for somewhere to rest, when he came to an old and beautiful tree. It spread its branches out like nurturing arms. In its age, it held

WISDOM

knowledge and wisdom. Its umbrella-like branches made a fitting place to pause and rest for a while. He nestled into the exposed roots that supported him like a comfortable armchair. Looking up through branches and leaves silhouetted against a clear sky, he felt a sense of timelessness in the tree and fell asleep.

The afternoon drifted into night, and he continued to slumber until he was suddenly awakened by a strange commotion. What could possibly be happening? Silently, he peered around the large trunk of the tree. Hundreds of eyes—animal eyes—lit the darkness. Without a sound, he lifted himself into the branches of the tree to gain a better view of this strange gathering. Every animal of the forest was represented. This was the Great Council of Animals.

From what he heard, it appeared the Council met regularly under this very tree to discuss those things important to all animals on the planet. Complaints about humans and the way they treated animals were high on the agenda. Animal after animal told tales of how humans were always taking from them and rarely giving in return.

Said the hen, "They take my eggs. I keep laying them hoping to have a family, but before I can sit on them long enough, the humans come along and snatch them away."

"I know," said the cow empathetically. "I suppose I at least get to have a calf, but then they take away my new born babe. They do that so they can take even more. They also want the milk I have produced to feed my young."

"They take my wool," said the sheep. "I spend a whole year growing it to keep me warm through the cold winter months. Just when it gets to the length I need, they come and shear it off. They leave me shivering so they can be warm."

"You're lucky," replied a forlorn elephant. "They hunt me. They kill me so they can use my tusks to make into piano keys and ornaments."

Typically the snail waited until last. There was no hurry; he knew he would be heard. Life did not need to be rushed. Even before he spoke, the traveler, still quietly observing the scene, was impressed by the snail's attitude. He saw so many of his fellow humans in a desperate rush, as though life itself depended on the next piece of paper to pass over their desk, or running a red light to save 10 seconds off their trip.

Life, he thought, easily can become so hectic that we are busy *doing* rather than just *being*. We start to prioritize the things we feel we *need* to do at the expense of what we *want* to do. We squeeze more and more things into our day, allowing less and less time for self-nurturing and self-caring.

The comments by the animals had touched him. He knew the truth in what they said. He also knew that wisdom was more than knowledge. Intellectual information was not necessarily sufficient to change what was happening. Just knowing the priority we give to work above self or family does not in itself change what we are doing. Knowing the stress we feel in rush hour traffic does not make us more relaxed, even if it highlights the need for us to do so. Wisdom is about knowing *and* doing, about taking knowledge and applying it, about being able to use what we have learned in a way that is helpful and beneficial.

The traveler had plenty of opportunity to think about these things while the snail was slowly mustering its words. When it spoke, it did so quietly and deliberately. "I have something that all humans want. I have something they would take if they could. Fortunately they can't. I have the ability to enjoy the pleasure of time. The irony is that, little do they know, they have it too."

STORY 80
CALL OFF THE SEARCH

Therapeutic Characteristics

Problems Addressed

- Depression and despair
- Stressful life style
- A quest for answers in the wrong places
- A lack of personal responsibility
- A desire for what can't be possessed

Resources Developed

- Starting to search for your own answers
- Learning to look in helpful places
- Exploring your inner resources
- Discovering how to give up what doesn't work
- Looking for simple solutions
- Finding what does work

Outcomes Offered

- Search appropriately for your answers.
- Look to the teaching rather than the teacher.
- Look for the answers within.
- Seek the simple solutions.
- Enjoy the pleasures of life.

When I met Lyndal she was on a journey of self-discovery and self-exploration. Until then she had had little time to explore the deeper questions of life or gain an understanding of herself. She had been too busy. Now she had time, and the desire, to discover herself.

Lyndal sought out several gurus, thinking that from the wise she may discover wisdom. Over time, these gurus were elevated to, and fell from, her pedestal of worship, for she was looking more to the teacher than the teaching. From the enlightened she had hoped to be given enlightenment, like a physician dispenses a pill.

On one occasion, a world-renowned guru came to visit her town. The guru was said to have evolved from a long teaching lineage, and she was revered by many. From this guru, Lyndal hoped to gain what others had failed to give. She sought a personal audience with the guru, and, much to Lyndal's surprise and delight, she granted her request.

"I have long been journeying on a path toward enlightenment," she explained to the guru. "I am a seeker of wisdom and self-awareness. I want to be of service to my fellow humans—in fact to the whole world, its animals, and its ecology. What advice can you give me to continue on this journey? What can you tell me that will help me reach these goals?"

The guru saw her sincerity, and also saw that Lyndal was expecting to be given an answer rather than find it for herself. Knowing that it is from our own experience that we learn the most, the guru recommended a path.

"To gain true enlightenment," she told Lyndal, "you must go into a life of retreat. You will need to give up all of your possessions, let go of your gurus, and relinquish all that you have been hanging onto from the past. You will need to devote yourself to prayer and contemplation. Only by doing this will you become enlightened. This is the path to the wisdom and self-awareness that you seek."

Lyndal did exactly as she was instructed. She severed herself from all worldly bonds. She let go of all she'd been hanging onto and went into retreat. At first it wasn't easy. She longed for many of the things that she had lost, but the more that she became used to her retreat, the more she appreciated her new life style. The months slipped by, and they turned into years. Year after year, she followed the guru's instructions. She was now comfortable with her new lifestyle, but she felt no wiser or no more enlightened.

One day she heard that the world-famous guru was returning to her town. Still not fully appreciating the difference between heeding the message rather then the messenger, Lyndal decided to leave her retreat and again seek the guru's advice.

"For years now," she explained to the guru, "I have followed your advice. I have given up all I possessed. I have lived a life free of the past. I have prayed and meditated devotedly, but still I feel no closer to attaining enlightenment. Tell me what more I need to do."

"I am sorry," said the guru. "I obviously gave you the wrong advice. You have devoted yourself diligently to the task. There is no question of that. The simple fact is that it hasn't worked. I have nothing more to offer, except to say there is no point in continuing to do what isn't working. I am afraid that now you will never be enlightened."

Lyndal was shattered. She fell sobbing at the guru's feet. "Years of my life have gone for nothing. I have lost everything I had. I have wasted my life." She begged for more guidance.

"I have no more to offer," repeated the guru. "There is nothing more that I can do."

Lyndal left. She had never felt so dejected and despairing. She had lost contact with all her friends and family. She had nothing—not even hope.

Depressed, she wandered back to her retreat. There was nothing else for her to do. She sat cross-legged on the floor and began to meditate. She knew how to do little else. As she did, a bird landed on a branch outside. It hopped along the limb, light and carefree. It darted off to pluck an occasional insect from the air. It sang its joy to the world. Why did this little bird seem so happy with its lot?

As she meditated, things became clearer. Wisdom, she thought, is not something a person possesses like a sack of gold or an overflowing bank account. Enlightenment does not come like a degree at the end of a school course. Wisdom is surely more about the combination of experience *and* knowledge. And, if it is about experience, wisdom is not something that someone else can have or do for you. To learn from your experiences, to test it against your knowledge, and to blend in a little of your heart's compassion: That is wisdom.

Enlightenment, she mused, has more to do with being free, like the little bird that continued to hop and sing within her vision. The bird was there now and could be gone in a moment. She found joy in appreciation of the moment, not worrying if it would go, or wishing to hang onto it when it did.

What she sought meant stepping away from the bounds of prejudice and superstition. It meant being free of rituals and the instructions of gurus. What she sought meant not seeking.

She arose and stepped out of her retreat. As she did she began to notice what had gone unnoticed. The earth smelled rich with life. The sweetness of flowers scented the air. She could hardly believe the clear, blue crispness of the sky. The sun gently warmed both body and soul.

Maybe, she thought, her drive to possess wisdom and enlightenment had been the very thing that prevented her from doing so. Whether others could see the difference as she returned to the world didn't really matter. What mattered was how she felt inside. What mattered was the knowledge that life could and would be different.

STORY 81
FINDING THE SOURCE OF WISDOM

Therapeutic Characteristics

Problems Addressed

- Self-importance
- Self-centeredness
- Assumption that we know the answers
- Narrow-mindedness

Resources Developed

- Developing a willingness to listen to others
- Being open to learning
- Seeking to find the simple solutions
- Taking a practical perspective
- Learning to have fun

Outcomes Offered

- Don't expect to know everything.
- Wisdom can come from many, and perhaps unexpected, sources.
- Relationships involve working together.
- Life is impermanent.
- Get out of your head and into fun.
- Appreciate life's simple enjoyments.

Once a great and famous teacher was walking home from a series of lectures. He found walking relaxing as it helped him to unwind after the concentration and energy of a day's teaching.

Of the several different routes available this particular day, he chose the beach. The scenery didn't hold his attention because he was too absorbed in his own haughty thoughts. He reflected on the accolades he received from his students. He relived the glory of signing copies of his latest book. His review of the day's lecture left him feeling proud. He patted himself on the back for what he had done well. Yes, he had certainly done well. It felt good to be good and know it.

Then something caught his eye. A young boy was building a sandcastle. This in itself was not unusual, but it was the largest and most elaborate castle the teacher had ever seen on a beach. The child respectfully scooped the sand up in his hands, then patted it firmly yet gently into place. He had carefully created towers and turrets, and he had raised flags from the parapets. His creation was an act of love.

The teacher sat on a promenade-side bench and watched the child. When the boy completed his impressive work of art, he rested back in the sand and seemed to admire it for a while. The teacher knew the emotion. It was exactly the same feeling he had sensed a moment or two before while walking along the beach reflecting on his own achievements of the day.

Suddenly, the child moved forward. He smashed down the castle, spread it over the sand, and watched as wave after wave washed away any evidence of its existence. The beach returned to how it had been before. The grains of sand washed back to the level of those around them. It was as though the castle had never existed.

The teacher wanted to cry out to the child to stop, but propriety restrained him. Nonetheless, the distress he felt was undeniable. What a waste! Why should such an achievement be obliterated? Why would a creator destroy his own work?

He wanted to ask the boy why he had done this, but hesitated. "Should I greet this little child?" the teacher asked himself. "I am a great teacher. He is just a young boy. Should I be seen talking to him?" However, his curiosity eventually won out. He walked across the sand and spoke to the child. "Tell me," he said, standing above the boy and looking down with the authority he knew was rightly his, "why are you playing in the sand?"

"Is this not what children do?" asked the boy. "Adults tell me that play is a way of learning, as though it should have some meaning other than just being fun. I am doing what a child does. I am playing."

"I am curious," asked the teacher, "why you spent so much time and effort building such a huge and elaborate castle only to break it down. You created your castle to the point of perfection then destroyed it, and watched the waves wash the beach back to what it had been before. You have left no evidence that your work ever existed."

"My parents have asked me the same question," confided the boy. "My mother sees something very symbolic in it, but then that is my mother. She tells me that each grain of sand is like each aspect of humanity. If we build them together, and pat them gently into shape, they form a relationship in which the whole becomes greater than the parts. She says there is no limit to our creativity when we work together. When we forget about our relationships and try to exist as a single, solitary grain of sand, our creativity is destroyed in much the same way that I destroyed the castle, or that the ocean breaks it up into millions of pieces and scatters it along the beach.

"My father says it is a way of learning about life. He says that nothing lasts forever. Sandcastles are an example. They are created and destroyed. They exist and vanish. They, like everything in life, are impermanent. Sandcastles represent our journey through life. Both are brief and temporary. When we appreciate this we can begin to enjoy the time that we have available. He says that building sandcastles is a way that children intuitively come to learn and understand these important lessons of life.

"For me?" asked the boy. "For me, I am just playing. Maybe my play has meaning, and maybe not. I just want to enjoy what I am doing. I want to experience the warm sun on my body, the sound of the lapping waves in the background, and the feel of the wet sand in my hands. I am just having fun."

The teacher realized how much he could learn from this small boy. He untied his shoelaces and cast aside his footwear. He peeled off his socks and rolled up his trousers. He unknotted his tie and sat down beside the boy. "May I stay?" he asked. "I would like to play too."

EXERCISE

In recording your own stories of wisdom or worldview in your notebook, make sure they include:

1. A sound and factual basis of knowledge.
2. Experience, for wisdom is about more than just knowing. It is a depth of understanding that comes from doing and having a first-hand awareness.
3. The combination of knowledge and experience, in a way that is practical, helpful, and replicable.
4. An element of compassion and caring, for wisdom has a completeness that is inclusive of head and heart, mind and emotion.

WISDOM

CHAPTER 12

📖 Caring for Yourself

While it is important that we care for others, we also need to nurture and care for ourselves. In therapy it is not uncommon to see clients experiencing problems in life because they are constantly caring for others, feeling guilty if they don't, and neglecting to nurture themselves.

Self-caring serves a preventative function in that the more we nurture and look after ourselves, the less likely we are to suffer from low levels of self-esteem or self-confidence. A balanced attitude toward self-nurturing can stave off depression, anxiety, and unhappy interpersonal relationships. Learning to care for yourself also has a curative function in that it can help shift attitudes and actions of self-denigration, self-rebuke, and self-directed hostility into attitudes and actions of self-nurturing. As such, it is an important goal of outcome-oriented therapy.

The stories in this chapter consider different aspects of self-nurturing, whether they are in the give and take of relationships, the need to fortify ourselves, adjusting to the flow of life, changing inappropriate beliefs, or adapting to our circumstances.

STORY 82
WHAT YOU GIVE IS WHAT YOU GET

Therapeutic Characteristics

Problems Addressed

- A tendency to jump to conclusions
- Lack of consideration for others

- A need to make assumptions
- Faulty communication

Resources Developed

- Remembering to think before you act
- Developing tolerance and consideration
- Learning to check the facts

Outcomes Offered

- What we give is what we get.
- Explore all options.
- Be wary of acting on assumptions.
- Be considerate to others.

I have a friend who once worked in Papua New Guinea for several years. He tells a story that takes some guts to admit, reflects his willingness to learn from his own actions, and highlights the benefits of being able to laugh at our own actions.

He and three colleagues shared a house with an adolescent Papuan housekeeper, whose task it was to do all the cooking and cleaning. Generally they were happy with his work, save for one concern. They had noticed the content of their brandy bottle was gradually dwindling and suspected the housekeeper was secretly nipping it. Liquor was expensive, and they didn't want to be responsible for introducing him to the problems of alcohol.

Seeking to be sure of their facts, however, they conducted an experiment. By marking how much brandy was left in the bottle, they would be able to see if the level dropped further. Sure enough, the contents continued to dwindle.

Jumping to conclusions or making assumptions is a major factor in faulty communication. Sometimes we may think the facts add up to a certain conclusion, but that doesn't necessarily mean the conclusion is right—as my friends were about to discover.

They came home from a party at the golf club late one night feeling a little on the merry side. Thinking to have a nightcap before they retired, they noticed the level of the brandy had dropped even further. In their somewhat inebriated state, they decided to teach the housekeeper a lesson. They would replenish the contents of the bottle by urinating in it, then put it back on the shelf and wait to see what happened next.

Several days passed and the contents of the brandy bottle continued to drop. Feeling guilty about their trick, they decided to confront the housekeeper. When they asked him if he had been drinking their brandy, he replied, "Not me, boss. I have been using it in your cooking."

CARING FOR YOU

STORY 83
GIVING YOUR BEST

Therapeutic Characteristics

Problems Addressed

- Lack of interest
- Failure to give appropriately
- Lack of energy
- Relinquishment of useful standards

Resources Developed

- Giving your best
- Practicing care of others
- Practicing care of yourself

Outcomes Offered

- What you give is what you get.
- Do the things you do well.
- Caring for others can be a way of self-caring.

A carpenter had spent his whole life building house after house. He had been a loyal and faithful employee, staying with one boss for his entire career, but now he was old and tired. Not only did he feel he could no longer keep going, but he looked forward to living a more leisurely life. He wanted to spend the remainder of his years in closer contact with his wife, children, and grandchildren.

His employer was sorry to hear the man announce his retirement. Despite his age the carpenter was still a good workman, indeed one of his best. He was very thorough and professional. The employer knew he could rely on him. When the man told his boss he was leaving, the boss asked for a last favor.

"Will you build just one more home?" At first the carpenter said no. He explained that he had lost interest and was ready to retire. "This home," explained the boss, "is for a friend. I would especially like you to build it as a personal favor."

The carpenter reluctantly consented and commenced work on his last home, but his heart wasn't in it. He no longer followed his practice of searching diligently for the best materials. Consequently, the timber wasn't always the straightest or the grain didn't run as true as it should. Not only were the materials inferior, but his workmanship lacked its former high standard of perfection.

When the job was finally completed, he stood back to look at his workmanship. He wasn't happy with it, but, thank goodness, it was over. He wished he'd retired when he'd chosen and not consented to the boss's request. This was not an illustrious finale to his career.

When the boss came to make his final inspection, he reached into his pocket and pulled out the key to the front door. He handed it to the elderly carpenter. "This," he said, "is my gift to you. It is a thank you for all your years of loyal work. It is now your home."

STORY 84
TOPPING UP YOUR RESERVES

Therapeutic Characteristics

Problems Addressed

- A tendency to feel emotionally drained
- A need to give without getting
- Neglect of our well-being

Resources Developed

- Deciding to model on good examples
- Learning step-by-step
- Choosing how to manage emotional reserves
- Developing self-caring strategies

Outcomes Offered

- Top up your emotional reserves.
- Find practical ways to care for yourself.
- Enjoy positive past experiences.
- Learn from practical mentors.

There is a theory of psychology that you won't find in any textbook. I call it the Rainwater Tank Theory.

Its origins, like many things, go back to my childhood. When I was at primary school, my parents purchased a beach house in a little seaside town where we spent our summer vacations.

When we arrived for the start of our holidays, the very first thing my dad always did was check the rainwater tank that held our water supply. Using his knuckle he tapped the corrugated rungs to determine the level of water the tank held. He put a chalk mark on it to monitor our consumption.

As a child, this fascinated me. What could my father hear? What did he learn from this ritual? What was the tank telling him?

As soon as the opportunity arose, I would sneak out to the rainwater tank and, with effort, pull myself up onto its wooden stand. Arching the knuckle of my index finger, just as my father had done, I started at the bottom of the tank, slowly tapping my way up each rung. I listened, rung after rung, to the dead sound of each tap muffled by the weight of water. Higher up the tank, I found it began to ring, vibrating with emptiness. I worked my way back down the rungs, listening to the subtle changes, then up again to determine the exact level of the unseen water in the tank.

I did it on the side opposite to Dad, so as not to be influenced by his chalk mark. Having found what I thought to be the level, I would walk around the tank stand, tracing my finger along the rung I had chosen, to check my assessment against his. At first I didn't do it as well as he did. It took a bit of practice over the years, but more and more my finger began to collide with his chalk mark.

This exercise was important because, unless we carefully monitored our water use, the tank could run dry. To ensure this didn't happen, we engaged in two processes. The first was preventative.

We had to learn to conserve and manage our reserves—using without overusing and meeting our needs without stressing our resources. Second, as there may be factors outside of our control, like a particularly hot, dry season, we had to be prepared to find ways to top up our reserves.

Through this experience I was learning about the importance of assessing and monitoring our emotional reserves. Now, I have this theory that we as people are a bit like emotional rainwater tanks. Although our emotions are not as finite as water in a tank, like the tank, we can turn our emotional faucet on and off. We can give to others, to family, to friends, to work, but, like the tank, if we keep giving and giving without topping up our reserves, there comes a point where we may run dry. Maybe there are ways to prevent it from occurring, or ways to top up the reserves if it does happen.

My father probably would have scoffed at the thought that his action contributed to my understanding of psychology. He just did what he did because it was practical. He did it because, for our survival, it needed to be done.

STORY 85
LEARNING TO CARE FOR YOURSELF

Therapeutic Characteristics

Problems Addressed

- Feelings of being stuck
- Feelings of powerlessness
- A concern for others to the detriment of self
- Lack of self-direction

Resources Developed

- Acknowledging the need for self-caring
- Acknowledging the need for change
- Developing self-caring strategies
- Finding direction and purpose

Outcomes Offered

- Learn to care for yourself.
- Look at what matters most.
- Discover self-empowering strategies.
- Circumstances can change for the better.

Philip is my teddy bear. Peta was a client. The two were destined to meet and have a conversation that would change Peta's life.

It was some time after their encounter that Peta invited me to talk on a radio program where she worked as a disk jockey. It was an interesting change as I had gone from interviewer to interviewee. With pleasure, I noticed the confidence and competence she brought into her work—qualities not obvious in Peta when we first met.

You see, Peta had been a drug addict. She felt caught in a trap, wanting to break free but feeling powerless to do so. Attempting to quit presented problems as well. She came from a very prominent family and didn't want to damage their reputation by seeking help from public agencies.

Her parents initially approached me about Peta's problem. They, too, were concerned about avoiding a scandal.

Peta made it clear on our first appointment that she felt confined meeting in an office. As a result, most of our consultations were conducted while walking through a nearby park. She was an intelligent young woman with a couple of university degrees behind her. She saw the problems of her situation, and acknowledged the need to change directions. Nonetheless, she felt stuck.

She wasn't the only one. Though I was not a substance abuse specialist, I drew on my list of therapeutic strategies, trying every intervention I could think of that would help alter or change her behavior, but it became obvious over the following sessions that she wasn't progressing. Both of us felt frustrated, and I didn't know what more I could do.

Returning to my office after one of our walks in the park, I looked across at my desk. Philip was sitting there, dressed in his tartan vest, with a red bow around his neck and a checkered cap on his head. A previous client had made him for me as a thank you gift at the end of her therapy. As a result, he was very precious.

In a spontaneous act that somehow seemed appropriate, I took him off the desk and handed him to Peta. I think I said something like, "This is Philip. He would like to spend the week with you. I don't know whether there is something that he has to teach you, whether you may teach him something, or whether there is something that you can learn from each other, but I look forward to hearing what you discover together."

When she returned the next week, Philip was wearing his checkered cap, red ribbon, and the tartan vest, but he also wore a pair of pants Peta had made for him.

I inquired about her week with Philip. She said, "I realized Philip was very special to you. At first I put him in the living room, but then my friends came over and I felt uncomfortable for him. They were smoking and I didn't want him polluted with the smell of their dope. I didn't want him seeing the sort of people I mixed with, so I moved him to the dressing table in my bedroom. He sat there looking kindly at me each night as I went to sleep and was there looking over me when I awakened in the morning. I thought he looked immodest without any pants, so I made him this little pair of trousers to wear."

"So, what's the most important thing that you have learned from him?" I asked.

She burst into tears, and the answer that she gave changed the direction of her life. Shortly afterward she checked into a substance abuse clinic and later spent some time at the agency's rehabilitation farm. She realized that kicking her habit was more important than protecting her family's reputation. The isolation allowed her several months in which to separate herself not only from drugs, but also from the social network that supported her habit.

So what had made the difference for Peta? What helped her to change when she and I had felt so stuck and powerless? What had taken place in that conversation between Peta and Philip, my teddy bear? When I asked her, tears flowed down her cheeks. She said, "I realized that I cared for him more than I cared for myself."

STORY 86
GO WITH THE FLOW

Therapeutic Characteristics

Problems Addressed

- A tendency to fight against the current
- Fear
- Uncertainty about what to do

Resources Developed

- Learning not to fight the unconquerable
- Discovering how to use what life brings
- Learning from role models
- Choosing to go with the flow
- Choosing your own directions

Outcomes Offered

- Go with the flow.
- Don't struggle if it is not necessary.
- Take care of yourself.

I always smile when I remember Uncle Tom, for he was both playful and wise, leaving words and experiences indelibly etched in my young mind. One summer day he, Dad, a couple of cousins, myself, and Rex, my dog, squeezed into my uncle's dinghy to go fishing.

We dropped anchor to fish on the river that ran down behind Uncle Tom's vineyard. Quickly becoming bored when the fish refused to bite, my older cousin picked up Rex and pretended to throw him overboard. I begged him not to. The dinghy rocked, he slipped, and Rex fell into the river. I was distressed. Rather than swim back to the boat, Rex swam away downstream. I called and whistled, but he kept swimming away.

This was no little stream. It was a strong, fast-flowing river and Rex was being washed away rapidly. I feared my longtime and close companion would drown. Again I called and whistled but Uncle Tom put a firm, comforting hand on my shoulder and told me to stop calling. "He is doing what is right," he said. "He is an intelligent dog. Let him do it his way. If he tries to swim back to the boat, he'd be swimming against the current. He'd wear himself out and could drown. Besides, he knows he wouldn't be able to get up out of the water. The sides of the dinghy are too high for him. He is doing is the right thing.

"Learn from him," continued Uncle Tom. "You don't fight against a force that is stronger than yourself. You go with it and use it. He is letting the current take him, while gradually making his way toward the bank."

Uncle Tom calmly pulled the rope starter on the outboard motor. It chugged into life, and we followed Rex downstream. As Uncle Tom predicted, Rex gradually edged across the current toward the shore. At last he made the bank and scrambled up onto flat land. He stood and shook himself, waiting for us to nose the dinghy to shore before he jumped aboard and rested his wet head on my lap. His wagging tail beat the wooden sides of the boat.

"See," said Uncle Tom, reassuringly, as he swung the dinghy back out into the stream. "He knew what he was doing. When you are in trouble, you don't reach out for something unstable. That's what the dinghy was for him. Look for solid ground where you can firmly plant your feet. Don't try and swim against the current. It may be more powerful than you. If you are out of your depth, be like Rex. He knows how to look after himself. Go with the flow—and use it to your advantage."

STORY 87
TURNING THE TIDE

Therapeutic Characteristics

Problems Addressed

- Lack of time for self
- Relationship conflicts
- Search for answers
- A difficult journey ahead

Resources Developed

- Appreciating the need to take time out
- Finding an acceptable way
- Looking at the big picture
- Getting issues in perspective
- Seeking resolutions
- Doing what feels good

Outcomes Offered

- The tide will inevitably turn.
- Choose your own way.
- Have time for yourself and for thinking.
- Time out may help you see things differently.
- Be open to new perspectives.
- Look at the big picture.

Joe set off on a beach walk. He needed time to think, especially to think about what Clare had said in her letter, for their relationship was in trouble.

Normally he didn't have time to think about his personal life. Driving to work, he had to concentrate on the traffic. At work he had to concentrate on his job. By the time he got home at night, he just wanted to rest, unwind, have a meal, watch a little television, and go to bed. Walking was his time to reflect on life, and himself.

Usually he could choose which way he walked, but today the tide was very high and the water turbulent. It was too dangerous to make his way around the rocky headland. Waves pounded against the slippery, rounded rocks and an undertow pulled plumes of sand back into the sea.

Instead of the smooth, sandy walk that the beach offered at low tide he was forced to take a more difficult route over the headland. "This," he thought, "is the way my life seems to be going at the moment." It was up and down, bumpy and rugged. He had to look ahead, planning his path around rocky chasms that were too wide to leap. He paused at times to look into rock pools, watch crabs scatter for shelter, and enjoy the pleasant distraction from his own thoughts for a while.

He had to watch where he put his feet on smooth, wave-drenched surfaces. He thought it was strange how symbolically it paralleled what was happening in his relationship. He had to be careful with each step. At that point he came to a large gap in the rocks. It was too wide to leap and too steep to descend. Waves dashed into it, licking up the rock walls like hungry tongues. There seemed to be no way around it. With a little patience and searching, he discovered an old track that cut across the headland.

The track had not been used recently, but at least it headed toward the sheltered beach that was his destination. Harsh dune vegetation had grown across the trail. Any passage along it would be hard won, forced through prickly scrub.

He stood for a while and contemplated his choices. He could take the easy way out, give up on his destination, and retrace his steps, or he could stick with his planned goal, accept that there may be some tough times, and forge ahead. Was it worth getting a few scratches along the way?

A part of Joe saw the advantage of beating a retreat. Another part was clear about where he wanted to go, and the pleasure he would have in arriving. Like all of us, there were times when he gave up and times when he was determined to forge ahead. On this occasion, he chose the overgrown path, even if it might be tough going.

It seemed no time at all before he reached his destination: a sheltered cove with protected waters that were clear, blue, and temptingly swimmable. A border of trees defined the gentle sweep of the shoreline and offered shelter from the warming sun. He sat cross-legged in the shade and looked out into the distance where sun and sea meet.

He and Clare had just had their first fight. It wasn't that they hadn't had differences of opinion before. Every relationship does and theirs was no exception, even though they liked to think they were different and a fight would never happen. They had a dream, and hope, of happiness forever after.

This one shattered it. It had been a real fight. Not a physical one, but one in which they felt like opposing boxers in a win-or-die conflict. Clare had moved out. Joe needed time to contemplate the direction of their relationship.

For some time a friend had been asking whether they'd had their first fight yet. He said that a relationship had not tested its mettle until a couple had faced conflict and learned effective ways of resolving it. He said it was like learning to walk. Taking a few falls helps a child learn how to stand.

Joe liked to think that such testing times were unnecessary. Their relationship had certainly been good and sound so far. Surely it was better if it continued in that direction. Was it not healthier if they got by without a fight at all? Could life not be one of complete harmony and happiness?

His eyes fell to the water's edge. The tide was gradually receding. It left its mark from where it had previously washed higher up the beach. As the lines of dampness began to dry in the sand, evidence of the high tide's presence faded and disappeared. Even the impression of the mighty ocean on the shore was temporary. The marks it left on the sand were soon to fade and disappear. Joe saw something symbolic in the wash of the water. "In various ways we all leave our marks on each other," he thought. The sand and the ocean wash back and forth, giving to and taking from each other. They swing in a balance of struggle and harmony that has, for millennia, shaped the shorelines with pristine beauty.

Conflict between the two sets of needs exists and always will. It seemed to Joe that it was not important that it happened so much as how the overall picture of balance and harmony could be maintained. He was eager to get home and reread the letter that Clare had left.

On the journey back, the tide had receded away from the rocks. Most of his walk was along smooth, damp, and firm sands. Occasionally he had to clamber over a rock. He mused with the thought that the tide would inevitably turn and the experience of the journey would become so different again.

When he got home he reread the words that Clare had left. He phoned her and invited her to a picnic on the beach the next morning. Carrying croissants and coffee, they climbed their way over the rocks, negotiating the various ups and downs. They pushed through the prickly scrubland and finally arrived at the sheltered cove.

Joe thought how the journey had seemed easier when it was shared. Had it been that the challenges he faced yesterday prepared him for this next encounter? Had the experience of discovering a route through the rocky and challenging circumstances meant that he knew the way that much better the next time? Had having Clare with him to share the experience shortened the distance and made the journey more enjoyable?

They sat together on the shore. The sand still retained some of its nocturnal coolness. An offshore breeze gently and warmly caressed their backs. They looked at the sea and observed the gradual change of the tide.

Joe pulled from his pocket the letter that Clare had left at home when she moved out. He wanted her to know that he understood what she had said. Inevitably the tide turns, forever moving back and forth. Though we may need to take into account the surge and wane of our emotional energies, what remains important is the big picture. He read back to her what she had written, but this time the meaning came from his own heart. "In our relationship," she had written, "I think we have now experienced all the emotions. Like the tide they ebb and flow. What remains is the ocean of constant love."

STORY 88
ACKNOWLEDGING AND USING OUR ABILITIES

Therapeutic Characteristics

Problems Addressed

- Indecision
- Uncertainty
- Procrastination
- Lack of self-appreciation

Resources Developed

- Seeking solutions
- Learning from others' experiences
- Assessing what works best for you
- Acknowledging your abilities
- Using your abilities

Outcomes Offered

- Look ahead.
- Be prepared to laugh at your foibles.
- Seek those who care for and nurture you.
- Set goals and go for them.
- Learn from others.
- Focus on abilities, not problems.
- Appreciate your uniqueness.

Charlie was a chameleon with a problem. He was constantly changing his mind. First, he couldn't make up his mind in the morning about whether to get out of bed. Once he had, he was faced with the decision of what to have for breakfast. Then he also had to choose when, where, and with whom he would eat it. The decisions were so numerous and complex that he began to dread the day ahead. Even deciding to make a decision was a challenge.

And with each changing emotion came a change in color. When he became angry, he turned a deep, blood red. If he felt cool on an idea, he would turn an aqua-bluish color. When he became excited, he would start to glow in a golden sun-like yellow.

All this wouldn't have been so bad were it not for the fact that Charlie's indecision and procrastination meant he often did nothing. Doing nothing wasn't the bad part. His indecision made him feel despondent, though, and when he felt despondent he turned a dark, despairing blue.

Charlie thought he needed help but, of course, deciding to seek it was another thing. Just when he was getting close to a decision, he felt so good that he almost inevitably decided he didn't need to decide. If he did get around to seeking help, there was then the question of from whom he should seek it. As soon as he thought of one animal friend with whom he could talk, he immediately thought of another. That turned him a motley pattern of hues.

Somehow, he got his feet out of the front door, but then he wasn't sure which way to go. If he looked to the right, he changed his mind and turned left. The first move to the left had him thinking he really should have turned right.

Each step forward was full of doubt, so he milled around in circles, going nowhere fast. "What are you doing?" asked a passing giraffe. When Charlie explained his problem, the giraffe gave him very sound and direct advice, "You need to stand tall like me," said the long-necked creature. "Look ahead and see where you are going. Don't get caught up in all the little things around you. You need to look beyond them. Then you can see where you are going."

Charlie tried to lift his head like the giraffe. He looked as far ahead as he could and actually made a few steps forward in the one direction. Then the doubts again set in.

He couldn't decide whether to move on or go home. He stepped back and forth, a little like a rocking horse. Suddenly his thoughts were interrupted by a peel of laughter. The chameleon looked up to see a hyena chuckling at his antics. "You look so silly," he said between bursts of laughter. "Don't be stupid. Just go and do what you want to do."

Charlie was humiliated. He felt so angry that he turned a deep, purplish red and stomped off, eager to get away from the hyena and his unsympathetic put-downs. He had gone three or four paces in a straight line before becoming unsure that was the direction he wanted to go.

Turning a leafy green like the foliage that had fallen to the jungle floor, he encountered a gorilla pushing her way purposefully through the undergrowth, a young babe gripping tenaciously to her fur. Stopping just before she trod on Charlie, she said, "I am sorry. I didn't notice you there."

"That's OK," Charlie responded. "Not many people do notice me and, if they do, they just order me about or laugh at me."

The mother gorilla sat on a fallen log and listened to Charlie's story. Her eyes were soft and empathic. Charlie felt as though he could talk about things he had never before said. "I can understand your dilemma," she said, "but I can't tell you what you have to do. You need to find your own way. The answers are within." Charlie's skin started to glow warmly. He felt the gorilla understood and cared for him. With a sense of peace, he made five or six steps forward. Then he began to doubt. The gorilla had offered nothing but caring. "Surely that alone doesn't give one direction," he thought. And he stopped short in frustration.

A cheetah was the next animal to encounter Charlie and hear his story. "It is simple," said the cheetah. "At first you just sit and watch. Choose what to set your sights on. When you have, make a bee-line for it. Go at it with every ounce of energy you've got. Don't hold back. That is the way to reach your goal." With that, the cheetah dashed off.

"That was a lot of help," he thought. "I am not a cheetah and never will be a cheetah." But, deep in thought, he had been following a straight path until a hoot from above distracted him. Gazing benevolently toward him was a wide-eyed owl.

The owl listened patiently to Charlie's tale, then sat pensively for a while. It was only after having contemplated all the issues that he finally spoke. His voice was deep, compassionate, and wise.

"You are right to have listened to the advice of your fellow creatures," said the owl. "Each has said something that has helped you a little on your journey. You are also right to discern that what works for them may not work for you. You are right to experiment with their suggestions to see how helpful they may be. But there is one thing that you have overlooked, you don't have to copy them. You have an ability that no other animal has.

"There is a saying in the jungle," continued the owl, "that the leopard cannot change his spots. That is true. Each animal is the color that they are and always will be. You, however, are unique and special. Of all the animals in the world, you are the only one who can change its color. Know your strengths and be proud of them."

Charlie had worried so much about his problems that he had forgotten how to appreciate his uniqueness. He felt excited and happy about the way the owl had valued him and the way he could now value himself. The knowledge filled him with confidence. All the way home he practiced changing color. He became dappled like the shades of the jungle, golden ochre as he crossed the dry savannah, and granite gray as he mounted some rocks. Caught up in this fun, he forgot to change his mind. In fact he had decided what he had wanted to eat for supper even before he arrived home. He

CARING FOR YOU

ate his meal and fell into a comfortable sleep. Of course he couldn't see what color he was when asleep, but he knew it was a nice one. It had to be. He was dreaming of Charlie, the confident chameleon.

STORY 89
GIVING WHAT YOU WANT TO RECEIVE

Therapeutic Characteristics

Problems Addressed

- Fear
- Confrontation with danger or possible death
- When life is a struggle
- When lack of resources feels limiting

Resources Developed

- Learning to care
- Learning to give
- Knowing that what you give is likely to be what you receive

Outcomes Offered

- Give as you want to receive.
- Who knows what may come from one good deed?
- Caring for others can be caring for self.
- Lack of resources need not limit your potential.

Have you ever noticed how one action invites a similar response? If someone pushes you deliberately, do you feel the urge to push back? If someone shouts at you, do you want to shout back?

The same process is true even if the content of the action is different. If someone gives you a hug, it is easier to hug back. If someone speaks affectionately to you, it is easier to respond in kind.

Consider the tale of a poor Scottish farmer by the name of Fleming. He was struggling to make a living for his family on their small property in the harsh Scottish countryside. One day as he was tilling his land, he heard a cry coming from a nearby bog. He instantly dropped his tools, forgot his work, and raced to the bog. A young boy had fallen in and was fighting to get free, but his struggles caused him to sink deeper in the quagmire. His eyes were wide in terror. He screamed in desperation, fearing the bog would swallow him up. There was nothing for him to grasp, no way to pull himself free.

Fleming rescued the lad from the bog, without regard for personal risk, and took him back to his humble cottage where, with the help of his wife, they calmed the boy's panic, cleaned him up, and saw him safely on his way home. In their act of caring they never inquired who he was or where he came from.

It was thus a surprise the next morning when an elaborate horse-drawn carriage pulled up in front of the farmer's humble abode. The driver dismounted and opened the carriage door for an expensively dressed nobleman to alight. The nobleman reached out and shook the broad, callused hand of the farmer.

"I am the father of the boy you saved," he explained. "To just say 'thank you' seems so trivial. Nothing in the world is more valuable to me than my son's life. How can I repay you? How can I compensate you for your kindness?"

"Thank you," said the farmer. "I appreciate your gratitude. That is sufficient reward. I cannot accept any payment. I did what anyone would have done. I am sure you would have done the same if you'd seen my son in the bog."

At this moment the farmer's son came to the door of the family cottage. He was curious to see the nobleman and the fancy carriage at their own little farm. "Is this your son?" asked the nobleman.

Stepping beside him and putting his arm around the boy's shoulder, Fleming replied proudly, "Yes."

"You saved my son," said the nobleman. "Let me do something for your son. I can take him and give him a good education. If he has the courage and heart of his father, he will grow into a man of whom you can truly be proud."

The farmer accepted, not for himself, but because he saw an opportunity for his son that he would never be able to offer. Fleming's son proved to be a keen and devoted scholar. After completing his basic education, he went on to medical school, where his passion to care for others led him into research—and a discovery that was to revolutionize the world of medicine. A single act of a kind farmer resulted in a discovery that continues to save the lives of millions. The farmer's son was knighted as Sir Alexander Fleming in recognition of his work as the discoverer of penicillin.

But our story does not end there. Some years later the nobleman's son faced another life-threatening situation. He was stricken with pneumonia, a condition that was, up until that time, almost always fatal. Penicillin conquered the illness and enabled him to live a life that also became famous.

The nobleman who provided for Fleming's son's education was Lord Randolph Churchill. The young man who was twice saved by the Fleming family was Sir Winston Churchill.

STORY 90
FORMING AND CHANGING BELIEFS

Therapeutic Characteristics

Problems Addressed

- The formation and desire to cling to unhelpful beliefs
- When beliefs lead to unwanted feelings
- When beliefs dictate inappropriate actions
- When beliefs effect relationships

Resources Developed

- Assessing the various possibilities
- Looking for all the facts

- Being open to new information
- Changing beliefs

Outcomes Offered

- Avoid leaping to conclusions.
- Don't mistake a thought for a fact.
- Let your thoughts evolve.
- Be open to new possibilities.

When my daughter was two years old, she formed a rather strange and inappropriate belief. It began with good intent. Keen, devoted, and enthusiastic about our new role as parents of a first child, we wanted to do the best for her. We sought to give her every opportunity and, as part of that commitment, we bought a pair of guinea pigs, hoping to teach her a love of animals and provide some of the necessary metaphors of life. It worked in a way that we hadn't expected.

The female guinea pig became pregnant and, just before she was to give birth, I had to leave for a convention in another city. As my wife and daughter were accompanying me, we returned the guinea pigs to the temporary care of the friends from whom we had initially purchased them.

When we returned from the meeting, our friends greeted us with two pieces of news. "We've got some good news and some bad news," they said. "The good news is that the mother has given birth to four babies. The bad news is that the father has died."

Our friends had separated the male and female when she was birthing. The male, seeking to return to the female, caught his neck in the chicken wire of the cage and was strangled.

Several months later our next door neighbor gave birth to twins, and we went to pay a welcoming visit to the new arrivals. Our young daughter looked delightedly for a while at the two young babies, then glanced up to their father and asked, "When is John going to die?"

Forming false beliefs is not just the prerogative of children. For years a colleague has stayed with us when he conducted workshops in our city. On his visits he has observed and followed our tradition of removing our shoes at the doorways—and formed a belief about the practice unknown to us for many years.

Our home has polished wooden and slate floors that needed to be resealed each year because of abrasions and scratching caused by footwear. One year I suffered a reaction to the sealant fumes, and my physician concluded I had become hypersensitive to the chemical fumes and should avoid using them. That left me in a dilemma—nicely polished floors or a few less brain cells each year. We solved this dilemma by removing our shoes at the doorway and wearing soft-soled slippers inside.

My colleague was amazed to hear this tale. "For years," he said, "I thought it was some religious ritual. You know, like people remove their shoes to enter a temple. I have told many people that you are such a spiritual person you even have a sacred ritual of removing shoes before you enter your own home!"

Some times such beliefs may be fairly innocuous, but other times they can be serious. I read a while ago how the Aztecs became terribly frightened that the descending winter sun was slipping closer to the horizon. As it dropped, the temperatures became colder and the land grew dormant. *Thinking* the sun might disappear, they made the mistake of *believing* their own false thought. Terror struck them. The sun *would* vanish completely and lead to their destruction. To appease the sun god and ensure its return they would have to offer the ultimate gift—the sacrifice of a human life. Their belief-driven action was validated, for the sun responded, climbed back into the sky, and again nurtured the land with warmth and life. Each winter solstice the Aztecs made a sacrifice, and each year the sun returned.

I don't know whether the Aztecs ever discovered that, just as false beliefs can be *formed,* so they can be *changed.* I hope that now my daughter has reached adulthood, she has discovered sufficient evidence to *know* that a child can be born without its father dying. For my colleague, receiving new information about his observations helped him develop a different way of looking at our ritual shoe removal. It is from my daughter, though, that I can give another example of how additional facts can change an existing belief.

It was just before Christmas and she was about four years old. We visited a department store where she had sat on Santa Claus's knee and told him all the presents she wanted. She came away with that jubilant energy of a child who has just been promised everything she ever wanted for Christmas from the season's number one authority.

A little while later we wandered into another department store where Santa was again seated on his throne dispensing sweets and wishes to admiring infants. She joined the line, sat on his knee, talked with him for a while, then walked away looking extremely dejected. I looked into her sad little face and asked her what was wrong. She said, "I don't think I am going to get anything for Christmas." "Why not?" I inquired.

"He asked me what I wanted for Christmas," she wailed. Thinking that was probably a typical line for Santa, I didn't understand her problem until she went on to explain. "I don't think I am going to get anything," she repeated, "because he can't remember what I told him fifteen minutes ago!"

STORY 91
NEGOTIATING TIME FOR YOURSELF

Therapeutic Characteristics

Problems Addressed

- Fixed, rigid patterns of behavior
- Family relationship problems
- Expectation that one approach should work in all situations
- A tendency to be highly principled
- Difficulty in adjusting
- Exclusive devotion to work
- Lack of time for self

Resources Developed

- Learning from others' experiences
- Looking for new alternatives
- Doing things differently
- Developing adaptation skills and flexibility

- Adjusting to the needs of others
- Taking time to care for yourself

Outcomes Offered

- Others may have things to teach us.
- Be flexible to life's needs.
- What works in one situation may not in another.
- Other possibilities may exist.
- Take time to relax.
- Caring for yourself is important in caring for others.

One of the delightful things about being human is our ability to share our experiences and learn from each other's tragedies and triumphs. I am sure my flying instructor had no idea, nor any intention, that something he shared with me would make a difference for Clinton and his family more than two decades later.

Clinton was in the Navy and loved it. His occupation had grown from a childhood dream to an adult career. Perhaps in part because of his training and in part because of what he was, he had become a military man, regimented in discipline, proper order, and correct procedures. This worked *very* well for him in the Navy, ensured his promotion, and guaranteed his success.

His problem was at home. What he had learned and used so effectively in his career didn't work with his wife and two young sons. He came home at the end of the day and, still in military mode, barked out orders to which he expected instant responses. He could not understand why his sons disobeyed him, why their rooms were untidy, and why he had no control. Clinton interpreted this as a rejection of him and his values.

If his wife forgot to cut his morning toast diagonally, he became irritable and short-tempered, not just because it hadn't been done the right way, but because he interpreted this to mean she didn't really care. His frustration grew to the point of anger, his anger turned into verbal abuse, and he flung down-putting comments toward his wife and sons. He knew what he was doing and hated himself for it, but he also thought of his principles as right and bore heavily the responsibility of raising his sons correctly. He loved them dearly, had no doubt about his feelings, and felt frustrated by the constant family tension.

As he was telling me his story, I remembered the words of my flying instructor, and related them to Clinton. We had been taxiing out to the runway at the beginning of a lesson when, out of the blue, the instructor asked me, "Do you know what I hate most about this job?"

I was hesitant to inquire further for I thought he might be critical of me, saying he feared for his life flying with inexperienced incompetents like me at the controls. But that wasn't what he said. "The thing that I hate most about this job," he continued, "is not going up with inexperienced people. I enjoy my work. The thing I hate most is getting home after flying all day long and being greeted by a son who says, 'Let's play planes Dad.'"

I knew exactly how he felt, for in my profession, too, I had that same sort of getting-home-at-the-end-of-the-day experience. Like my flying instructor, I generally enjoy my job. What I found most difficult was getting home at the end of the day and immediately having a wife and two children pounce on me with all the problems of their day.

I wanted to take off my work cap when I got home. The last thing I desired was to face the family's accumulated problems, so at one stage, I sat down with my wife to discuss how we might manage the situation. I could take time-out on the way home to visit the gym, have a swim, or down a few beers with the guys, thus giving me a bit of a buffer zone between work and family responsibilities. That, however, wasn't high on my priority list, and, as my preference was to be at home, we decided to experiment with me having time-out there. I would take 10, 15, or 20 minutes to sit back with a cup of coffee and read the paper, to put on some headphones and listen to my favorite music, to spend time meditating, or whatever.

Something interesting happened during our experimental period in that my wife and children probably adapted more than I. They discovered that, if they waited for me to switch off from work, I could be more focused and relaxed about listening to the things they wished to discuss. They learned that by allowing me time to put the day behind me and don a different cap, they got better value for their money out of the deal.

"I know what you mean," said Clinton. "I come home from work in my uniform. It is only a three minute drive. There's no time to switch off, and while I am in my uniform, I am still a sailor. What I can do is commute in 'civvies'. I can leave my uniform at work and change when I get there.

"In fact," he continued, "I have been wanting to get more exercise and was wondering how to do it. If I cycle to and from work, I can take a trip along the foreshore. It would take me about 15 or 20 minutes. That way I could begin to think about work as I cycle in and begin to think about the family as I cycle home."

Over the years I have lost contact with my flying instructor, but I have wondered whether he may be interested to know how sharing his experience made a difference for me and my family, and how sharing that in turn made a difference for Clinton and his family. And who is to know what impact Clinton's story may have on others?

EXERCISE

What stories of self-caring have you heard, witnessed in your clients, or encountered in your own experiences?

Use your notebook to jot down these ideas:

1. Keep clearly in mind the client's goal for self-caring or self-nurturing.
2. Define the desired therapeutic outcome with your client in a way that is specific, positive, and achievable.
3. Outline a metaphoric tale aimed at attaining this goal, and providing the means to do so.

CARING FOR YOU

CHAPTER 13

Enhancing Happiness

Happiness—a state of contentment in which a person experiences well-being and enjoyment with themselves, in their relationships with others and in the environment in which they live—can serve as a preventative of depression, anxiety, phobias, and dysfunctional relationships. If we feel contented, we are less likely to seek the mood altering effects of drugs, blame others for the things that happen to us, or adopt a position of helplessness.

Like depression, happiness is made up of many components and, hopefully, many of the healing stories offered in the preceding chapters will help contribute to this state. Developing a realistic sense of personal empowerment, learning to accept, what can not be changed and reframing negative attitudes are all component parts of well-being, as are the abilities to modify unwanted patterns of behavior, learn from our experiences, and strive toward attaining what we want. If we can help clients learn to care for themselves, have a caring or compassionate approach toward others, and adopt these qualities into a considered worldview, we are assisting them to acquire those aspects of contentment that will be both curative and preventative.

The ability to have fun—one of the components of happiness—can serve as a reciprocal inhibitor of anxiety, depression, and fear and is thus a legitimate means of, and outcome for, therapy. It is possible to use humor and humorous experiences as a way of communicating a salient therapeutic message that may be relevant to the client's desired outcome—in fact in humor it may be possible to say something to your client that you may not choose to do directly. The indirection of humorous communications makes them useful mataphor material.

The following stories include examples of using jokes and humorous tales but, as with all stories, one needs to be sensitive to the values, morals, and sense of humor of the client to avoid the risk that they may be perceived as offensive or denigratory. With this caution it becomes possible to bring home a therapeutic message in a way that is light, fun, and salient.

STORY 92
THE SECRET THAT WILL NEVER BE KNOWN

Therapeutic Characteristics

I have not listed the Problems, Resources, and Outcomes offered by this story for the simple reason that, although it is one of my favorite tales, it is not a story that I have ever used therapeutically. I have, however, frequently told it in workshops, and reproduce it here because it illustrates some important aspects about storytelling.

First, by retelling this tale, you can practice the Guidelines to Effective Storytelling presented and discussed in Chapter 2. Because I enjoy the story, it is one I can tell with enthusiasm and involvement. It is one that gives the scope to use and develop a variety of sensory experiences for capturing the listener's attention and enhancing the intrigue of the tale.

Second, it is a story that, if well told, engages and entrances listeners so powerfully that the teller will be able to observe easily the characteristics of their entrancement and search processes. Listeners typically exhibit a relaxed yet absorbed posture. Their focus of attention is fixed on the teller, their rate of respiration slows, their eye blinking is reduced, and their motor activity shows the stillness of a statue.

Two knights of old once set out on a quest to find the Holy Grail. In those days knights engaged in long and arduous pilgrimages to holy destinations, sought the meaning of life, searched for what no one else had yet attained, and yearned to make the ultimate conquest. Our knights were no exception to that illustrious and committed cause.

One cold and miserable evening, after uncountable days of strenuous riding, the knights sought a place to rest. Claps of thunder shook the heavens and bolts of lightening intermittently illuminated the gloomy trail ahead. On a hillside, through the distant mist, they saw the rising turrets of a welcoming castle.

As they approached, a creaking drawbridge mysteriously lowered over the still, lily-filled waters of the moat in front of them, almost as if anticipating their arrival. Their horses clip-clopped across the echoing wooden bridge, and, as soon as they stepped off into the cobblestone courtyard, the bridge creaked up behind them and clunked solidly shut. The sharp hammer of hooves on centuries-worn stone cracked through the reverent silence as they led their mounts to the open stables on the far side of the barren, battlement-protected courtyard. Entering, the comforting mix of earthy aromas, sweet-smelling animal sweat, and fresh-mown hay that awaited them and their horses produced the familiar homecoming sensations yearned for by any horseman after a long day in the saddle.

Having tethered their beasts, the knights approached the main arched doors to the castle. They rapped with the wrought iron knocker and heard the sound reverberate through the vestibule. When no one answered, they tried the lock, and the door swung open, permitting them to enter a wooden-paneled chamber decorated with gloomy portraits of past generations that watched their arrival in solemn suspicion. Trying another door, they found themselves in a dining room with a chandelier dangling decoratively from the ceiling and lighting the walls with the flickering dance of its candles. A long wooden table stretched down the middle of the room, and a frail old man with a long, white, wispy beard sat at the far end.

"Welcome," he greeted them. "I have been awaiting your arrival." He fed them sumptuously, then directed them to their accommodation in the west wing of the castle. There, two rooms offered hospitable comfort in comparison to the raging storms outside that still clapped with thunder and dashed the roof with pelting rain. Deeply fatigued, they fell into bed anticipating a heavenly night's sleep, but barely had they dozed off when they were awakened by bloodcurdling screams. Groans of agony silenced the raging storm and raced through the castle's corridors. The knights, not knowing what to do, were on edge all night and gained barely a wink of slumber for their wearied bodies.

In the morning they could not restrain their curiosity. Even before they sat to the elaborate breakfast already spread on the table, they began to question the frail old man who remained seated, as he had the night before, at the table head.

"What were the sounds?" they asked. "What was the groaning and screaming that went on all night and kept us awake?"

"That," replied the old man, "is the secret of the castle." The knights asked him about the secret, but he said, "I can't tell you. You see, I swore a vow to guard the secret of the castle, but I am getting old and don't expect to live much longer. If you come back in one year's time, then I will tell you the secret."

The knights resumed their journey in search of the Holy Grail, and, in time, memories of their night in the castle faded but, perchance, one year later to the very day, they found themselves seeking shelter on a cold and miserable night. They had been in the saddle for uncountable, strenuous days. With claps of thunder shaking the heavens and bolts of lightening illuminating their gloomy trail, they spied, through the mist, the rising turrets of a familiar castle.

Again the creaky drawbridge lowered for their horse to clip-clop across its worn, wooden planks, then clunked shut behind them. Sweet-smelling hay was freshly laid out in the warm stables, and in the dining room the old man, a little older and frailer, sat in the same position as though he had not moved since they last visited. He welcomed them back, fed them sumptuously, then directed them to the same rooms in the west wing.

That night amidst the claps of thunder, bolts of lightening, and beating rain, the knights were once more awakened by the bloodcurdling screams and groans that echoed through the castle's stone-walled corridors. They could not wait to get down to breakfast the next morning.

"You remember," they reminded the old man, "that you promised if we came back in twelve months you would tell us the secret of the castle. Here we are to the very day. Please tell us about those screams and groans that have now kept us awake on two occasions."

"You are right," said the old man through his long, wispy beard, his voice almost as creaky as the drawbridge. "I did give my promise. Now, I am even older and frailer. I don't expect to be around much longer, so I will share the secret with you, but first I should point out that I took a vow never to tell anyone else. You must also promise never to tell another soul."

And they never did.

STORY 93
GIVE AND TAKE

Therapeutic Characteristics

Problems Addressed

- Anxiety of unfamiliar places
- The hustle and bustle of life
- A desire to want things to be all our way
- Lack of reciprocal sharing

Resources Developed

- Learning from others
- Learning through humor
- Appreciating the need to give if we want to receive

Outcomes Offered

- Life is give and take.

Kathmandu is an ancient capital that lies in the base of a valley ringed by Himalayan hills. The first time I arrived there, I remember hearing a pilot at the airport say it was like trying to land in a teacup. The hills form the sides of the cup. Clouds often cap it like a saucer placed on top. Buildings are haphazardly spread over the valley floor like accumulated tea leaves at the bottom of the cup.

Now serviced by jet airlines, Kathmandu is a tourist hub, but in times gone by, this isolated valley was serviced only by mule trains and barefooted porters. Then it was the intersection of trade routes that exchanged valued and necessary goods across the mountains from the subcontinent of India to the high plateaus of Tibet and the vast lands of China.

Durbar Square, the crossroads of these oriental trade routes, flourished and became the center of commerce and religion. Temples rose in the square, storey upon storey of thin red bricks to pagoda-style roofs supported by elaborately carved, and sometimes colorfully painted, wooden struts. Window shutters on the temples opened to reveal painted wooden effigies of Hindu deities peering down on the masses of traders that gathered below. Today they still look out on vegetable sellers, butchers, barbers, clothes merchants, and flute hawkers who spread their wares among the wandering cows and camera-laden tourists.

I mention this because I was one of the camera-laden tourists who happened to be in Durbar Square early one morning hoping to catch the first golden rays of light as they lit up the earthen red bricks of the temples. At that time of the day, the square bustled with local activity: women in colorful saris; men with brocaded hats; farmers with weather-beaten faces; tall Tibetans with high, rosy cheekbones; skinny Hindu holy men wrapped in grubby, white cloth; and only a few sleepy tourists.

The light fell beautifully on one temple that worshipfully faced the rising sun. Large slabs of gray stone formed steps that seemed to invite one up and away from the hustle and bustle of everyday commerce. To enter the realm of the spiritual, one would not only have to climb the stairs but pass through the portal of majestically carved doors, deeply etched in symbols and effigies that apparently held significance for the believer.

Standing in the shade of another building, I leaned against its wall, steadying my body and camera to capture a shot of the intricately carved woodwork. As I did, a holy man walked across the square. His maroon robes seemed to flow with the combined motion of his gait and the gentle wind. He walked with a staff as tall as himself and as intricately carved as the door. His long flowing beard was plaited with golden flowers as fresh as the morning sunlight. Strings of wooden beads hung, layer upon layer, around his neck and his hair was plaited and coiled upwards into a spiraling turban. His face was painted with white lines and a red thumb print, symbolizing the third eye in the center of his forehead.

He crossed the square through the preoccupied crowd of traders, seeming quite oblivious of others, including me, hidden back in the shadows of another building. He walked to the temple on which I had my lens focused, climbed the stone slab steps that I had been admiring, and turned to sit right in front of the very door I wanted to photograph. He positioned his body perfectly symmetrically in the doorway. He turned to face my direction without his eyes ever making contact with mine or showing any indication that he was aware of my presence. He sat in a meditative pose, his legs crossed, his gaze up, and his thoughts apparently on some higher plane.

This was a front-page, National Geographic photograph. It was the shot of a lifetime, one of those of which any shutterbug would be proud. Here it was, right in front of me, an exhibition award-winning snap. I zoomed the telephoto lens in. I adjusted the focus and lifted my finger to the shutter button. Simultaneously, as if our actions were divinely coordinated, the holy man lifted his hands. Between them he held a worn, old piece of cardboard that now obliterated his face. On it was etched a message. Curious, I zoomed the lens in closer to read what it said. *Life is give and take,* it began. This is nice, I thought, the holy man is giving me a holy message, so I read on. *You take photograph you give me 50 rupees!*

STORY 94
KEEP IT SIMPLE

Therapeutic Characteristics

Problems Addressed

- When life gets complex
- Caught in the "analysis paralysis"
- A tendency to be philosophical rather than practical
- When an important point is missed

Resources Developed

- Seeing the problem clearly
- Looking for simple, practical answers

Outcomes Offered

- Don't make things more complex than necessary.

- Seek practical solutions.
- Keep it simple.

Sherlock Holmes and Dr. Watson went camping. As they lay back on their camp beds, snuggled into their sleeping bags, and looked up at the stars, Holmes addressed Watson. "Watson, dear fellow. When you look at the starry sky, what does it tell you?"

Watson studied the celestial bodies that lit the darkness with their sparkling dots and deliberated a while before responding. "Well," he said, "from a meteorological perspective the clear, cloudless sky tells me we can expect a crisp, rainless night. There is no sign of haze around the moon, so I venture to forecast that tomorrow will be as fine and fair as it was today. We may have light winds but the sky shows no sign of foul weather.

"From a nautical perspective, I gain comfort from watching the stars. Their formations have been charted and their courses observed with such scientific scrutiny that they are immensely practical navigational aids. The stars have guided sailors safely around the world. They have enabled explorers to reach into the darkest and most forbidding parts of our planet. They serve as a reference point for people to identify where they are and where they are going. Their contribution to safety and exploration has been so immeasurable that we could never have discovered our world without guidance from their world.

"Aesthetically, the starry sky reminds me of the beauty that is so inherent in our world. We gaze at the stars, and admire their twinkling array of patterns and formations that transport us into the mystical realm of the distant and unreachable. Generation upon generation has enjoyed the familiar constellations and pointed them out to each new cycle of children: They are a reminder of the beauty that is intrinsic in our world and the things around us.

"From an astronomical perspective, the stars tell me there are billions and billions of worlds out there we will never get to know. There is galaxy upon galaxy that stretches away for thousands and millions of light years, in a time frame our brief existence cannot permit us to measure. Our solar system is just one small part of a great universe—a universe beyond our comprehension and understanding.

"Spiritually, it tells me that if there is such a vast creation out there, it is logical to deduce there must be a creator. Given that there must be a god or deity who has formed all these stars and planets, looking at them awakens in me a deep sense of spirituality.

"From a personal perspective, they remind me of something about myself. They make me feel insignificant, as though I am just a mere speck, or the tiniest of dots, on the immense face of the universe. I look at the stars and am humbled by any previous thoughts of self-importance or pride. They remind me of my place in the world and my place in relation to other people."

So, for a while, Watson carried on, describing the many, many things the stars told him as he lay on his back and looked at the heavens. Finally, at the end of his monologue, he rolled his head over, shifted his gaze from the twinkling canopy above, looked at Holmes, and asked, "When you look at the starry sky, what does it tell you, Holmes?"

Holmes inhaled deeply on his pipe, paused for a moment as he slowly expelled the smoke, and replied, "It is elementary dear Watson. Someone has stolen our tent."

STORY 95
IF YOU ARE FEELING HAPPY

Therapeutic Characteristics

Problems Addressed

- Feeling down
- Tardiness
- Procrastination
- Indecision
- Anxiety
- Rebelliousness

Resources Developed

- Listening to sound advice
- Making appropriate decisions
- Enjoying humor

Outcomes Offered

- Discovering self-insight is possible.
- Be aware of the consequences of your actions.
- Learn acceptance.
- Learn self-caring.

There is a story of a little sparrow who decided *not* to fly south for the winter. Perhaps the sparrow had heard the sound advice of its fellow birds and just didn't care. Maybe he was enjoying where he was and couldn't be bothered to make a change. Perhaps he was a procrastinator, always putting things off for no good reason. Maybe he was scared or apprehensive about being in crowds, or could have just been angry and rebellious.

But these are only guesses. The fact is that the sparrow refused to go. It wasn't long, however, before he began to rue his decision. Winter set in. The weather turned cold. Food was in short supply. To stand by his principles could be fateful, so, reluctantly, the sparrow took to the air and began the flight south.

Unfortunately, he had delayed too long. Winter was upon the land, snow covered the fields, and the wind blew harshly. When ice began to form on his wings, the sparrow wasn't sure which weighed the heavier, the burden of frozen water or the heaviness of his heart. No longer able to keep up the battle, he dropped from the sky, falling into a farmyard paddock.

As chance would have it, a cow happened to reside in that very paddock. Being preoccupied with a delicious bale of hay in which she had her nose deeply buried, the cow neither saw nor heard the frozen sparrow fall behind her. She just did what any cow would do with a delicious bale of hay. She ate and, having eaten, she defecated—right on top of the sparrow.

"This," thought the sparrow, "is truly the end!" But it was not as fateful as the little bird had anticipated. The warm manure melted the ice from his wings and raised his temperature. In fact, he felt so snug and warm the sparrow burst into song.

However, the farmer's cat was lurking behind the corner of the barn. When the cat heard the sparrow's chirping, she could not believe her luck. Using the bale as a shield, the cat crept forward to investigate the sounds. The sparrow sat in the manure singing. He wallowed self-indulgently in the muck, too absorbed in his own feelings to be aware of potential danger.

The cat didn't need to think twice. She stuck swiftly and accurately. She whisked the bird from the manure and ate it.

So, you may ask, what is the point of this tale? Well, it is said that all good stories have a moral. This one has at least three.

The first is that not everyone who craps on you is your enemy.

Second, not everyone who rescues you from the manure is your friend.

And, third, if you're happy in the muck, then keep your mouth shut.

STORY 96
THINGS COULD BE WORSE

Therapeutic Characteristics

Problems Addressed

- Pessimism
- Depressive thinking
- A need to see the worst possible scenario
- A desire for others to rescue you

Resources Developed

- Accepting what life brings
- Relying on your own resources

Outcomes Offered

- Things could be worse.
- Accept your circumstances.
- Trust yourself and your judgments.

In the days of missionary fervor, a young, enthusiastic priest journeyed halfway around the globe in his zeal to take the Word to the pagan, head-hunting tribes of darkest Borneo. With little more than a Bible under his arm and scant supplies in his pack, his faith provided him with the fortitude to face the challenges of paddling up raging rivers, portaging around roaring rapids, and fighting through near-impenetrable jungle. Eventually he reached his journey's destination: a lost tribe of cannibals who had never seen a white person.

As he approached the village, 200 ferocious warriors leaped from the jungle and surrounded him.

They raised their spears, pulled them back over their shoulders, and aimed two hundred barbed points at his heart. He was unarmed, powerless, and in dire straights. Not knowing what to do he cried out, "Oh God, I'm in trouble!"

From the heavens, a voice answered the good missionary. "You are *not* in trouble. Look down at your feet. There is a rock. Pick up the rock and beat the chieftain to death."

The chieftain was not hard to identify. He was the one who wore a headband of elaborate plumage and carried a staff topped with a human skull. The missionary picked up the rock, walked over to the chieftain, felled him with the first blow, and proceeded to beat him to death.

At first the warriors stepped back in fear and disbelief. Their chieftain's body lay lifeless at the feet of this pale intruder. As the missionary breathlessly dropped the rock and raised his head, he again saw himself encircled by the 200 spear-bearing warriors. Ferocity grew on their faces. The 200 barbed points which were about to be launched at his heart quivered with anger.

Again a voice came down from the heavens. "*NOW* you are in trouble!"

STORY 97
THE PROBLEM OF LOOKING FOR PROBLEMS

Therapeutic Characteristics

Problems Addressed

- A habit of only seeing the problems
- Inability to see possible outcomes
- Lack of regard for personal well-being

Resources Developed

- Discovering how to accept the positive
- Developing an outcome-oriented perspective

Outcomes Offered

- Accept good fortune.
- Focus on outcome rather than problems.

During the French revolution an attorney, a physician, and an engineer were all sentenced to death. When the day of their execution arrived, the attorney was first onto the platform that supported the guillotine. He stood tall and proud, uncompromising of his principles.

"Blindfold or no blindfold?" asked the executioner. The attorney, not wanting to be seen as fearful or cowardly in the face of death, held his head high and answered, "No blindfold." "Head up or head down?" continued the executioner. Still there would be no compromise. "Head up," said the attorney proudly.

The executioner swung his axe, cleanly severing the rope that held the razor-sharp blade at the top of the scaffold. The blade dropped swiftly between the shafts and stopped just half an inch above the attorney's neck.

"I am sorry," said the executioner. "I checked it just this morning, like I always do. This should not have happened."

The attorney seized on the opportunity. Although willing to die for his principles, he preferred to live. "I think," he addressed the executioner, "if you check The Procedural Manual For Execution By Guillotine, you will find there is a clause that states if the guillotine malfunctions, the condemned is permitted to walk free."

The executioner checked his manual, found the attorney to be correct, and set him free.

The doctor was the next to be led to the platform. "Blindfold or no blindfold?" asked the executioner. "No blindfold," said the doctor as proudly as the attorney. "Head up or head down?" asked the executioner. "Head up," said the doctor standing tall and defiant.

The executioner swung his axe, cutting the rope cleanly. Once again the blade stopped just half an inch above the doctor's neck.

"I can't believe this," exclaimed the executioner. "Twice in a row! I checked it out thoroughly this morning, but rules are rules and I have to abide by them. Like the attorney, your life has been spared and you may go."

The engineer was the third to mount the stand. By this time, the embarrassed executioner had double-checked the guillotine and everything looked operational.

"Blindfold or no blindfold?" he asked the engineer. "No blindfold," came the reply. "Head up or head down?" asked the executioner. "Head up," said the engineer.

For the third time, the executioner swung back his axe to slash the rope that supported the blade. Just as he was about to bring the blow forward and sever the line, the engineer called out, "Stop! I think I can see the problem."

STORY 98
BEING ONE WITH EVERYTHING

Therapeutic Characteristics

Problems Addressed

- Self-improvement
- Seeking answers

Resources Developed

- Learning to do it your own way
- Finding what works best
- Finding sources of happiness

Outcomes Offered

- We are interactive beings.
- Happiness and well-being depend on being one with everything.
- Good relationships are the basis of well-being.
- Find your own way.
- Use what works best for you.

A novice monk approached the master about his impending retreat. As part of his apprenticeship to monkhood, he was required to spend the next two years alone in a high mountain cave living the life of an ascetic and practicing those traditions that would enhance his enlightenment.

"Master," he asked his guru before departing, "on what should I meditate during the next two years of my retreat?"

His master replied, "You should meditate on any subject or symbol that will help you attain enlightenment. Enlightenment is an individual journey, and each must find his own way."

The novice climbed high into the rugged mountains with his meager possessions and sought out the cave he would call home for the next 24 months. Despite his preparation, the novice was unsure what to expect, and had no idea what subject of meditation would help him survive, let alone achieve enlightenment.

The master had doubts about the apprentice. He expected that he would not last two years in isolation. However, contrary to the master's expectations, his student did not return to the monastery until after the full term of his retreat. As he walked down the mountain slopes, the master took note of the young man's relaxed gait. As he neared, the master could detect a serenity of face and peacefulness of spirit that confirmed the success of the novice's sojourn in the hills.

"I see, my son," he said in greeting, "that you have been successful in your retreat. Tell me, on what did you spend your time meditating?"

The young disciple replied, "On a pizza supreme, Master."

"A pizza supreme!" exclaimed the master. "Why did you choose a pizza supreme?"

The young novice answered with his new air of enlightenment, "Because I wanted to be one with everything!"

STORY 99
MAKE USE OF WHAT LIFE OFFERS

Therapeutic Characteristics

Problems Addressed

- Wasted opportunities
- Failure to use available resources
- Missed opportunities for happiness
- Failure to contribute to the happiness of others

Resources Developed

- Discovering how to be aware of opportunities
- Using available resources
- Learning to develop the self
- Learning to contribute to the happiness of others

Outcomes Offered

- Don't let valuable opportunities slip by.
- Take responsibility for your own happiness.
- Contribute to the happiness of others.
- Make use of what life offers.

Once an abbot received a very auspicious incarnation. His birthright had placed him as head of a large monastery where he was surrounded by men of high learning and a vast library of the most valued texts. He was afforded every opportunity to ensure his growth in knowledge and wisdom. The abbot, however, failed to make use of what he had been given.

Many described him as lazy, whereas others labeled him idle. The abbot let opportunity pass by him and when he died, many agreed he had wasted his life.

A peer of the abbot's, who lived a far less ostentatious life in a humble cave on a mountain that overlooked the monastery, had spent much time praying for the abbot. The ascetic hoped the abbot would see the error of his ways and make the most of what life had given him.

When the abbot died, the ascetic left his cave to wander the countryside, crossing mountains and valleys until he came to a particularly rich, verdant valley. Here, cattle, sheep, horses, and donkeys munched lazily on the green grasses. A stream bubbled along a rocky course and, as the ascetic wandered its banks, he noticed a beautiful young maiden drawing water. He approached the woman and asked if she would marry him, but his request frightened her, and she dropped her pail and ran away. The ascetic sat on a rock beside the singing stream and waited.

In the meantime the girl ran home and told her mother about this old, unkempt man who had the audacity to ask her to marry him. Her mother wondered who this man might be. None of the men of the valley would ask her daughter's hand in marriage without first approaching her parents or following the appropriate rituals of courtship.

When the woman described the old man, her mother immediately recognized him as the famed ascetic who lived in a cave overlooking the monastery several valleys away. She said to the daughter, "He is a very famous and spiritual man. If he asks for your hand in marriage, he must have his reasons. Go back, talk with him, and find out more about what he wants and why."

The young woman returned to the stream-side rock where the ascetic sat meditating. "Forgive me," she said. "I did not know who you were. My mother has explained and asked that I come back and talk more about your proposal."

"Thank you," replied the ascetic. "I approached you out of deep concern for the abbot of the monastery several valleys away. He was given many opportunities to enrich and benefit the lives of others. Unfortunately, he ignored those opportunities and passed on without taking advantage of what might have been.

"I was concerned that he did not waste another opportunity. I had hoped that we would marry and provide the abbot with an appropriate reincarnation. Unfortunately, you returned too late. While I sat waiting for you to come back, the two asses in this paddock have just mated."

STORY 100
CELEBRATE LIFE

Therapeutic Characteristics

Problems Addressed

- Restrictions of principles and dogma
- Lack of enjoyment of life
- A tendency to treat life too seriously

Resources Developed

- Learning to relax and enjoy
- Being open to humor and happiness

Outcomes Offered

- Celebrate life.
- Have fun.
- Enjoy.
- Laugh.

When the Pope died he was welcomed to heaven as a very distinguished guest. To ensure an honored reception, St. Peter had assembled the archangels at the Pearly Gates and greeted the Pope personally. "We are so pleased to have you here, your Holiness," said the Saint. "You have devoted your life to God and humanity. We would like to give full recognition to your service and dedication. If there is anything we can do to make your stay comfortable and enjoyable, please let us know."

"Well," said the Pope, "All my life I have been interested in God's original commands to humankind. Over time, however, these have probably been distorted and misinterpreted. We don't always hear what was intended, and our own perceptions and priorities tend to distort what we did hear, so that the final message may be very different from the original.

"I have been fascinated with this phenomenon all my life. I have a passionate interest in how, or if, this has happened with the Holy Scriptures. How closely do the teachings of today's Church conform to what God originally taught us?"

"As you can imagine, we keep very detailed records up here," St. Peter responded. "All the archives are stored in the library, and I will personally ensure you have full access to whatever you want, whenever you want it."

The Pope could not have dreamed of any better way to spend his retirement. He buried his head in the archives, searching his way through dusty documents, so absorbed that he lost track of time. He read day and night. He found God's words of instruction and compared them with current dogma and doctrine. Truly, this was heaven.

After weeks, or it may have even been months or years, the whole of heaven was awakened by screams from the library. "Aargh, aargh, aargh," came the scream that shattered the stillness of the night, awakening saints, angels and archangels from their slumber. Led by St. Peter, the disturbed residents raced to the library to find the Pope was leaning over an ancient, musty-smelling manuscript. His papal finger stabbed at the page. "Aargh, aargh, aargh," he shouted.

"What is the matter?" asked the perplexed St. Peter.

The Pope's gaze was fixed on a single word, his finger stabbing at it repeatedly. "Aargh, aargh, aargh," he kept crying. "There is an R in it. God said, 'Celeb*R*ate.'"

EXERCISE

Jokes, humor, and funny experiences in our own lives often communicate a message that may be relevant to the outcome goal of a particular client. Using humor in therapy is not only a fun way of learning, but also a potent teaching tool. We can often use humor to express a message we might not wish to communicate directly.

Record your own humorous stories with outcome messages in your notebook, following the example I have offered of defining the Therapeutic Characteristics of each tale:

1. Note the types of Problems it addresses.
2. Record the sort of Resources, abilities, or means it seeks to develop for overcoming the problem.
3. Define the Outcomes it offers to listeners.

Be careful, for humor can be deprecating, so it is important to ensure that humorous stories facilitate a goal-oriented outcome without denigrating the listener.

PART THREE

Creating Your Own Metaphors

CHAPTER 14

How to Do It and How *Not* to Do It

Of the many things my father used to say to me as we hammered some wood together, constructed a handmade gift for Mother's Day, or dug in the vegetable patch was, "Don't do what I say, do what I do." Little did I realize then that he was teaching me about the difference between words and actions, or content and process. He was educating me not to slavishly follow his commands but to find my own ways of developing skills crucial for my eventual independence. In this last section I want to teach you *not* to do what I have done but show you how you can create your own effective metaphoric stories. So, first matters first.

DON'T DO WHAT I HAVE DONE

I have now recorded 100 of my favorite healing stories, with a final one following this section. I have done so mainly at the request of trainees who often ask, "Where do I find the themes or ideas around which to create metaphors?"

These stories, I hope, will serve as a trigger for creating and developing your own teaching tales. You may have found some of them to be salient, you may have felt some grab you with the poignancy of their message, you may have found some to be unenlightening, and you may have found some you would not retell. This is part of your own search for relevance in these tales, and it is an important part of learning what feels comfortable to you in this form of therapy. Be aware that your clients will have similar individual responses to healing stories.

As well as creating a personal association, some of the stories may have provided themes that are worth storing in the memory banks for future use. I encourage that you read them from the perspective of a distressed client as well as from your own associations. Think in terms of how your depressed, phobic, or substance-abusing client might hear them and respond, because the stories that are salient for your clients may not be the ones that appeal to you, and vice versa.

Now that you have read these stories, I want to say one thing very clearly: Do not read or repeat them verbatim. I don't—and would encourage that you don't. This caveat is based on the need to find your own "voice" for telling stories.

In communicating what *not* to do in using metaphor therapy, let me say there are a number of surefire steps you can take to ensure your successful failure.

Step 1. Use these healing stories exactly as you have read them.

When we tell metaphors in therapy we do so as part of the conversation or communication that takes place in a therapeutic relationship. In other words, therapeutic stories are part of a context in which it is more helpful to be interested in the process and function of the communication than in a verbatim repetition of a particular story.

I remember once hearing a computer expert say that most people buy their computers in the wrong order. "They buy the hardware first," he said, "purchase the latest whiz-bang software, and then try to figure out how to use it." He claimed that people should first ask what purpose or goal a computer would serve and then search for the software that fulfills that function. Only then should they select the hardware that would support it.

Using metaphors effectively follows a similar process. First, conduct an appropriate goal assessment with the client and consider whether metaphors may be appropriate and relevant for reaching that goal—or whether some other therapeutic approach may be more effective. Then search for the resources necessary to reach that goal. Finally, find the tale that corresponds with the problems that need to be addressed, the resources necessary to reach that goal, and an ethical, appropriate outcome. I refer to this as the PRO (Problem, Resources, and Outcome)-approach and discuss it in more detail in the next chapter.

Repeating these stories as you have read them here does not follow this process; consequently, they are unlikely to be specific, client-centered, goal-focused, or individually relevant for your listener.

Step 2. Use metaphor therapy with every client, for every problem.

I believe it was Maslow who said, "If you give a person a hammer, they will see every problem as a nail." Having a story, no matter how good, insightful, or brilliant that story may be, does not mean that it will be effective for every client. If the goal is to unite two pieces of wood, one needs to consider the most effective way of achieving that goal. Can they be glued? Do they need to be jointed? Is it possible to screw them together? Will stapling do the job? Would they be better nailed?

Although stories have a universal appeal and have long formed a basis for human interactions, metaphor therapy is not for everyone. Some clients may see it is condescending or evasive. Because metaphor therapy is an indirect approach to treatment, it may not be appropriate for clients who prefer, and respond to, more direct approaches. You can avoid therapeutic failures by developing a clear, goal-oriented assessment, an appropriate selection of therapeutic interventions, and the awareness that this one tool may not be sufficient to resolve every problem.

Step 3. Use these stories like a medical prescription.

Think depression, conclude Prozac. Think abuse, conclude analysis of repressed memories. Think low self-confidence, conclude an ego-strengthening hypnotic script. Think empowerment, conclude story number 10. Such prescriptive thinking can be inappropriate and even dangerous, for it does not allow the therapist to acknowledge or adapt to the client's individual needs and resources.

If you are going to work effectively with metaphors, do not use them like a medical prescription or hypnotic script, but rather, consider the PRO-approach as a process for focusing on the outcome rather than the pathology and its prescriptive treatment.

Step 4. Expect that a single story will fix a lifetime of trauma.

Sometimes a single, well-crafted story will change a lifetime of traumatic problems or ensure a client will reach a long-desired, but as yet unachieved, goal. In Story 91, "Adjusting To Circumstances," I spoke of a real-life client I chose to call Clinton. The metaphor that I told him in that story served as a solitary intervention that opened the opportunity for him to create some simple changes in his life, enabling him to arrive home feeling more relaxed and in a different mental mode. This, in turn, ensured that he reached his therapeutic goal of better family relationships.

It does not always work that way. In Chapter 1 under "The Power of Stories," I wrote about Phillipa, who was one of the most phobic people that I have ever encountered. The story that she and I created collaboratively (Story 11, "Soaring to New Heights") led to her painting a series of pictures that illustrated that metaphor. It exposed a creative talent and allowed us the opportunity to develop that talent in a way that indirectly assisted in overcoming her phobia.

Yet, metaphor therapy was not the only therapeutic intervention. Phillipa and I shared many metaphors in the course of her therapy. However, she also learned self-hypnosis, completed a program of *invivo* desensitization, and practiced strategies for managing her feelings of depression. In other words, the metaphors were an adjunctive part of a total therapeutic plan that included several other interventions.

The story of the little octopus wrought no miracle in and of itself. It provided no magic—perhaps apart from what the client may have perceived in it. The story, however, offered an element of hope and a recognition that the means were there for her to change. It was a facilitative part in the total therapeutic program.

Step 5. Use these stories as if they are fixed and immutable.

Traditionally, stories are oral and, as such, are mutable, interactive, and adaptable. In therapy, I view the metaphor as an idea or theme around which the tale may adjust, adapt, or be modified to match the client's experience and desired results. Teaching metaphors in workshops also follows the oral tradition in that trainees do not leave with a verbatim account of a particular story, but instead learn metaphor ideas and a replicable process for creating their own healing stories.

Putting them in print changes that tradition, giving them a sense of being fixed and biblically immutable. If you read this book five years from now, the stories will be exactly the same, but, if I use one of these story themes five years from now, it will be told very differently.

Step 6. Believe that 101 Healing Stories *contains the ultimate or the best metaphoric tales.*

The 101 stories in this volume just happen to be some of my favorites at the time of writing. I do not know how many thousands of stories I have heard or read throughout my life. I do not think I would want to count the many thousands of experiences I've had or incidents I have observed that also have metaphoric significance. Sometimes I see a client who returns for therapy after several years and reminds me of a story I told them previously. I had forgotten that I used that story at that time. It may have been one that slipped out of my repertoire, as new stories and new experiences become part of my evolving personal and professional life.

Story 41, "Are You Better Now Than You Used To Be?" is drawn from a personal experience of mine and describes a little of how we change and adapt over time. As our experiences—both as people and therapists—change, so what we have to offer our clients also changes. The nature of all stories is as fluid and flexible as life itself.

So, unless you want to be a metaphoric failure, do not take the tales that you have read here and use them in a verbatim style, like reciting a hypnotic script. How then, you may ask, can I use them most effectively? In the following section, I go through, step-by-step, the processes I employed in building some the stories in this book and offer guidelines for the creative development for your own stories.

HOW TO CREATE HEALING STORIES

There is an old proverb that says, "Give a person a fish and he or she will feed for the day. Teach that person to fish and he or she can eat for a lifetime." I have given you a metaphoric fish or two—in fact 101. Even that supply is exhaustible, and the diet may not best suit your needs, or the needs of those with whom you wish to share the stories. However, showing you the processes that I went through to obtain the catch I have presented here may help you develop the skills you want to go on providing yourself with metaphor stories.

To do this I will revisit a number of stories from Part 2 and illustrate where I found the source of the story, how I developed the idea into a metaphor, and the processes by which I constructed the teaching tale. This demonstrates how to create metaphors from a variety of sources such as an idea you encounter, imagination, client cases, evidence-based literature, observations, and everyday life experiences. In the next chapter I outline the PRO-approach for constructing, administering, and following up metaphor interventions. The function is to show how you can create and use your own effective metaphors.

I. Develop metaphors from an idea.

You can find ideas for metaphors in many sources. The idea for "Looking Up" (Chapter 6, Story 22) came from a small four-liner I read in Anthony de Mello's *The Song of the Bird* (1988).

Said a Zen monk,
"When my house burnt down

I got an unobstructed view
Of the moon at night!"

What a delightful little tale! What a wonderful basis upon which to develop a metaphor about reframing experiences! It has a forceful message that illustrates there are other outcome possibilities beyond those that you would usually expect. It teaches that we can view a given circumstance from different perspectives. It clearly shows the possibility for adopting a positive mental attitude in a situation of loss. It communicates that grief, sadness, or anger are not our only emotional choices for dealing with loss; nonetheless, the tale—as it stands—has several deficits that limit its potential as a healing story.

First, the outcome is magical and mystical in that there are no apparent causal links between the problem of the burned-down house and the attitude that the monk can now view the sky at night. It does not follow the usual patterns of cause and effect: that a significant loss will result in some sort of negative or unpleasant emotional response.

Second, it is a story with a clear *beginning* (the monk's house burned down), and it also has a good *ending* that may be salient for clients in therapy. What it lacks is a *middle*—it gives no indication of how the monk arrived at his conclusion, or what process of thinking brought him to that end. Consequently, there is no replicable pattern or model for clients to follow.

Third, the story implies that to reach such a conclusion you need to have attained the enlightened status of a Zen master. This puts the outcome outside the realm of mere mortals such as your client who may be a truck driver, a housekeeper, student, shop-assistant, or business manager.

Fourth, it has an unreality by which listeners could easily discount the story as not applicable to them. What average person would think like the Zen monk? Who would find happiness in losing everything?

Fifth, the outcome of the story is very specific and does not communicate any process of generalization. It talks about a monk's reaction to the particular loss of a house and, as it stands, is limited in its applicability to other situations of loss.

My version of the story (as retold in Story 22), has sought to overcome these deficits and to weave the idea into a metaphor that provides more recognition of the problem, the responses a person may experience in similar circumstances, and the processes for adopting a more positive perspective. It seeks to demystify the original story by describing typical reactions to such situations and the types of skills the listener can replicate. "Looking Up" also gives the story a middle, so that the client has a map to successfully reach the end of the journey. Finally, the version in Story 22 describes a variety of emotions that we normal human beings (who are not enlightened Zen masters) are likely to experience if faced with a similar situation of loss. It strives to engage listeners in a way that enables them to identify with the problem, processes, and outcome of the story.

In adapting the Zen monk tale, I wanted to focus not on *content* (a burned-down house) but on *process*. "Looking Up" brings into the tale the experiences, feelings, emotional conflicts, and struggles that a person may go through when suffering a significant loss. By retaining the house as an object of metaphoric loss, but becoming more descriptive of the processes associated with loss, the metaphor may be equally as relevant for someone who has lost a house, a job, or a loved one. The tale could be made more personally relevant by the therapist listening to the grief experiences of the individual client and weaving those struggles into the metaphor.

To make the original story effective as a teaching tale the therapist needed to address its biggest

EXERCISE 14.1   DEVELOPING METAPHORS FROM AN IDEA:

- Be constantly mindful of possible metaphor ideas.
- Look for what metaphoric ideas you may encounter in books, client comments, social conversations, jokes, and so on.
- Note the ideas. Keep a record of them and build up a store of metaphoric messages that you can draw on when appropriate.
- Develop the problem, challenge, or crisis that needs to be resolved in a way that enables the client to identify with the process.
- Develop the resources that the client may need to achieve his or her outcome.
- Develop appropriate possible outcomes.

deficit: It needs a how-to-do-it process that would enable listeners to develop skills for managing their feelings, shaping their thinking, and reframing their attitudes. It has only one outcome, but one of the most important goals of therapy is to open up possibilities and allow a client to see that there are different ways of thinking, feeling, and responding in their current repertoire. In "Looking Up," the monk, as the main character, was given possibilities, thus drawing the client's attention to the possible options and choices that may be helpful for them at that time and in those circumstances.

2. Develop metaphors from imagination.

I have often heard trainees complain that they lack the imagination or creativity for developing metaphoric stories. The good news is that one does not need the creative genius of an imaginative novelist to be able to tell a therapeutic tale. Sources of most therapeutic stories can be found in our own experiences, our observations of other people, our client cases, and day-to-day events. Weaving these into creative tales follows a step-by-step, developmental process as I shall illustrate with "Soaring To New Heights" (Chapter 4, Story 11).

This metaphor evolved collaboratively with Phillipa whose case I mentioned in Chapter 1. To recap, Phillipa had a decades-old, debilitating phobia that resulted in her spending hours and hours each day standing on the front lawn of her home. She could not bear to be alone inside the house and was too fearful to go outside of the yard.

Initially, she was too scared to talk to me, hanging her head forward so that her hair fell like a veil and cloaked her face. There was no point asking her questions, for they elicited little response and seemed to make her even more fearful. Stories therefore seemed a better means for communicating and "Soaring To New Heights," the tale of a little octopus, was the metaphor that developed.

Selecting and Developing the Story's Character

I selected an animal story after her husband described Phillipa as a gentle person who would not stand on an ant or dust away cobwebs because they were the homes of living creatures. I theorized that using an animal character was likely to engage her attention, involve her interest, and, hopefully, attain some identification in the therapeutic process.

Choosing a little octopus as the animal was the product of several factors. First, as her concern was for small animals, making the story's character small was a way of engaging the client in the metaphor. Second, people might have described Phillipa as "clingy." She hung on to her husband for her security, and the front lawn was her only safe territory. When I began to contemplate what sort of small animal would replicate these characteristics, an octopus filled the role. With eight tentacles it could be very clingy.

Third, by presenting it as a *little* octopus, it seemed not only small, but also weak and helpless. This paralleled both the client and the client's problem, for Phillipa hung her head low, made herself look small, and presented as a helpless individual, unable to change her unhappy circumstances.

Finally, an animal with eight tentacles afforded an opportunity not just to match the client and problem, but also to match the means of resolution and the outcome. With eight tentacles, there is a variety of choices about how it could let go of that to which it clung. It could do it suddenly and completely, or gradually and carefully, by peeling one tentacle off at a time.

Developing the Plot of the Metaphor

The little octopus began life in warm and comfortable waters, but she had always been a little clingy (hopefully matching the client). As she grew and ventured further afield, the waters grew darker and deeper (and made her feel out of her depth). The anchor (like the lawn for Phillipa) was the only small space in a big universe where the little octopus felt safe, but even that had its ambivalence. She was afraid to hang on and afraid to let go (replicating Phillipa's fear).

The first fish to swim by represented her physician. The little octopus called out for help. The fish said it could not help, but it recommended a bigger fish that could (the referral to a clinical psychologist). That fish gave her some directives and accompanied her on her journey until she felt comfortable and confident enough to continue the progress herself.

Reaching an Outcome

The outcome did not finish with the little octopus swimming on independently, but had her crawl up onto the beach and then climb the cliffs beyond, where she spread her tentacles like an eagle, lifted on the air, and began to soar to new heights.

In many ways the metaphor's outcome offered a map that Phillipa followed. She had migrated from England as a child and had long wished to return to her roots, but this seemed impossible for somebody who was too frightened to venture beyond her front lawn. In time, she experimented by taking short trips and was finally able to return to England.

During therapy she sketched our metaphor into a series of color pictures. The sketches showed talent, and, in therapy, she was encouraged to take art lessons. Later, her teacher organized a one-person exhibition of her work, to which I was invited. She has since staged other exhibitions, painting fable-like works that include mainly animal characters and little creatures.

Phillipa's story, like that of the little octopus, did not stop there. She has soared on to even greater heights. She began to create teddy bears that have become international collectors' pieces due to their quality and character. She has formed a group of caring people who supply teddy bears to children's hospitals and police cars, so they are available as a source of comfort to children in distress. Her work has been recognized in the press and on television. I think that it is appropriate that Phillipa named her first teddy bear Peregrine, after a bird that can soar to unbelievable heights.

HOW TO, HOW NOT TO

EXERCISE 14.2   DEVELOPING METAPHORS FROM IMAGINATION:

Select a current client for whom metaphor therapy would be appropriate.

- Take time to think about creating the metaphor, maybe even jotting your thoughts down on paper.
- Think about what sort of character is likely to match the characteristics, qualities, and resources of your client. What sort of character is likely to experience a similar problem and go through similar processes to achieve a similar outcome as desired by your client?
- In developing the storyline or plot, take into account how you can:
    - Describe the crisis or challenge.
    - Develop the necessary resources.
    - Provide an appropriate resolution.
    - Facilitate the relevant processes of learning and discovery.
- Determine a viable and realistic goal for the character to achieve in a way that would match the client's desired outcome.
- Write out these key elements to the story.
- Tell the story to your client, watching carefully for the search phenomena and processes that the client uses during the telling.

3. Develop metaphors from client cases and a basis of evidence.

The bottom line to all therapy is that it needs to be helpful and not harmful. To be certain we provide the most effective and efficient assistance to our clients, we need to ensure that there is a good basis of evidence to support the interventions that we use with a given client. Researchers have spent a considerable amount of time and energy to clarify the question of what treatments work and what treatments do not (e.g., Nathan & Gorman, 1998).

What applies to therapy in general also applies to metaphor therapy. Metaphors need to be grounded in effective strategies for clients to develop appropriate resources that will lead to goal attainment. Metaphors also need to be realistic about what the client is capable of doing as well as realistic about the attainability of the outcome. There is no point in offering a metaphor that does not have a reality base, does not present pragmatic means for achieving the desired end, and does not offer an attainable outcome. The therapist requires the same ethical basis in using metaphors as in using any other therapy, and one aspect of that is a sound and deep understanding of the condition being treated. Only on the basis of such an understanding can a therapist offer an appropriate metaphor.

For example, when using metaphors with a depressed client, the therapist should understand the symptoms that need modification and the processes by which these changes are best facilitated. Metaphor therapy, as any other treatment for depression, needs to assess the individual client to determine whether to treat feelings of hopelessness and helplessness, improve poor interpersonal skills, increase low levels of frustration tolerance, or deal with feelings of worthlessness and guilt. Do the interventions need to address the improvement of sleep patterns, the enhancement of concentration, or the restoration of lost energy? Do they need to help modify thoughts about death and suicide or distorted cognitive patterns?

Much has been written about the cognitive distortions of depressed people (Beck, 1967, 1972, 1976; Beck, Rush, Shaw & Emery, 1979; Beck, Brown, Berchick, Stewart, & Steer, 1990), their learned patterns of helplessness (Seligman, 1989, 1990, 1993, 1995), and their attributional styles (Yapko, 1985, 1988, 1992, 1997, 1999). A sound knowledge of these facts and a sound understanding of the relevant principles of treatment are crucial for effective metaphor interventions with a depressed client.

"Good Follows Bad" (Story 24 in Chapter 6) is an example of where a client's story and the literature on attributional styles combine to allow a listener with similar problems to identify with the metaphor, appreciate the understanding of the therapist, and begin to find strategies for change. This particular story focuses on the style of attribution often observed in people with depression and may thus be appropriate for someone with similar symptoms, but not necessarily for a client with other features of depression. This is why a goal-oriented assessment and knowledge of evidence-based therapies are important to any treatment, including metaphor therapy.

Attributional style refers to what attributes we give to events, or how we explain the things that happen in our lives. This, in turn, affects the way we feel and how we act on the basis of those feelings. The outcome of our actions may then validate the attributions we hold.

Creating a Metaphor to Match the Client's Attributional Style (the Problem addressed)

In "Good Follows Bad," Maria, the client on whose story the metaphor was constructed, initially expressed a statement that typified a common depressive attribution. She said, "whenever something good happens, something bad always follows." The first attribution a therapist will note in this statement is that *things happen*. They are outside of the client's area of control and, because of this perception, she feels powerless. That powerlessness fuels a sense of helplessness—another common symptom and cause of depression.

Always is the clue to the second attribution. Bad events *always* follow. They are permanent, unchangeable, and constant. With this immutability, there is no hope or anticipation of improvement.

Her third style of attribution is global: *Whenever* something happens, something else always follows. It covers every possibility, allows for no exceptions, is inevitable, and denies hope of any possible change. Again, we see it contributing to one of the major characteristics of depression: hopelessness.

Tracing the Development of the Attributions in Metaphor

"Good Follows Bad" succinctly traces how such attributional styles develop over a series of unfortunate events. In the first one, Maria's husband leaves. Her response is specific: He is a bastard, and life, at times, is unfair. When the second situation occurs and her male boss fires her, her attitudes become more generalized: Men are bastards and life is not treating her fairly. By the time we get to the third event and her new lover has left, her response becomes global and all inclusive: *All* men are bastards and life *never* gives her a fair go. The global attribution has become stable as well. It has taken on the quality of circumstances having been and always being that way.

Presenting Strategies for Change (the Resources developed)

Here the metaphor needs to facilitate the discovery and use of those processes and strategies that contribute to healthier and more constructive patterns of thought. Under the heading "Breaking Your Patterns of Attribution," Yapko (1997) lists three such strategies: correcting the self, judging each situation on its own merits, and being more responsive to external, rather than internal, stimuli.

In the metaphor, "Good Follows Bad," Maria modeled self-correction by examining her own attributions with the question of whether there are exceptions to her "rule" that *all* men are bastards. She began to judge situations on their own merits when she started to explore *each* man and *each* life event for its individual characteristics.

Maria also shifted her inwardly focused depressive thoughts to looking at, and thinking about, the pleasurable experiences in the world around her—a summer's swim, a blossoming springtime bulb, or a newborn bird descending into her garden. She learned methods to shift her focus from depressive ruminations to the joyful, comforting, and enriching experiences that can exist in interaction with the natural environment. (For more strategies on facilitating this inner to outer focus in depression, see Burns, 1998, 1999.)

Attaining the Therapeutic Goal (Outcomes Offered)

Having provided strategies that will help the client reach his or her goal, the metaphor's next step is to attain the goal. "Good Follows Bad" shows that a shift in attributional style is possible, then proceeds to have Maria model those attributions that are less likely to lead to a state of depression. At the follow-up session she asked, "Do you know what I have discovered?" The *I* indicates a shift to an internal locus of control, contrasting with the powerlessness she felt at the beginning of the story.

EXERCISE 14.3   DEVELOPING METAPHORS FROM A BASIS OF EVIDENCE:

- Note the condition of your client and particularly those specific symptoms, characteristics, or features that he or she displays.
- Study the evidence-based literature for that condition, examining in particular the therapeutic interventions that work.
- Examine which of those particular interventions are most likely to help your client reach his or her therapeutic goal.
- Structure a metaphor around the utilization of those effective interventions in a way that will make them relevant to year client.
- Bear in mind:
  - The character should match the challenge and model the outcome.
  - Consider the particular aspects of the problem that to need to be addressed.
  - Elaborate the resources necessary for the client to reach his or her outcome.
  - Look at the evidenced-based interventions that will lead to new learning and discovery.
  - Offer a valid and obtainable client–desired outcome.

When she went on to say *if* something happens, she was thinking of things more specifically and less globally. It is not now *whenever* they happen, but *if* they happen, acknowledging that life events are not permanent or invariably predictable. In saying they *may* happen, Maria allowed the possibility that they *may not*. "That's life," she said, now expressing an unstable attribution and modeling an attitude of acceptance.

Her final comment, "It really depends how you see it," summated a healthy style of thinking that is likely to ensure her current and future well-being.

Just telling a client what research shows to be effective is not necessarily helpful. The language of research articles, or even the style of communication we use with colleagues may not be the language a client understands. Wrapping the sound, evidence-based principles proven effective in our discipline in a story of human experience can communicate better the message, and means, of change.

4. Develop metaphors from life experiences.

Perhaps the best source of healing stories is life itself. All story ideas, whether they come from different traditions, case histories, research data, or imagination, are based in life. Life itself is a metaphor, and life's experiences offer a vast pool of resources for developing new metaphors.

For example, you may meet a client who is in constant and severe pain. Although you may not have suffered the same illness or have been involved in the same motor vehicle accident, you do know something about the feeling of pain and have, to some degree, experienced those sensations. No one goes through life without pain, and so we learn to know the things that exacerbate it and the things that ease it. We learn something about our mental attitude toward pain and the effect that attitude has on the sensations of pain. The *content* of our experiences may be very different but the *process* of that experience can be very similar.

If we look at the processes, there are many aspects of everyday life experience that can provide sources for metaphors. We may learn from our parents, such as in "My Dad" (Story 21) and "Topping Up Your Reserves" (Story 84). We can see metaphoric messages by observing children as they shape their beliefs about life ("Forming and Changing Beliefs," Story 90) or engage in journeys of discovery ("A Journey of Unexpected Learning," Story 18). We can learn from challenging or difficult circumstances, such as in "Empowering Joe" (Story 10). Experiences of overcoming difficulties in a relationship, like "Going With the Flow" (Story 86) or "Recognizing and Using Absurdity" (Story 34) may hold ideas that are helpful to others encountering interpersonal difficulties.

Traveling not only permits us to *be* in a different context but also to *see* things differently. Examples of using these experiences as a basis for metaphor development can be found in Story 42, "Use What You Have," Story 45, "Problems May Open New Options," Story 46, "Finding Treasures in Tragedy," Story 50, "Trusting Your Own Abilities," and Story 93, "Give and Take." Onerous chores ("Adjusting Your Sails," Story 25), the challenge of a large task ("Writing a Book," Story 56), or the poignant messages discovered while walking through the neighborhood (Story 21, "Life Is Not What It Should Be") are all part of those life experiences from which a story can emerge.

Consider the story that emerged from taking a group of boys hiking in the backcountry (Story 60, The Secrets of Success). It has a tinge of naughtiness, playfulness, and humor, yet woven into it are practical directives about managing situations of rivalry and competition, as well as striving toward a goal.

EXERCISE 14.4   DEVELOPING METAPHORS FROM YOUR OWN LIFE EXPERIENCES:

- Be mindful of your client's desired goal.
- Seek an experience that describes the attainment of that outcome. Ask yourself, "When did I obtain a similar goal?"
- Seek to develop the resources, learning, and discoveries necessary for the goal attainment. Ask yourself, "What abilities or means did I need to reach that goal?"
- Define a metaphoric problem. Ask yourself, "What experience did I encounter that encapsulated or paralleled the key characteristic and processes of the problem my client faces?"
- Tell the story beginning with the problem and working through the resources, learning, and discoveries to the outcome.
- Tell the story in your own words because it is based on your own experience, but you should relate the story in a way that is highly relevant to the experience and needs of the client.
- Tell it using the techniques of storytelling described in Chapter 2.

Creating a Metaphor to Parallel the Client's Challenges (the Problem)

The client to whom I originally told "The Secrets of Success" felt that he was not doing as well as some of his peers. He was struggling with competitiveness in the workplace and wanted to improve his performance, but he felt helpless to do so. Listening to him brought to mind the delight I saw in my grandson's attainment of a goal that seemed to epitomize the joy of achievement. The *content* of the story was far removed from my client's concern, but the *process* of reaching the outcome was something with which my client could relate in a way that was both meaningful and humorous.

The story described the rivalry and competition that existed between Daniel and Thomas—part fiction and part fact. Through the story the issues of rivalry fade and what becomes more important is achieving your personal best. In a tale that may apply to work, sports, or study, the content of a metaphoric challenge is not as important as the process through which the protagonist meets the challenge. Although the content may be unrelated, the metaphor needs to describe similar processes that clients can use to face and overcome their unique challenges while negotiating the various obstacles along the way.

Using and Developing Strategies for Success (the Resources)

The story of Daniel and Thomas sought to develop strategies that may be helpful and effective for the listener. First, from the goal-oriented assessment, I discovered that having a mentor was one factor that previously helped this client along his journey to success. As a result, the story introduced a mentor (Grandpa) and a trainee (Thomas) delivering a message that it is possible to learn from those who have trod the path before you.

The story also talked about strengths and abilities, about recognizing weaknesses, and about

EXERCISE 14.5 DEVELOPING METAPHORS FROM OBSERVATION OF OTHERS' EXPERIENCES:

- Identify the goal or desired outcome. Keep it as the central focus of attention in developing the metaphor.
- Ask yourself when you had observed or heard someone relating a story about achieving a similar goal. Look for how well the message or outcome of that story relates to your client's objective.
- Though you may be relating the story in the third person, make it yours. Tell it in your words but in a way that is specifically relevant to your client's wants and needs.
- Look at what means were or could be used to reach the goal. What does the client have available, or what does he or she need to develop, to help him or her along the journey?
- How can the original challenge or problem faced by the character in the story be adapted to match the experiences of the client?
- Remember you are not just relating a story as you heard it but purposefully adapting it to a specific therapeutic purpose.

learning to capitalize on one's strengths. This opens up choices about how to develop personal strengths.

Third, the metaphor described what to do once we have decided where to place our efforts. We cannot obtain a goal without putting in some effort to make it happen. Thus, the story delivered a message of training and application to reach one's goal.

Finally, it advocated the necessity of shifting the focus from competing against others to developing our own ability. The message is one of self-improvement and struggle to attain one's personal best.

Achieving Your Personal Best (the Outcome)

To match the outcome desired by the client to whom I told this tale, Thomas attained his goal by using both the resources he had available and those he needed to enhance. He learned from his mentor, acknowledged what he was not so good at, developed what he could do well, applied himself to training, and strove for his personal best. His success was a sweet and well-deserved victory.

GUIDELINES FOR USING PERSONAL LIFE STORIES

Workshop participants at times inquire whether self-disclosure in storytelling a good thing. The question itself raises some assumptions about what we mean by the term *self-disclosure*. Self-disclosure is a concept that comes from some early approaches to therapy, in which the client is encouraged to "self disclose" whereas the therapist reveals nothing of him or herself. The therapist variable is seen as an interference in the therapeutic process of free association and, consequently, the therapist remains an omniscient nonentity in the background. Such therapeutic roles reflect an inequality in the relationship between therapist and client.

Other schools of thought consider an effective, interactive, and equal relationship to be a significant consideration in terms of therapeutic outcome, and that communicating about shared personal experiences is one of the ways we have of relating meaningfully. This is evidenced in Chelf, Deschler, Hillman, and Durazo-Arvizu's study (2000) of cancer patients that showed that 85% of patients who attended a therapeutic storytelling workshop reported gaining hope from hearing the personal life experiences of others who had faced and coped with the same illness.

Using stories from personal life experiences is not a question of self-disclosure when those stories are designed to meet the needs of the client and move toward the client's designed outcome. In other words, the purpose and function of telling a therapeutic tale is to facilitate the client's goal attainment rather than disclose material about the therapist. If something from the therapist's life experience is relevant to the outcome process, it can be woven into a metaphor in much the same way as a client case, a cultural story, or evidence-based data about a certain condition.

Stories of personal life experiences, as with all therapeutic tales, become metaphoric when they meet certain conditions or guidelines to facilitate an effective, interactive therapeutic relationship in which the client's story, rather than the therapist's, is the core objective. Throughout our history, teaching stories has always been about sharing of experiences. Similarly, metaphors are about communicating from a basis of human experience. Thus, they are not an act of disclosure so much as a process of sharing.

To ensure the effectiveness of using personal life experiences as therapeutic teaching tales, it may help you to keep several guidelines in mind.

- **Be mindful of the story's purpose.** Its function is not to disclose something about the therapist but rather to create a beneficial learning experience for the client that will facilitate acquisition of the necessary skills or processes to overcome a current challenge and better cope with similar situations in the future.

- **Remember for whom the story is intended.** The metaphor should be specifically designed for the client and, therefore, should not be told as a casually related account of the therapist's personal memories, nor as a game of one-upmanship about who has the worst symptoms, nor as one may flippantly tell a story at a dinner party. It is *not* your story that is relevant but how clients will hear it, adopt it, and employ it for themselves.

- **Keep the goal of the story in mind.** The purpose of the story is to provide clients with meaningful therapeutic experiences that will contribute to their management and enjoyment of life. A story from your own experience, or indeed any source, works best if it closely matches the client's issues and desired outcome.

It may be that you have experienced an appropriate outcome-oriented metaphor. Nevertheless, making the story about you may distract from its message, or it may not be relevant to speak of your own foibles, grief, or pain. In such situations, shifting personal stories from the first to third person can be a good solution. That way therapists can distance themselves from the story yet still communicate the metaphoric message of that experience.

- **Ensure the story is relevant to the context.** Stories of personal experience are more likely to be accepted when they are part of the context of conversation. If a client is discussing his or her children, it may be contextually appropriate to tell a childhood tale based on your own experiences. If a client is talking about hobbies, sporting, or recreational interests, it may be relevant to offer a metaphor originating from a recreational activity of your own.

■   **Use props if they help.** I have a number of objects in my consulting room: a rug from Nepal, a carved wooden shaman's totem from Sarawak, as well as various framed photographs of my childhood family, triumphant college swimming team, and travels—behind each are several potential therapeutic tales. If a client inquires about these, it provides the opportunity to relate a relevant metaphor in response to the client's question rather than initiating the metaphor myself. The rug, for example, allows me to talk about meeting a challenge, facing the unexpected, climbing to new heights, overcoming a problem, making new self-discoveries, and attaining a long-held goal. An old black and white family photograph, spanning three generations, opens the opportunity to discuss relationships, growth, change, and personal development.

■   **Follow the PRO–approach (which will be discussed more fully in the next chapter).** Tell the story in a way that addresses the issues and problems relevant to the client, accesses the types of resources appropriate for his or her resolution, and provides a satisfactory outcome or outcomes.

■   **Observe the client's responses carefully.** Assess the relevance of the story by observing how well it holds the client's attention. Note whether there are signs of disinterest or distraction that may suggest the story is not salient or interesting enough for that person.

■   **Discontinue using personal metaphors (or any others) if they are not helpful.** As I have mentioned previously, metaphor therapy may not be for everyone and it is not the only effective therapeutic intervention. If your stories do not hold the client's attention or if they do not seem to be relevant, there may be two potential problems. First, the nature of personal, life-experience stories may not fit comfortably for the client. In this case, it is helpful to examine whether case histories or evidence-based stories might be a more beneficial approach to using metaphors. Second, the indirect approach of metaphors may not be relevant for that particular client or problem, in which case it is better to select a different therapeutic intervention. Part of the art and science of any effective therapy is matching the intervention to the individual client, the particular problem, and the desired outcome.

HOW TO, HOW NOT TO

CHAPTER 15

Using the PRO-Approach to Create Your Own Healing Stories

While the last chapter demonstrated how metaphors can be constructed from different sources, this one outlines a process for creating your own metaphors. Throughout the book, I have offered a common format for structuring and presenting the metaphor that I call the PRO-approach. This approach was summated under the heading Therapeutic Characteristics for each of the stories presented in Part 2 and so should be familiar by now. PRO is the acronym for Problems, Resources, and Outcomes.

STRUCTURING A PRO-APPROACH

The PRO-approach refers to the sequence in which the story is usually presented to the client. First, the story describes the client-matched Problem. Second, it portrays how the character accesses appropriate Resources for resolving the Problem, and, third, the story presents a successful Outcome. In planning the structure of the metaphor, however, it is helpful to use the reverse process. That is, define the outcome first. This approach helps keep a clear focus on the therapeutic goal and the direction of the story.

Often I have observed that trainees in the early stages of learning metaphor therapy identify the client's problem very clearly and relate a story that matches the problem very well. It may communicate a deep level of understanding and awareness by the therapist, but it does not facilitate movement beyond the problem, or provide the means for change. If the therapist does not know where to go and stops at a clear, even if empathic, understanding of the problem, the mechanisms are not there for the client to learn how to move forward. For this reason I recommend that you first have a clear understanding of the outcome and where your story is going to lead you and your client.

Once you have defined the outcome, it is easier to explore what resources, abilities, or means the client (and metaphor character) needs to reach the desired outcome, and to consider what problem the metaphor needs to move away from. In the remaining part of this chapter, I use this approach to draw together the threads of effective communication through metaphor that have been presented throughout the book.

STEPS FOR ADMINISTERING THERAPEUTIC METAPHORS

Step 1. Focus on an Outcome-Oriented Assessment

The primary function of a therapeutic metaphor is to lead or guide a person along a path to a desired destination. By keeping the destination or goal clearly in mind, a person is less likely to be sidetracked into the issues of the problem or the seemingly insoluble perception of it that the client may have. If there is one golden rule for developing and using metaphors in therapy, I would say it is this: *Be clear about the objective and keep the story moving toward it.* To do so means that the therapist needs a clear and accurate assessment of what clients want to gain from treatment. The following steps may be helpful for obtaining this.

Take an Outcome-Oriented Approach

The focus of this book, and the collection of metaphors contained herein, is on outcome. The metaphoric ideas offered are designed to help a client move toward, and attain, his or her specific therapeutic goal. These are not stories about analyzing or understanding the past so much as tales designed to teach the skills and means for healthier functioning in the present and future.

Therapists adopting this approach will, in their assessment and therapy, be looking toward the future. Their approach will be pragmatic, aimed at providing the means or resources the client requires in the present to reach that goal. Like when we drive an automobile, we need to look where we are going in therapy. If we keep our attention on the road ahead, it is much easier to follow the road that will lead to our destination, whereas if we keep looking behind us, it is easy to veer off course. In assuming a goal-oriented approach, we adopt a perspective that is most likely to help our clients move ahead in the most efficient and effective manner.

Make an Outcome-Focused Assumption

In listening to what clients say, I make an assumption. I readily acknowledge that my listening is biased, and I consciously choose to have it that way because I do not always accept that what my clients say is what they desire. Therefore, one of the first questions I ask clients is what they want to achieve in the time that we spend together. With such a question, I invite clients to start looking immediately toward the goals or outcomes that they desire.

If a client replies by saying "I am depressed," I assume that what he or she is really saying is, "Tell me about feeling happier." If a person says, "I feel anxious," I assume that he or she is really saying, "Teach me about relaxation," "Show me ways to feel calmer," or "Talk to me about tranquility." If a couple says, "We are having relationship difficulties," I assume that they want to know about effective relationships or ways of relating more enjoyably and more comfortably.

CREATING STORIES

Examine the Client-Expressed Goal

An initial client-expressed goal may not clearly define what the client is seeking. A client may say, "I want to know why I am feeling this way," but is this his or her therapeutic objective? For a long time our profession has been teaching people that they need to understand why something has happened to be able to change it. The image tends to be perpetrated by media and movies that portray therapy as a process of analysis, or seeking to understand the reasons behind our behavior and emotions.

If I stop to explore this statement with a question like, "Is it more important for you to understand why you are feeling this way, or is it more important for you to develop some means and skills to be able to feel better?", the response usually is something like, "It would be nice to know why, but, obviously, what I want is to feel better."

Shift the Negative to the Positive

Often clients express goals in negative terms: "I *don't* want to be frightened," "I *don't* want to be depressed." If we accept this as the client's goal, we are in the position of removing something from the client's realm of experience and offering nothing in its place. I am concerned that often therapy is directed more toward symptom removal, rather than enhancement of well-being. If the therapeutic goal is to take away depression and anxiety, to eliminate a phobia, or to eradicate inappropriate patterns of behavior, what does the client have left? This excising of an emotional or behavioral pattern, analogous to the way the surgeon may remove a tumor, is both unrealistic and impractical.

First, it is unrealistic because we do not live in a state of neutrality. We are emotional beings who are constantly experiencing feelings in the full range of their variety and intensity. It is not possible for us to be without emotions, whether our value judgements define them as positive or negative. One way or another, we feel and will go on feeling. To direct therapy toward a goal of emotional neutrality by doing no more than removing a negative feeling does not fit with the laws of emotions and is, therefore, destined to fail.

Second, removing symptoms is impractical. It is more practical to help a person *create* a desired goal than it is to *eliminate* a problem with which he or she has been struggling, unsuccessfully, for a long time. It is more practical to move forward in the desired direction than to move backward before you move forward. It is more practical to perceive happiness, relaxation, enjoyment, and effective relationships as appropriate therapeutic goals. After all, all are achievable, and there are pragmatic means by which they can be attained.

To encourage a client to make this shift, I am inclined to ask questions that presuppose the positive. If a person says, "I don't want to be frightened," or "I don't want to feel depressed," I ask, "If you don't want to feel that way, how would you like to feel?"

Question a Global Goal

A client's response to the former question may be global. For example, it may be, "I want to feel happier." For an outcome-oriented approach to therapy, this answer is not sufficiently specific or clear enough to design the appropriate therapeutic interventions.

Consider the person who presents for therapy saying, "I am depressed." We may assume that person wants to feel happier and, on the basis of that assumption, use a presuppositional question inviting that person to focus on a more positive goal. If the response is "I want to feel happier," we have taken a step forward, but not quite far enough. If we choose a metaphor approach, a story on a global theme of happiness may not be specifically relevant to that person's needs and, therefore, may not provide the means to facilitate the shift to a state of greater happiness.

Explore Specific Outcomes

Explore what has helped clients experience their global goal in the past. What specific things have they done previously to feel happier, relate better, or sleep more peacefully? What sort of things might help them reach those goals now?

A person who reports feelings of depression and has a global goal of being happier more specifically may want to develop constructive techniques for managing guilt. Such a person might find it helpful to learn ways to set boundaries or enhance feelings of personal empowerment. He or she may want to feel more hopeful, increase pleasant stimuli, or make some cognitive shifts toward a more positive attitude. The person may want to learn how to accept a loss, improve sleep patterns, or change ruminative thought processes. The specific goals may be various and vast. If we accept the global goal as the direction of therapy, we may miss the subtleties of these specifics and thus steer treatment along an inappropriate path.

Once client and therapist have defined the specific goal, it is easier to direct therapy (no matter what therapeutic interventions we choose) toward the attainment of that specific goal. If we are working with metaphors, this may require a series of different metaphors designed to help develop and enhance those specific goals that cluster together to create a state of happiness.

Anticipate Outcome

An outcome-oriented approach anticipates goal attainment. When a therapist anticipates a client's ability to reach a goal, it is easier for the client to do so. Positive expectations of outcome by the therapist have a significant effect on actual goal attainment.

If we believe the goal is attainable and that the client has or can develop the means to attain that goal, then we communicate an anticipation of achievement. We may also help to build the client's own anticipation by asking questions that presuppose the attainment of that outcome. Such questions may ask, "How will you feel when you have reached this goal?", "What difference will it make to your life when you are feeling more hopeful?", "When you have learned how to accept losses, how will you look at circumstances more positively?"

Ratify Outcome

It is helpful to ratify or confirm with clients the achievement of each step in the process of reaching the desired therapeutic goal. This validates their immediate achievement, confirms their empowerment, and reassures them that they are capable of setting and attaining future objectives.

The means for ratifying the achievement may be asking a client who has been phobic of travel to send a postcard from the first destination of a trip. It might be to encourage a client to take a photograph of something that verifies the achievement. Even the act of writing a letter, making a phone call, or sending an e-mail to the therapist helps confirm the experience that things are different or have changed.

CREATING STORIES

An Example of an Outcome-Oriented Assessment

Jamie, a twenty-year-old, sought therapy for an injection phobia and was seen by a colleague I was supervising. She took a goal-oriented approach at their initial meeting, asking, "What do you want to achieve by being here?" Using such a question immediately helped the client focus on the purpose or reason for being present in a way that was positive and outcome-oriented.

Jamie responded as many clients do. He wanted to tell his story and related at length his fear of syringes and needles. He was concerned because he was about to join the army and knew that there would be times in the future when he would need medical treatment or be required to have blood tests.

My supervisee listened respectfully to his story. She assumed, implementing a goal-oriented approach, that Jamie was not there to talk more about the problem but rather to find a resolution. In saying that he was afraid of needles, she assumed he was really asking for assistance to feel appropriately relaxed when requiring such medical treatment. Thus, she again asked, "Given that this is the problem you have been experiencing and that you would like to see it change, what do you want to gain from this consultation?"

Jamie responded in negative terms by saying, "I *don't* want to feel panicky when I need to have a needle." My supervisee responded with an outcome-focused approach: "If you do not want to feel panicky, how would you rather feel?"

As stated earlier, the purpose of this question is twofold. First, it helps clients keep their focus on the outcome in a way that is positive, constructive, and practical. Second, it gives the therapist clear directions about which way to orient therapeutic interventions.

When clients can be specific about their goals, especially in a positive way, the therapist can determine the direction of treatment more easily and more accurately. If Jamie had said he would like to be more relaxed in those previously anxiety-arousing situations of coming in contact with an injection, the therapist may have elected to desensitize Jamie systematically to such situations. If he said that he would like to be distracted or to think about something else, the therapist may have taught him some dissociative techniques. If he had problems with fainting and wanted to be free of such spells, then the therapist may have taught him to apply tension, rather than relaxation, to counter the rise and fall of blood pressure that occurs with blood or needle phobias.

What Jamie said was that he wanted to be more comfortable—a globally stated goal. My supervisee sought to help him define this more specifically. "When you are comfortable, how does that feel?" she asked. "What sort of things have you done in previous situations of tension to be more at ease?"

The question helped Jamie form a more specific definition. He said that to be comfortable would mean to be calm when anticipating an injection or blood test. Being comfortable also meant that he would feel more relaxed in the clinic. He would be calm in his mind and relaxed in his body. The specifics of this now gave a clear focus to the direction that Jamie could go as well as an idea of what therapeutic interventions would be most helpful. For him the problem now had shifted from an overwhelming and seemingly uncontrollable set of symptoms to attainment of specific goals that seemed more readily within his reach.

My supervisee sought to facilitate the anticipation of a goal achievement. She asked, "When you are feeling calmer prior to an appointment, and when you are feeling more relaxed in the clinic, what difference is that going to make for you? How will life be better? In what ways will things have improved?" Although this helps the client to think beyond the problem and toward the solution, such questions also have a presupposition. They presuppose that the problem is soluble and communicate indirectly to the client that the therapist believes, and anticipates, that the client will resolve the problem. Once we have an appropriate goal-oriented assessment then we can look at selecting the relevant type of metaphor and structuring it to meet the client's needs.

Step 2. Formulate the PRO-Approach

Begin at the End: Defining the Metaphor's Outcome

It should be relatively easy to structure an outcome for your metaphor on the basis of a clear and appropriate goal-oriented assessment. Defining the Outcome provides a roadmap for steering future therapeutic interventions necessary to achieve the therapeutic goal.

Find the Middle: Developing the Necessary Resources

Once you have defined your goal, you can then consider what you need to do to get there. The resources are the means to the end. They are the road, the vehicle, and the fuel that makes the journey possible. The previous chapter provided examples of how to build resources into metaphors from a variety of sources. It also illustrated how to access and use those abilities necessary for clients to take the appropriate steps of learning and discovery along the road to their destination.

- **Assess existing abilities.** Find the skills your clients already have that will help them to attain their goal. It is more therapeutically efficient to use existing abilities than to create new ones.
- **Use those existing abilities.** Once you have discovered how a client has learned or acquired a skill in the past, it may be possible to tap into those processes and employ them in learning what is necessary to reach the current desired outcome.
- **Build what resources are necessary.** If you are dealing with adult clients, they have already encountered a variety of life experiences and learned to overcome many difficulties and challenges. Consequently, these abilities can be built on or adapted to reach the current goal.

   Sometimes clients need to develop new skills. For example, a depressed person who has a long-term pattern of processing events in one cognitive style may need to learn new patterns for processing those same types of events.
- **Create experiences for new learning.** Hopefully the objective, and art, of any therapy is to show that it is *possible* to bring about change. As therapy's aim is to alter experiences, whether at a cognitive, emotional, or behavioral level, metaphors may need to create learning experiences that clients have not encountered in their own lives, but from which they can benefit through others' experiences.
- **Open options for new discoveries.** When the patterns of the past do not prove helpful in dealing with the present, we need to open up new options or new possibilities. Most of the story ideas presented in this book give examples of this process and specifically address the creation of new possibilities for modifying old issues.

CREATING STORIES

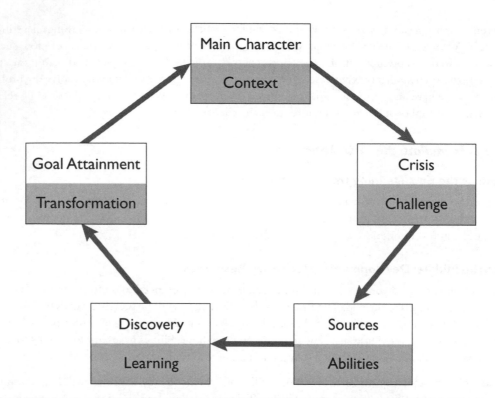

FIGURE 15.1   A FORMAT FOR CONSTRUCTING AND PRESENTING METAPHORS

End at the Beginning: Finding a Matching Problem

Finally, investigate what hurdles or obstacles you need to overcome. This is the Problem. My father used to say, "A problem is just an excuse to help you find a solution" (see Chapter 6, Story 21). The crisis or challenge that the character in a metaphoric story encounters is simply the vehicle for creating new experiences and thus enriching life. It is part of the means toward the end.

Step 3. Construct and Present the Metaphor

Although I have recommended that you *plan* your metaphors in the reverse PRO-approach (i.e., Outcome to Problem), you should *structure and tell* your story following the PRO format. Present the Problem first, followed by the Resources (i.e., learning and discoveries), before concluding with the Outcome (see Figure 15.1).

Create the Main Character and Context

Develop a character with whom the client is likely to identify. A matching character can engage the client in a way that is both empathic and empowering—just as in the example given of the little octopus in Story 11. At this point, the primary objective is for the key character to parallel those characteristics of the client that will best help that person identify with the story and develop a personal relationship with the outcome. This can be done in several ways. The tale may match its character to similar client attributes such as age, gender, cultural background, occupational activity, and types of interests, or, more diffusely, it may create a character who shares similar personality features, styles of thinking, or patterns of behavior.

Once the listener has identified with the character, problem, or both, it is much easier to identify with the processes of change and the outcome that can be achieved. In this way matching the character to the client employs presuppositions of change and offers guidelines of how to shift problems into solutions.

Although the aim of this book focuses primarily on outcome-based metaphors, matching client characteristics and the processes of identification are also essential aspects of engaging the listener and ensuring a satisfactory therapeutic outcome. If you want to explore this aspect of metaphors further, you may find Lankton and Lankton (1983, 1989), Yapko (1990), and Kopp (1995) to be helpful.

The character in the story needs to be set in a context, and the situation in which the story is constructed can add to the listener's identification with and, consequently, the reality of the story. The context is best selected on the basis of what the story is trying to communicate. Thus, if its purpose is to facilitate relaxation, it may be set in a relaxing environment such as a peaceful day at the beach or on a hilltop watching a sunset. If it is to aid the client's identification with the story, it may replicate something of the listener's own environment at home or work. If the story is designed to arouse curiosity or be a little mystical, it may be set in an unusual location or a different cultural context.

Describe the Crisis or Challenge

In a metaphoric story the character usually experiences a problem, encounters a crisis, or faces a challenge similar to that of the listener. As such, the crisis or challenge may be as diverse as our clients and the stories they relate to us about their experiences. It could involve encountering a loss, managing a situation of fear, or dealing with a relationship problem.

The story may make a direct match to the problem the client presents, such as telling an overweight client a story of another person you have seen who experienced a similar struggle—before losing weight. The story may make an indirect match, reflecting aspects of the struggle and the difficulty, though not describing the specific problem.

At this point, the metaphor simply presents the problem but does not offer any solutions because there are other processes that we need to go through before reaching a successful outcome. In the next steps, the metaphoric story guides the listener through those processes.

Develop Resources and Abilities

This part of the story helps the client access abilities he or she already has, reactivate past skills, or develop new means to overcome the current problem. It assists clients to acknowledge and be aware of what tools he or she has available.

Facilitate Learning and Discovery

The next step is about discovering how to use available resources to reach a satisfactory outcome. Simply having the tools is not sufficient to do the job if you do not know what to do with them. The processes of adaptation, change, and discovery are what lead the listener to the final step.

Reach the Therapeutic Goal

The final step is about transformation, modification, and attainment of the goal. Here the story is likely to describe the experiences and feelings of having reached that objective, as well as the ongoing benefits that the character of the story is likely to gain.

As stories evolve and change with our clients, the story may not necessarily end at this point. It may return to the main character or introduce another character who also matches with the listener. Thus, the story may continue within that consultation or at subsequent appointments.

In telling therapeutic stories, recall the art of storytelling discussed in Chapter 2 and revisit the Ten Guidelines for Effective Storytelling as aids to your story preparation and storytelling. Practice using the Six Guidelines for the Use of the Storyteller's Voice to enhance the effective communication of the therapeutic message. Experiment with these guidelines when presenting metaphors, seeking to find and use those tools that most involve and assist your listener.

Step 4. Observing and Using the Search Process

A metaphor, like a projective test, is an ambiguous stimulus for the listener, even though the teller may have structured it with a defined purpose. Although the therapist may present a tale with a clear therapeutic objective, the therapist should remember that there is no correct or right way for a client to interpret the story. The interpretation most meaningful for the listener is usually the one he or she ascribes to it.

When presented with any ambiguous stimulus, we search for meaning or relevance. We seek structure, and explore how it may relate to us. The same process occurs when a person listens to a metaphor.

In therapy the search process is enhanced by certain characteristics of the therapeutic setting. A client seeks therapy to gain something from it and thus has a different set of motivations and expectations from listening to a tale told in a social context or watching a story unfold on a movie screen. In different contexts we look for different meaning. In a theater we seek to be entertained, whereas in therapy we search for the relevance a story may hold for our lives. Given this motivation, clients invariably begin to wonder how therapeutic metaphors apply to them and their reason for being in therapy. The therapist may be perceived as an "expert" or a source of wisdom and knowledge from whom the client hopes to gain answers and solutions. When the therapist tells a story, the client may wonder, "Why am I being told this? What purpose does my therapist have in relating this tale?"

From the therapist's point of view, the answer should be clear. There should be a solid rationale and sound ethical reasons for telling each and every healing story. In terms of the therapeutic contract with the client, the metaphor needs to provide the means for facilitating the client's movement toward the desired outcome—but be prepared for the fact that the intent or purpose with which the therapist tells a tale may not be the meaning that the client attributes to it.

Do not deny any client's interpretation of a story, for his or her interpretation is what is likely to be most meaningful for that client, even if it is different from what you had intended. Use the client's interpretation to confirm and facilitate his or her progress in your subsequent metaphors and therapeutic interventions. See your tale as a projective test, understanding that different people are likely to see different meanings in the same story, and be flexible enough to build on their meanings in a way that constructively moves them toward their goal.

In my filing system I keep a letter from a client that forcefully reminds me of those individual processes in the search for meaning. At the age of 50 she experienced many life events that were outside of her control; as a result, she began to feel powerless and depressed. Because one of her specific goals was to have a greater acceptance of those events, I told her the story, "Learning To Accept Our Circumstances" (see Story 13). She listened to the story intently, and whether it was a product of the tale or not, for the next few weeks she seemed to handle her circumstances better. A while later she suffered a relapse. Having forgotten that I had already told her a version of this story, I retold it to apply to her current situation.

Before our next session she wrote me a letter. She said, "I have worked out the story about the stonecutter (as she referred to it). It is told once while people are sick, then again when they are feeling better. It stops them from relapsing, because they know that if they do, you will tell them the damn thing a third time!"

I had not retold the story deliberately, but my doing so had stimulated a search in her for some meaning or purpose in the second recounting. She concluded something so important that she needed to put it in writing. What she found was both constructive and therapeutic for her. She was going to get better before she had to listen to it a third time!

Step 5. Ratify the Metaphor

Ratification is a process of confirmation and validation. Setting the story and its outcome in a personally relevant context can help validate or remind the listener of both the story and its conclusion.

Cathy was a Buddhist who lived in a Tibetan Buddhist center and devoted herself to her faith. She was also a competent and capable artist. Her two strong interests brought her into conflict. On the one hand, she wanted to live the simple life of a Buddhist, but, on the other, she wanted to develop her artistic talent and enjoy the fame and fortune that would possibly accompany it. Her ambivalence about these conflicting interests made her—as she described it—feel she was "about to explode."

I told her a story that I hoped would help her to identify with both the character and challenge, as well as mobilize her resources toward reaching a constructive decision. It also provided the opportunity for a metaphor that could be ratified in her day-to-day activities and religious practices.

I reminded her of the story of Chenrezig, the thousand-armed Buddha of Compassion. Like Cathy, Chenrezig was torn between two conflicting feelings. He had taken a vow to save all beings from suffering, but he felt he lacked the ability to achieve what he most wanted to do. Realizing the enormity of his task and the conflict in which it put him, his head exploded into countless pieces. Combining their powers, the Buddha of Infinite Light and the Buddha of Powerful Energy came to his assistance. They reassembled his body into a more powerful form with eleven heads and a thou-

SUMMARY: STEPS FOR USING METAPHORS IN THERAPY

1. Adopt a goal-oriented assessment that defines specific outcome objectives. This will make it easier for you to structure relevant metaphoric interventions (or indeed any therapeutic intervention) and for clients to confirm their goal attainment.
2. Formulate the metaphor on the PRO-approach, beginning with the desired Outcome, then developing the appropriate Resources, and finally defining a relevant Problem.
3. Structure the metaphor by creating the character, describing the crisis or challenge, developing the necessary resources, facilitating new learning, and attaining the goal. Follow the pattern for structuring metaphors in Figure 15.1 if this is helpful. Present the metaphor to the client using (a) the guidelines for effective storytelling, and (b) characteristics of voice described in Chapter 2.
4. Observe the client's search processes and use the meanings that he or she finds in the story to facilitate the journey toward the desired outcome.
5. Ratify the story, validate the outcome, and encourage ongoing learning.

sand arms. Each hand had an eye in the center of the palm, thus symbolizing the unity of wisdom (the eye) and skillful means (the hand). Using his resources of *both* wisdom and skillful means, the Buddha of Compassion was able to resolve his dilemma. It was not a question of one *or* the other (as Cathy had been perceiving her situation), but rather a matter of constructively blending *both*.

The more expanded version of the story I told to Cathy engaged her in a process of identification and helped lead to a resolution of her dilemma. She discovered how to use her resources: the skillful hands of the artist and the wisdom of her compassionate philosophy. Each time she prostrated herself before the image of Chenrezig or looked at a photograph of the Dalai Lama (considered to be a reincarnation of Chenrezig), she may have remembered the story, and this, in turn, ratified her outcome. The last time I saw Cathy was at a fund-raising exhibition to which I had been invited. She had painted some beautiful works of art that were on sale to support a charity. If we base metaphoric stories in a context with which our clients are familiar or add something of the reality of their world in a way that links it to the desired therapeutic outcome, there is an ongoing confirmation of the therapeutic tale and a ratification of the metaphoric goal.

A CONCLUDING COMMENT

At the beginning of Chapter 2, I mentioned a conversation I overheard between two therapists. One expressed his desire to learn more about using therapeutic metaphors with clients: "I watch the experts and they somehow seem to pick up on just the right story for that particular client. Their ideas are so creative. I struggle to begin. I do not know where to get the material for metaphors, or how to tell them effectively."

I never addressed these issues with him. Instead, I wrote a book. My hope is that, in its pages, you have found—and continue to find—helpful hints for telling tales effectively, means for matching them to your clients and their desired outcomes, and ideas for stimulating possible metaphoric themes. In addition, I have provided a structure for creating healing stories and a means for communicating metaphorically with clients.

Our lives, like our clients' lives, are not *a* story, but rather are *packed full* of healing stories. We listen to other people's tales of life, we read them in books, we find them in different cultures or traditions, we hear them from our clients, and we experience them in our own life journeys. In telling them, we share experiences with others. In hearing them, we find lessons that facilitate our own journey, enhance our well-being, and contribute to our growth. Enjoy.

CREATING STORIES

Why Do You Teach in Stories?

Once a young man approached a learned teacher hoping to discover the answer to the many questions that concerned him. Somewhat brashly, and in a hurry to gain the ultimate in knowledge, he leaped in with his most challenging question first.

"Tell me," he demanded, "if I am to find the secret of life, where should I begin my search?"

"Once," replied the teacher compassionately, "God surrounded himself with his council of angels. He had just sat back in his heavenly throne, pleased with his creation. Beneath him lay a beautiful universe. He felt particular pleasure with the planet Earth, for there he had created life. Leaves danced in the breeze, birds chorused to the rising sun, and whales hummed an underwater harmony. The planet would go on creating and sustaining life. It was a proud achievement.

"He congratulated the council of angels for their diligent assistance, then continued, 'Our job is complete, save for one remaining task. We must find a place to hide the secret of life so that humans cannot abuse it.'

"One angel immediately came up with an idea. 'Let's place it on the top of the highest, most inaccessible mountain.'

"For a moment God pondered. 'No. I foresee that humans will climb to the top of even the tallest and most inaccessible mountain. When they do then they will discover the secret of life. We must find somewhere else to hide it.'

"A second angel contributed, 'Then let us place it at the very bottom of the sea. Surely, that will be out of their reach.'

"Again God contemplated. 'I have given humans the intelligence to create machines,' he said. 'I can foresee that they will create machines that will take them even to the bottom of the deepest oceans.'

"A third angel came up with yet another idea. 'I know,' he said. 'Let us hide it in the humans themselves.'

"God was delighted. 'What a great idea! They will never think to look there.'"

The student was a little puzzled by the story, but he was not deterred from his quest. To each new question he received not a direct answer, but yet another parable. Finally, he could contain his disappointment no longer and blurted out, "Why, when I ask you a direct question, do you always reply in stories? Why not just tell me the meaning directly?"

"Once," answered the teacher in a style the young man had now come to expect, "an apple grower wished to give an apple to a young man. This was no ordinary apple. It was a very special gift for a very special person.

"The apple grower had, over the years, learned his trade, observed his teachers, and developed his skills. This special apple he had grown himself. He had taken the seed and nurtured it. He had planted it in the best conditions of soil, shelter, and sunlight. He had fertilized the ground, pruned the branches, chased away the invading birds, and plucked the fruit when it reached perfection. Now he handed it to the young man, a glistening, ruby red apple with sweet, crisp flesh.

"Do you think that if he had also chewed it for the young man, the young man would have had any personal experience of the apple's qualities, or just how special the gift had been?"

Resources

REFERENCES AND PROFESSIONAL LITERATURE ON METAPHORS

In the professional literature there are many books and journal articles about metaphors that provide research into metaphor processing, offer case histories, and give examples and sources of metaphors. I have attempted to minimize the amount of referencing and reiteration of other people's research in the text of this book so as to give maximum space to the stories and the techniques for using them. This book alone does not begin to cover the whole tapestry of metaphor therapy, and so I have sought to provide a comprehensive bibliography for you to explore in greater depth the science, theory, styles, and applications of healing stories. Listed below is a broad cross section of the literature (some of which, you will find, take a different orientation than my own) that hopefully will build your knowledge, understanding, and practice in this fascinating field of therapy. Also in this section are the articles and books I have cited in the text.

Angus, L. E., & Rennie, D. L. (1988). Therapist participation in metaphor generation: Collaborative and non-collaborative style. *Psychotherapy, 25,* 552–560.

Angus, L. E., & Rennie, D. L. (1989). Envisioning the representational world: The client's experience of metaphoric expression in psychotherapy. *Psychotherapy, 26,* 372–379.

Barker, P. (1985). *Using metaphors in psychotherapy.* New York: Brunner/Mazel.

Beck, A. (1967). *Depression: Causes and treatment.* Philadelphia: University of Pennsylvania Press.

Beck, A. (1973). *The diagnosis and management of depression.* Philadelphia: University of Pennsylvania Press.

Beck, A. (1976). *Cognitive therapy and the emotional disorders.* New York: International Universities Press.

Beck, A., Brown, G., Berchick, R., Stewart, B., & Steer, R. (1990). Relationship between hopelessness and ultimate suicide: A replication with psychiatric outpatients. *American Journal of Psychiatry, 147,* 190–195.

Beck, A., Rush, J., Shaw, B., & Emery, G. (1979). *Cognitive therapy of depression.* New York: Guilford Press.

Bettelheim, B. (1976). *The uses of enchantment: The meaning and importance of fairy tales.* New York: Knopf.

Bettelheim, B. (1984). *Freud and man's soul.* New York: Vintage.

Black, M. (1962). *Models and metaphors.* New York: Ithaca.

Burns, G. L. (1996). *From coconuts to cocktails: A sociocultural study of tourism on a Fijian island.* Unpublished Master's Thesis, University of Western Australia, Perth.

Burns, G. W. (1998). *Nature-guided therapy: Brief integrative strategies for health and well-being.*Philadelphia: Brunner/Mazel.

Burns, G. W. (1999). Nature-guided therapy: A case example of ecopsychology in clinical practice. *Australian Journal of Outdoor Education, 3* (2), 9–16.

Campbell, J. (1986). *The inner reaches of outer space: Metaphor as myth and as religion.* New York: Harper & Row.

Campos, L. (1972). Using metaphor for identifying life script changes. *Transactional Analysis Journal, 2* (2), 75.

Chelf, J. H., Deschler, A. M. B., Hillman, S., & Durazo-Arvizu, R. (2000). Storytelling: A strategy for living and coping with cancer. *Cancer Nursing, 23* (1), 1–5.

Close, H. T. (1998). *Metaphor in psychotherapy: Clinical applications of stories and allegories.* San Luis Obispo, CA: Impact.

Cohen, T. (1979). Metaphor and the cultivation of intimacy. In S. Sacks (Ed.), *On metaphor* (pp. 1–10). Chicago: University of Chicago Press.

Combs, G. & Freedman, J. (1990). *Symbol, story, and ceremony: Using metaphor in individual and family therapy.* New York: Norton.

Cox, M., & Theilgaard, A. (1987). *Mutative metaphors in psychotherapy: The aeolian mode.* London: Tavistock.

Dolan, Y. M. (1986). Metaphors for motivation and intervention. *Family therapy collections, 19,* 1–10.

Donnelly, C. M., & Dumas, J. E, (1997). Use of analogies in therapeutic situations: An analogue study. *Psychotherapy, 34* (2), 124–132.

Donnelly, C. M., & McDaniel, M. A. (1993). The use of analogy in learning specific scientific concepts. *Journal of Experimental Psychology, 19,* 975–986.

Duhl, B. (1983). *From the inside out and other metaphors: Creative and integrative approaches to training in systems thinking.* New York: Brunner/Mazel.

Erickson, M. H., Rossi, E. L., & Rossi, S. (1976). *Hypnotic realities.* New York: Irvington.

Evans, M. B. (1985). *Metaphor, personality, and psychotherapy: An individual difference approach to the study of verbal metaphor.* Unpublished doctoral dissertation, University of North Carolina, Chapel Hill.

Evans, M. B. (1988). The role of metaphor in psychotherapy and personality change: A theoretical reformulation. *Psychotherapy, 25*(4), 543–551.

Fantz, R. E. (1983). The use of metaphor and fantasy as an additional exploration of awareness. *Gestalt Journal, 6,* 28–33.

Gardner, R. (1971). *Therapeutic communication with children: The mutual storytelling technique.* New York: Science House.

Gonclaves, O. F., & Craine, M. H. (1990). The use of metaphors in cognitive therapy. *Journal of Cognitive Psychotherapy, 4* (2), 135–149.

Gordon, D. (1978). *Therapeutic metaphors: Helping others through the looking glass.* Cupertino, CA: Meta.

Groth-Marnat, G. (1992). Past Cultural Traditions of Therapeutic Metaphor. *Psychology: A Journal of Human Behavior, 29* (3/4, 1–8)

Grove, D. J., & Panzer, B. I. (1989). *Resolving traumatic memories: Metaphors and symbols in psychotherapy.* New York: Irvington.

Haley, J. (1973*). Uncommon therapy: The psychiatric techniques of Milton H Erickson.* New York: Norton.

Hammond, D.C. (Ed.). (1990). *Handbook of hypnotic suggestions and metaphors.* New York: Norton.

Harris, J. J., Lakey, M. A., & Marsalek, F. (1980). Metaphor and images: Rating, reporting, remembering. In R. R. Hoffman & R. P. Honeck (Eds.), *Cognition and figurative language* (pp. 231–258) Hillsdale, NJ: Erlbaum.

Haskell, R. E. (Ed.). (1987). *Cognition and symbolic structures: The psychology of metaphoric transformation.* Norwood, NJ: Ablex.

Hesley, J. W., & Hesley, J. G. (1998). *Rent two films and let's talk in the morning: Using popular movies in psychotherapy*. New York: Wiley.

Hillary, E. (1975). *Nothing venture, nothing win*. London: Coronet Books.

Hintikka, J. (Ed.). (1994). *Aspects of metaphor*. Boston: Kluwer Academic.

Hoffman, L. (1983). Imagery and metaphor in couples therapy. *Family Therapy, 10* (2), 141–156.

Honeck, R. P., & Hofman, R. R. (1980). *Cognition and figurative language*. NJ: Hillsdale.

Hunter, M. E. (1988). *Daydreams for discoveries: A manual for hypnotherapists*. Vancouver: Seawalk.

Ingal, C. K. (1997). *Metaphors, maps, and mirrors: Moral education in middle schools*. Greenwich, CT: Ablex.

Jung, C. G., & von Franz, M. L. (Eds.). (1964). *Man and his symbols*. New York: Dell.

Kingsbury, S. J. (1994). Interacting within metaphors. *American Journal of Clinical Hypnosis, 36* (4), 241–247.

Kirsch, I. (1997). Hypnotic suggestion: A musical metaphor. *American Journal of Clinical Hypnosis, 39* (4), 271–282.

Kohen, D. P., & Wynne, E. (1997). Applying hypnosis in a preschool family asthma education program: Uses of storytelling, imagery, and relaxation. *American Journal of Clinical Hypnosis, 39* (3), 169–181.

Kopp, R. R. (1995). *Metaphor therapy: Using client-generated metaphors in psychotherapy*. New York: Brunner/Mazel.

Kopp, R. R., & Craw, M. J. (1998). Metaphoric language, metaphoric cognition and cognitive therapy. *Psychotherapy, 35* (3), 306–311.

Kopp, S. (1971). *Guru: metaphors from a psychotherapist*. Palo Alto, CA: : Science & Behavior Books.

Kuttner, L. (1988). Favorite stories: A hypnotic pain-reduction technique for children in acute pain. *American Journal of Clinical Hypnosis, 30,* 289–295.

Lakoff, G., & Johnson, M. (1980). *Metaphors we live by*. Chicago: University of Chicago Press.

Lankton, C., & Lankton, S. R. (1989). *Tales of enchantment: Goal-oriented metaphors for adults and children in therapy*. New York: Brunner/Mazel.

Lankton, S. R. (1988). *The blammo-surprise book: A story to help children overcome fears*. New York: Magination.

Lankton, S. R., & Lankton, C. (1983). *The answer within: A clinical framework of Ericksonian hypnotherapy*. New York: Brunner/Mazel.

Lankton, S. R. & Lankton, C. (1986). *Enchantment and intervention in family therapy: Training in Ericksonian hypnosis*. New York: Brunner/Mazel.

Martin, J., Cummings, A. L., & Hallberg, E. T. (1992). Therapists' intentional use of metaphor: Memorability, clinical impact, and possible epistemic/motivational functions. *Journal of Consulting and Clinical Psychology, I,* 143–145.

Matthews, W. M., & Dardeck, K. L. (1985). Construction of metaphor in the counseling process. *American Mental Health Counselors Association Journal, 7,* 11–23.

McCurry, S. M., & Hayes, S. C. (1992). Clinical and experimental perspectives on metaphor talk. *Clinical Psychology Review, 12,* 763–785.

McNeilly, R. B. (2000). *Healing the whole person: A solution-focused approach to using empowering language, emotions and actions in therapy*. New York: Wiley.

Mills, J. C., & Crowley, R. J. (1986). *Therapeutic metaphors for children and the child within*. New York: Brunner/Mazel.

Muran, J. C., & DiGiuseppi, R. A. (1990). Towards a cognitive formulation of metaphor use in psychotherapy. *Clinical Psychology Review, 10,* 69–85.

Nathan, P. E., & Gorman, J. M. (Eds.). (1998). *A guide to treatments that work*. New York: Oxford University Press.

Norton, C. S. (1989). *Life metaphors: Stories of ordinary survival*. Carbondale: Southern Illinois University Press.

O'Hanlon, B. (1986). The use of metaphor for treating somatic complaints in psychotherapy. *Family Therapy Collections, 19,* 19–24.

Ornstein, R., & Sobel, D. (1971). *The healing brain.* New York:: Simon & Schuster.

Ortony, A. (Ed.). (1979). *Metaphor and thought.* New York: Cambridge University Press.

Pert, C. (1985). Neuropeptides, receptors, and emotions. *Cybernetics, 1* (4), 33–34.

Pert, C. (1987). Neuropeptides: The emotions and the body-mind. *Neotic Sciences Review, 2,* 13–18.

Radman, Z. (Ed.). (1995). *From a metaphoric point of view: A multidisciplinary approach to the cognitive content of metaphor.* New York: W de Gruyter.

Remen, R. M. (1996) *Kitchen table wisdom: Stories that heal.* Sydney: Pan Macmillan.

Rosen, S. (1982). *My voice will go with you: The teaching tales of Milton H. Erickson.* New York: Norton.

Rossi, E. L. (1993). *The psychobiology of mind-body healing: New concepts of therapeutic hypnosis* (2nd ed.). New York: Norton.

Rossi, E. L., & Cheek, D. B. (1988). *Mind-body Therapy: Methods of ideodynamic healing in hypnosis.* New York: Norton.

Rossi, E., Ryan, M., & Sharp, F. (Eds.). (1984). *Healing in hypnosis. Vol I. The seminars, workshops, and lectures of Milton H. Erickson.* New York: Irvington.

Sacks, S. (Ed.). (1979). *On metaphor.* Chicago: University of Chicago Press.

Seligman, M. (1989). Explanatory style: Predicting depression, achievement, and health. In M. Yapko (Ed.), *Brief therapy approaches to treating anxiety and depression* (pp. 5–32). New York: Brunner/Mazel.

Seligman, M. (1990). *Learned optimism.* New York: . Knopf.

Seligman, M. (1993). *What you can change and what you can't.* New York: Knopf.

Seligman, M. (1995). *The Optimistic Child: How learned optimism protects children from depression.* New York: Houghton Mifflin.

Siegelman, E. Y. (1990). *Metaphor and meaning in psychotherapy.* New York: Guilford Press.

Sommer, E., and Weiss, D. (1996). *Metaphors dictionary.* Detroit: Visible Ink.

Sommers-Flanagan, J., & Sommers-Flanagan, R. (1996). The wizard of oz metaphor in hypnosis with treatment-resistant children. *American Journal of Clinical Hypnosis, 39* (2), 105–114.

Sontag, S. (1991). *Illness as metaphor and AIDS and its metaphors.* London: Penguin.

Sternberg, R. J. (1990). *Metaphors of mind: Conceptions of the nature of intelligence.* Cambridge: Cambridge University Press.

Stevens-Guille, M. E., & Boersma, F. J. (1992) Fairy tales as trance experience: Possible therapeutic uses. *American Journal of Clinical Hypnosis, 34* (4), 245–254.

Thiessen, I. (1983). Using fairy tales during hypnotherapy in bulimerexia and other psychological problems. *Medical Hypnoanalysis, 4,* 139–144.

Thiessen, I. (1985). A new approach with fairy tales as anchoring devices in hypnotherapy. *Medical Hypnoanalysis, 6,* 21–26.

Tilton, P. (1984). The hypnotic hero: A technique for hypnosis with children. *International Journal of Clinical and Experimental Hypnosis, 32,* 366–375.

Turbayne, C. M. (1991). *Metaphors of the mind: The creative mind and its origins.* Columbia: University of South Carolina Press.

Ullman, J. R. (1956). *Man of Everest: The autobiography of Tenzing.* London: Reprint Society.

Vaisrub, S. (1977). *Medicine's metaphors: Messages and menaces.* Oradell, NJ: Medical Economics.

Wallas, L. (1985). *Stories for the third ear: Using hypnotic fables in Psychotherapy.* New York: Norton.

Walters, C., & Havens, R. A. (1993). *Hypnotherapy for health, harmony, and peak performance: Expanding the goals of psychotherapy.* New York: Brunner/Mazel.

Welch, M. J. (1984). Using metaphor in psychotherapy. *Journal of Psychosocial Nursing and Mental Health Services, 22,* 13–8.

White, R. M. (1996). *The structure of metaphor: The way the language of metaphor works.* Oxford: Blackwell.

Wynne, E. (1987). Storytelling in therapy. *Children Today, 16* (2), 11–15.

Yapko, M. (1985). Therapeutic strategies for the treatment of depression. *Ericksonian monographs, 1,* 89–110. NY: Brunner/Mazel.

Yapko, M. (1988). *When living hurts: Directives for treating depression.* NY: Brunner/Mazel.

Yapko, M. D. (1990). *Trancework.* New York: Brunner/Mazel.

Yapko, M. D. (1992). *Hypnosis and the treatment of depressions: Strategies for change.* New York: Brunner/Mazel.

Yapko, M. D. (1995). *Essentials of hypnosis.* New York: Brunner/Mazel.

Yapko, M. D. (1997). *Breaking the patterns of depression.* New York: Brunner/Mazel.

Yapko, M. D. (1999). Hand-Me-Down Blues: How to stop depression from spreading in families. New York: Golden.

Zeig, J. K. (1980). *A teaching seminar with Milton H. Erickson.* New York: Brunner/Mazel.

Zeig, J. K., & Gilligan, S. G. (Eds.). (1990). *Brief therapy: Myths, methods and metaphors.* New York: Brunner/Mazel.

Zeig, J. K., & Munion, W. M. (Eds.). (1990). *Ericksonian approaches.* San Francisco: Jossey-Bass.

METAPHOR THERAPY FOR CHILDREN

Metaphors are easily, and appropriately, incorporated into therapy for children. While this list is far from comprehensive, it is a starting point to give you an idea of the sort of literature available and the places you can begin to look for additional resource material.

Amos, J. (1994). *Brave.* Austin, TX: Raintree Steck-Vaughn.

Amos, J. (1994). *Happy.* Austin, TX: Raintree Steck-Vaughn.

Amos, J. (1997). *Lonely: Stories about feelings and how to cope with them.* Bath, UK: Cherrytree.

Amos, J., & Spenceley, A. (1997). *Owning up.* Bath, UK: Cherrytree.

Brett, D.(1997). *Annie stories: Helping young children meet the challenges of growing up.* Sydney, Australia: Hale and Iremonger.

Brown, L. K., & Brown, M. (1998). *How to be a friend: A guide to making friends and keeping them.* Boston: Little, Brown.

Johnston, M. (1996). *Dealing with insults.* New York: Powerkids.

Lankton, C., & Lankton, S. R. (1989). *Tales of enchantment: Goal-oriented metaphors for adults and children in therapy.* New York: Brunner/Mazel.

Lankton, S. R. (1988). *The blammo-surprise Book: A story to help children overcome fears.* New York: Magination Press.

Mills, J. C., & Crowley, R. J. (1986). *Therapeutic metaphors for children and the child within.* New York: Brunner/Mazel.

Moses, B. (1997). *I'm worried.* East Essex, UK: Wayland.

CHILDREN'S STORIES

Children's stories often contain metaphoric content and may be good sources for stimulating creative ideas. In addition, they illustrate the nature of stories, the process for structuring stories, and the art of communicating them. Here are just a few examples.

de Saint-Exupery, A. (1993). *The Little prince.* London: Mammoth.

Jackson, J. (1981). *Tawny scrawny lion.* Rancine, WI: Golden.

Milne, A. A., & Shepherd, E. H. (1999). *Winnie-the-pooh's little book of wisdom.* London: Methuen.

Nyokabi, S. (1974). *The chameleon who couldn't stop changing his mind.* Nairobi, Kenya: Transafrica.

O'Mara, L. (Ed.). (1991). *Classic animal stories.* London: Michael O'Mara.

Powell, M. (1994). *Wolf tales: North American children's stories*. Santa Fe, NM: Ancient City.
Shipton, J., & Foreman, M. (1991). *Busy! Busy! Busy!*. London: PictureLions.
Williams, M. (1991). *The Velveteen rabbit*. London: Heineman.

FOLKTALES, CROSS-CULTURAL MYTHS, LEGENDS, AND STORIES

Folktales contain the whole history and tradition of communicating through stories, whether to inform, teach, or entertain. In them are stories that are universal, transcending cultures, religions, and the generations. There is no more delightful method to appreciate the nature of stories than to read these tales—or even better, sit with traditional storytellers—with an eye or ear open for possible therapeutic themes.

Akello, G. (1981). *Iteso thought patterns in tales*. Dar Es Salaam, Tanzania [formerly Tanyanyika]: Dar Es Salaam University Press.
Bruchal, J. (1991). *Native American stories*. Golden, CO: Fulcrum.
Bruchal, J. (1993). *Flying with the eagle, racing the great bear: Stories from native North America*. Mahwah, NJ: Troll Medallion
Caduto, M. J., & Bruchal, J. (1994). *Keepers of the night*. Golden, Colorado: Fulcrum.
Chophel, N. (1983). *Folk culture of Tibet*. Dharamsala, India: Library of Tibetan Works and Archives.
Hatherley, S. (1991). *Folk tales of Japan*. South Melbourne, Australia: Macmillan.
Hull, R. (1992). *Native North American stories*. East Essex, UK: Wayland.
Hull, R. (1994). *Indian stories*. East Essex, UK: Wayland.
Ingpen, R., & Hayes, B. (1992). *Folk tales and fables of the Middle East and Africa*. Surrey, UK: Dragon's World.
In-Sob, Z. (1979). *Folktales from Korea*. New York: Grove.
Kamera, W. D., & Mwakasaka, C. S. (1981). *The compliment: East Africa folktales*. Arusha, Tanzania [formerly Tanyanyika]: East Africa Publications.
Lall, K. (1991). *Nepalese book of proverbs*. Kathmandu, Nepal: Tiwari's Pilgrims Bookhouse.
Morgan, W. (1988). *Navajo coyote tales*. Santa Fe, NM: Ancient City.
Njururi, N. (1975). *Tales from Mount Kenya*. Nairobi, Kenya: Transafrica.
Retan, W. (1989). *Favorite tales from many lands*. New York: Grosset & Dunlap.
Roberts, A., & Mountford, C. P. (1980). *The first sunrise: Australian Aboriginal myths in paintings*. Adelaide, Australia: Rigby.
Sakya, K., & Griffith, L. (1980). *Tales of Kathmandu: Folktales from the Himalayan kingdom of Nepal*. Brisbane, Australia: House of Kathmandu.
Scheffler, A. (1997). *Silent beetle gets the seeds: Proverbs from far and wide*. London: Macmillan.
Schultz, G. F. (1968). *Vietnamese legends*. Tokyo: Charles E. Tuttle.
Scott, M. (1988). *Irish fairytales*. Dublin: Mercier Press.
Sherman, J. (1993). *Rachel the Clever and other Jewish folktales*. Little Rock, AR: August House.
Te Kanawa, K. (1997). *Land of the long white cloud: Maori myths, tales And legends*. Auckland, NZ: Viking.
Urton, G. (Ed.). (1985). *Animal myths and metaphors in South America*. Salt Lake City, UT: University of Salt Lake City Press.
Zipes, J. (1979). *Breaking the magic spell: Radical theories of folk and fairytales*. Houston: University of Texas Press.

RELIGIOUS AND SPIRITUAL STORIES

Religions have long taught through parables. The spiritual literature contains many stories of strong moral values, positive reframing, constructive management of relationships, and healthy worldviews. Here is just a small sample.

Berg, L. (1999). *The God Stories: A celebration of legends*. London: Frances Lincoln.

de Mello, A. (1988). *The Song Of The Bird*. Anand, India: Gujarat Sahitya Prakash.

Feldman, C., & Kornfield, J. (1991). *Stories of the spirit, stories of the heart: Parables of the spiritual path from around the world*. San Francisco: Harper.

Friedlander, S. (1987). *When you hear hoofbeats think of a zebra: Talks on Sufism*. New York: Perennial Library.

Hoff, B. (1989). *The tao of Pooh*. London: Mandarin.

Hoff, B. (1993). *The te of Piglet*. London: Mandarin.

Jensen, L. (1999). *Uncovering the wisdom of the heartmind*. Wheaton, IL: Quest.

Martin, R., & Soares, M. (1995). *One hand clapping: Zen stories for all ages*. New York: Rizzoli.

Redhouse, R. W. (Trans.). (1977). *Legends of the Sufis*. London: Theosophical Publishing House.

Shah, I. (1970). *Tales of the dervishes*. New York: Dutton.

Shah, J. (1979). *The Sufis*. London: Allen.

VIDEOTAPES

There are a number of good videotapes available that demonstrate skilled practitioners of metaphor therapy working with this medium. These are useful to watch as they show aspects of interactions with the client, styles of communication, and use of the voice that are not readily observable in the printed word.

The Milton H. Erickson Foundation has a comprehensive selection of videotaped demonstrations recorded at their congresses over the last 20 years. The Foundation's contact details are:

The Milton H. Erickson Foundation. Inc.,
3606 N. 24th Street, Phoenix, AZ 85016, USA
E-mail: office@erickson-foundation.org

INTERNET WEBSITES

There are a number of interesting websites for storylovers and those seeking stimulating ideas to adapt into metaphor therapy. Just as for all of the sources I have listed above, you may need to wade through many tales before an idea that may suit a particular client, presenting problem, or desired clinical outcome leaps from the vast pool. As websites are subject to change—and sometimes rapidly—I am hesitant to say these were correct, even at the time of publication. I hope they serve as the first wave to help you surf onto many more stories.

Afterhours Inspirational Stories. Available at http://inspirationalstories.com.

Ah-life Stories. Available at http://www.ah-life.com.

Inspirational Stories: Sufism. Available at http://inspirationalstories.com/2_sfm.html.

Kid Stories. Available at http://home.netrover.com/~kinskid/108.html.

Lakoff On Conceptual Metaphor. Available at http://www.ac.wwu.edu/~market/semiotic/metaphor_toc.html.

Metaphors In Language And Thought. Available at http://garnet.berkeley.edu:4247/metaphor.html.

Metaphors We Talk By. Available at http://www.stanford.edu/~dib/metaphor.html.

Stories Of Nasrudin. Available at http://www.csclub.uwaterloo.ca/u/tamulder/nasrudin.html.

Story Arts. Available at www.storyarts.org/library/nutshell.

Story Palace: Inspirational Stories. Available at http://storypalace.ourfamily.com/inspirational.html.

Success Stories. Available at http://www.success-stories.digital.com.

Sufi Stories. Available at http://www.ias.org/sufi_stories.html.

Work On Metaphors. Available at http://www.le.ac.uk/psychology/metaphor/abstracts.html.

Worldwide Stories. Available at http://www.enimagnaphics.com/stories/stories/world.html.
Zen Pursuer. Available at http://sungag.buddhism.org/14enlight/looking.html.
Zen Stories To Tell Your Neighbors. Available at http://www.rider.edu/users/suler/zenstory/nature.html.
Zensufi Story Park. Available at http://www.zensufi.com/story.html.
Zen Workshop. Available at http://www.acc.umu.se/~aramis/zenworkshop/koan.html.

Index